*The County Books Series*

GENERAL EDITOR: BRIAN VESEY-FITZGERALD, F.L.S.

# THE LOWLANDS
## OF
# SCOTLAND
### *Glasgow and the North*

# THE LOWLANDS

## OF

# SCOTLAND

*Glasgow and the North*

*by*

## MAURICE LINDSAY

SECOND EDITION

## Robert Hale & Company
63 Old Brompton Road London S.W.7

© Maurice Lindsay 1953 and 1973

First published 1953 in "The County Books" series
This revised edition 1973

ISBN 0 7091 3884 9

Printed in Great Britain by
Lowe & Brydone (Printers) Ltd., Thetford, Norfolk

# CONTENTS

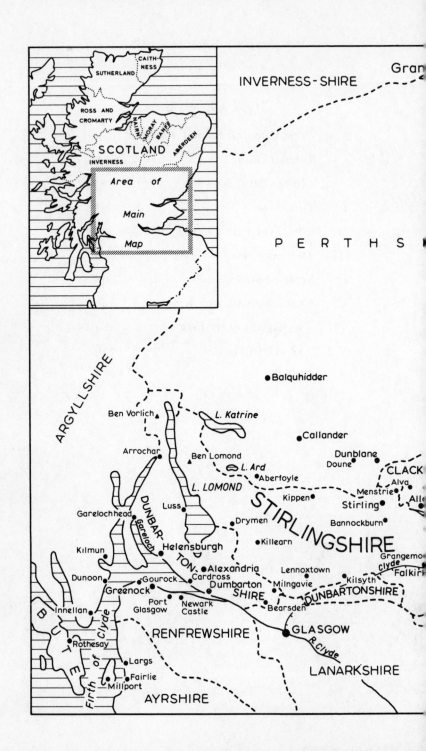

# ILLUSTRATIONS *Facing page*

ACKNOWLEDGEMENTS

The illustrations above numbered 11, 15 and 16 were provided by the *Scottish Field*; numbers 1, 2, 3, 6, 8 and 13 came from the library of the now defunct daily newspaper *The Bulletin and Scots Pictorial*; 5, 12 and 14 were provided by the *Scottish Tourist Board*; 9 and 10 by Mr Eric L. Palmer; 7 by Mr James MacEwen; and 4 by W. Ralston Ltd., the latter being taken from my book *Portrait of Glasgow* (1972).

# PREFACE TO THE SECOND EDITION

I T is thirty years since the idea of writing this book was conceived under the somewhat unusual circumstances described in the Introduction, and twenty years since it was first published. Since *The Lowlands of Scotland* was neither intended to be a guide-book nor simply a verbal topographical survey, but rather one man's sense-impression of that part of the world he knew and loved best, the fundamentals of the approach have not much altered, any more than have most of the value judgments. The purpose of this Preface is to add to the picture some notes and comments on features, buildings and attitudes that have undergone change.

Twenty years ago, Scottish history and Scottish literature were not taught in Scottish schools as systematically or as extensively as they are now. During the years between there has been an astonishing increase in the number of serious studies on Scottish themes published, and a gratifying number of reprints of Scottish texts of merit made re-available. Not even the growth of television and its establishment at a far lower level of cultural and imaginative achievement than the B.B.C. in Scotland managed to sustain with radio in pre-television days, has affected such gratifying developments as the emergence of the Scottish National Orchestra under Alexander Gibson to become one of the finest orchestras in Europe, or the even more astonishing rise in ten years of Scottish Opera, like the S.N.O. another of Mr Gibson's artistic achievements and based in Glasgow (which also provides a home for the more recently adopted Scottish Theatre Ballet.)

So far as the man-made fabric of the Lowlands is concerned, there have certainly been some major changes. Vast areas of crumbling Victorian tenements have been bulldozed down, and the first of Glasgow's twenty-seven Comprehensive Development Areas—that at Pollokshaws—has been virtually completed. Such redevelopment projects displace sixty per cent of the population, dispersing them mostly to the New Towns: to the "garden city" Mark I new town of East Kilbride; or to the more concentrated closer-built Mark II new town of Cumbernauld, high rise and low rise houses covering its wind-swept ridge straddled by an enormous shopping-centre—an international award-winner of a place, though for reasons apparently less clear to some of those who live in it than to its distant admirers. Nevertheless, a warm sense of community has been nurtured in both these New Towns, as will doubtless in due course also be manifested in Irvine, attached to the famous old Ayrshire Royal Burgh, and to Livingstone, halfway between Edinburgh and Glasgow, in both of which thousands of future Glaswegians are destined to settle.

The Civic Amenities Act of 1967 and other post-war planning legislation consolidated in the Town & Country (Scotland) Planning Act of 1972, have created the concept of the Conservation Area—an area of high environmental quality—and given increased protection to individual buildings listed as being of outstanding architectural or historic interest. The chapter on Glasgow reveals my failure—a fairly common one twenty years ago—to appreciate fully the richly inventive qualities of Victorian architecture: qualities which recently led Lord Esher to describe Glasgow as "the finest Victorian city in the United Kingdom". I should certainly have devoted more space to the Park Conservation Area (as it now is), with its Circus, Crescents and Terraces by Charles Wilson, John Baird, George Smith and others, prettily set out upon one of Glasgow's many interesting built-over hills. I should have written at greater length of "Greek" Thomson's outstanding contributions; in the domestic range, Great Western Terrace and Moray Place, among others; and in public buildings the Egyptian Halls (his "Greekness" was really always rather suspect, Old Testament rather than strictly classical influence playing an important part in the moulding of his style) and St. Vincent Street Church. I should certainly have felt more warmly towards such varied Glasgow architectural riches as Charles Wilson's Royal Faculty of Procurators building, a miniature Venetian *palazzo* with a sumptious library interior, the great carved sweep of Sir J. J. Burnet's Stock Exchange building (re-built internally) and his Charing Cross Mansions. It now stands above the Western Flank of the Inner Ring Road; itself, like W. A. Fairhurst and Partners' Kingston Bridge, a new source of visual pleasure as well as of usefulness. And of course there is the unique and curiously dateless freshness of Charles Rennie Mackintosh's Glasgow School of Art.

Because of the pressures of land shortage, Glasgow has built many high rise towers, altering the skyscape of the City as seen from the surrounding hills. Some, like the mixed block of housing and shops in the Hutchesontown-Gorbals redevelopment, by Sir Basil Spence, Glover and Ferguson, wear their distinction obviously. Others look like all-too-real-life Lego. Anyone who thinks that our cost-conscious concrete-bound age cannot ever again achieve creative architectural excitement, however, should take a look at the Library of Glasgow University by William Whitfield of London; or Frank Fielding & Associates' School of Architecture for the University of Strathclyde; or Gillespie, Kidd & Coia's St. Charles R.C. Church, one of several buildings for religious use designed by this originally-minded firm. The finest example is St. Peter's Seminary at Cardross.

Shipbuilding has managed to hang precariously onto the narrow reaches of the Upper Clyde, a part of the famous river really neither wide nor deep enough to accept the launching of major ships of modern tonnage. The most celebrated yard of them all—John Brown's of Clydebank, builders of the liners *Queen Mary* and *Queen Elizabeth I* and *II*—has been taken over by an American firm to build oil-rigs which will assist in the retrieving of the newly-found harvest of energy beneath the shallow but easily stormed-up waters of the North Sea.

Shipbuilding on the lower· reaches of the Clyde, though not in receipt of the subsidies given mainly for social reasons by both Labour and Conservative Governments to Upper Clyde Shipbuilders (and, after the bankruptcy of that concern, to Govan Shipbuilders Limited) has managed to maintain economic viability.

The famous fleet of Clyde pleasure-steamers, which had already begun to dwindle twenty years ago, is now reduced to two ships—the last sea-going paddle-steamer in the world, the *Waverley*, built in 1946, and the turbine *Queen Mary II*, built in 1936 but reconstructed to carry only a single funnel after the war. For the rest, their places have been taken by car-ferries, and the classic "doon the watter" sail from Glasgow's Broomielaw has been cast off into the silence of the past, like so many of the yards whose clattering, flash-point welding activities made this sail so memorable an experience.

On the South bank, Greenock has secured for itself an important container terminal and a large dry dock that did not survive its first decade of existence without financial difficulty. Inverkip has had intruded upon it an electricity generating station; unhappy long-term mis-planning leaving the Secretary of State of the day no choice but to approve reluctantly its construction to ensure an adequate future supply of electricity in the Clyde valley. The realisation of the potential of the deep water flowing past the Hunterston—an area of outstanding scenic quality which should really have been designated as a National Park—has brought to it two atomic power stations, and may yet result in the construction of a general cargo port, an ore terminal, an oil refinery, a petro-chemical complex and possibly also some kind of steel mill.

On the North side of the Estuary, the Gareloch now houses the British atomic-submarine base, while over the hills, in the Holy Loch, lies the American Polaris submarine base. Shandon Hydro has made way for a caravan park and housing development.

If Dunoon, Innellan and Rothesay no longer attract the number of local visitors from Glasgow they once did, some of their tourist trade has been sustained by holidaymakers from the North of England and abroad. Rothesay Castle has been splendidly restored by the Marquis of Bute.

A motorway now connects Glasgow and Stirling, by-passing that town as it leads North towards Perth. Stirling University, set in the grounds of Airthey Castle, must certainly be one of the most beautiful sites available to any post second-war academic development. A well equipped theatre, the MacRobert Centre, occupies part of the campus. Speculative and council house build-ing has disastrously disfigured the treeless slopes of the southern approach to the cathedral town of Dunblane, although the old houses around the cathedral have been well restored.

In Stirling Castle, the Great Hall has been magnificently rest-ituted to its original state by the Ministry of Works, and a former hotel just below the Castle esplanade has become a Landmark Centre. Replica buildings and some restoration have improved the appearance of Broad Street and John Street, which aroused complaint in me twenty years ago.

The motorway from Edinburgh to Perth passes within sight of Loch Leven. Fife is now linked by a road-bridge to Edinburgh over the Forth, and to Dundee over the Tay. The decline in the demand for coal has resulted in a less vigorous development of the Fife coalfields than one seemed likely to ensue.

Rossend Castle became the subject of a demolition order, and a public inquiry upheld the objectors, who felt it should be conserved. Plans are afoot to convert it into high-amenity flats.

Kellie Castle is now in the care of the National Trust for Scot-land. The sixth Earl, about whose music I was somewhat scathing twenty years ago, has now had his reputation reinstated by the discovery of fresh scores. Although no Haydn, nevertheless he was clearly a much more gifted and interesting composer than I then believed him to have been.

St. Andrews has been lovingly conserved, and many more of its little houses restored. Even the provision of additional students' residences and a large hotel on the approach from the North West have not seriously altered the quality of its environment.

Dundee, in spite of some much-needed central redevelopment, remains a monument to lost opportunity. All along the North East coast, including Orkney and Shetland, economic life may soon be affected by the discovery of oil beneath the North Sea. It is, of course, vital that in places where amenity considerations are important the utmost strictness of control should be exercised by Central and Local Government authorities if long-term environmental damage is not to be the high price paid for short-term economic gain. Our grandchildren will not bless us if an exhausted oil industry leaves behind it dereliction besides which the concentrated wasteland of 19th century iron and steel exploitation might seem an environmental paradise.

More personal changes must be recorded. Where changed facts necessitate, minor adjustments to the text and footnotes have been made. Two of my poems which seem to me to be not wholly bad, "In Scotland Now" and "The Salmon Loup at Gartness", have been substantially revised and now appear in their new form. Two other verses of my own represent the lost enthusiasm of youth in such a way as to make major revision impossible. One piece has been deleted. Though I would not include the other in any collected edition of my poetry, should such a thing ever be contemplated, it seemed best to let it stand in its context with the excising of the final stanza.

The book of twenty years ago was dedicated to that remarkable Scot and dual personality, J. M. Reid and his literary other self "Colin Walkinshaw", under whose kindly editorial auspices, from 1947 until its demise in 1960, I was Music Critic of *The Bulletin*, the daily paper he edited. He, alas! is now dead, as are others acknowledged in my Introduction including Mr. George Emslie, Mr. D. M. Cowie and my father, Matthew Lindsay, a distinguished Glaswegian. Although modern circumstances have forced a reduction in the number of photographs originally included, I have introduced only one new picture—a dramatic illustration of Glasgow's 'seventies look—most of the others reflecting that which is unchanging; what Hugh MacDiarmid so aptly describes as "the old loveliness of earth that both affirms and heals."

11, Great Western Terrace,
Glasgow.    November, 1972                    MAURICE LINDSAY

# INTRODUCTION

## I

ONE cold, raw night in the winter of 1943, I found myself standing on the doorstep of a comfortable Chelsea flat wishing my host and hostess, without much conviction, a peaceful night. I was at that time a junior staff officer in the War Office, working long days which left me little time and less energy for leisure or recreation. But I had stolen some hours from sleep to visit these people—artists who lived in an atmosphere of cheerfully spontaneous bohemianism—and we had enjoyed a lively evening. A warm fire crackled in the hearth, its glow reflected in the garish-red fabrics with which the house was furnished. *Objêts d'art* were liberally distributed about the room—a varnished branch mounted on a pedestal, labelled "Sea-God Arising"; the tip of an aborigine's spear; a Polynesian native necklace; and contemporary paintings galore. Above the mantelpiece, an interweaving of loudly coloured triangles occupied the place of honour. But from the shadows of the back wall, a futuristic nude dominated the room. It was impossible to escape from the piercing stare of her one mad eye—the other eye had been put where the laws of anatomy would normally have favoured a breast! She was called Calliope, the caricature of a lyre woven out of her hair being supposed to establish the epic connection.

Over sipped beer and slow-drawn tobacco, reputations had been splintered by an epigram; perversions ruthlessly parodied. We had talked about the war; about Picasso and the "arty" French Communists; about William Blake and the Englishness of his mysticism; finally, about Scotland. I was the only Scot in the company.

To my hostess, Scotland was a place where it was hardly safe for a civilized Londoner to venture unaccompanied, except at the height of the summer season. At least, so she said. But I could not be sure; for like almost every Southern Englisher I have met, she did not take Scotland seriously. It was a primitive, half-savage land which England had somehow acquired in the normal process of preserving the general peace: a kind of near-hand colony mainly administered from London: a land where the fighting capabilities of its soldiery could always be usefully harnessed: a sports-ground where the wealthier and more intrepid English gentry could tweed themselves in Autumn.

These views seem extraordinary to Scots folk. But they are quite commonly held, or claimed to be held. It is difficult, often impossible, to get the English to appreciate that Scotland the Nation does still exist. To the average Englishman, Scotland is not really a nation at all. She is dead history.

Naturally, I mustered such factual defences as I could against the onslaught of the whole party. To my host and his clever, brittle-witty young guests, my earnest defences were doubtless but a bettering of the joke. To myself, they were a revelation; for I suddenly discovered that I knew singularly little about my own country; little, at least, that mattered. I was a mass of stock responses.

As I set out alone along the Embankment, my mind alternated between an examination of the shame I felt at my intellectual vanquishment, and the more urgent task of not losing my way in the gathering fog.

It leered round every creeping, muffled bus-light. It scraped the eyes and the throat. It swirled and thickened to a stinking, shiversome, yellow mucus. Finally, it even obscured the pavement's edge. There was nothing for it but to stand still and hope that someone who knew the district might stumble past. Then the air-raid warning cut through the fog, swelling and swooning, swelling and swooning, louder than ever in the traffic-stilled, thickened darkness. In the distance, ack-ack guns roared. I blundered on.

Suddenly a voice loomed up in front of me. "'Ere you," it thundered. "Come out o' that. You can't stay there. Stuff'll be fallin' about these parts very soon. You come erlong with me, Jock." The helmeted figure swept me past a high wall and round a sharp corner. "Now you stay there till it's orl over," it commanded firmly; then it disappeared as mysteriously as it had arrived.

I found that I was in a stoutly built public lavatory along with half a dozen other men. We had just time to exchange those simple observations anent the weather, which English punctiliousness demands, when the "stuff" began to fall. Guns barked angrily upwards. Far above, the enemy planes droned slowly round and round, as if deliberately probing aside even this artificial concealment which the fog had lent to the sprawling city. Then the bombs came whining down, striking the earth with a sickening, disintegrating thud. I thought of the crowded miles of poorish brick homes across the river, lying open to destruction; of the shattered walls, the broken bodies, and the ghastly smell of destruction.

A small man who had taken no part in the meteorological exchanges sidled up to me and mouthed huskily, in the unmistakable accents of the Gorbals: "Whaur d'ye come frae, mister?"

I told him. My voice was trembling. I was experiencing an overwhelming desire to run and to keep on running—away from this absurd, odoriferous sanctuary; away from the whole damned war, and from the degradation it imposed on human values.

"Cigarette, mister?" he suggested, stuffing a crumpled Woodbine into my hand.

"Thanks," I said.

By the light of his match as it momentarily licked away the darkness, I could see the lines of his face. He was squat and wiry, with the bitten-and-chiselled features of the industrialized Clydeside Celt. His hand was as firm and steady as Dumbarton Rock.

During the rest of our stay in this improvised shelter, we talked of home: eagerly, but in a damp-voiced whisper, for the cold fog had seeped into our throats. To him, Glasgow was mainly Argyle Street on a Saturday night, the shop-lights magnetizing the drifting crowds with a coloured fascination which added magic to their desire for the gaudy things in the windows. To me, Glasgow was first and foremost a Victorian west-end terrace-house looking out on to a garden with a pink chestnut tree in it. To both of us, Glasgow meant Scotland; and Scotland was home. To the three Londoners, and the tall, tubercular-looking sailor from Portsmouth, who chattered amongst themselves, and who, when the noise slackened, threw occasional jokes about our Scots voices over the jumping glow-spots of their cigarettes, Scotland was nothing in particular; remote and probably as impersonally uninteresting as Honolulu or Peru.

When eventually I reached my "digs" in Maida Vale, I took stock of my own position. Clearly, it was not enough to know only the vague legends and the filmified episodes of one's country's history; not enough to have read only those few Scottish authors whose works happen to have been appropriated by the English for inclusion in English literature; not enough—not for me, at any rate—to go through life as an Anglified half-Scot, accepting and unquestioning.

I was neither a peculiarly unobservant, nor a particularly indolent person. I was merely a product of the Scottish educational machine, operating, indeed, at one of its more exclusive levels. There are to-day thousands of Scottish boys and girls who enter adulthood without ever having heard more than the sketchiest outline of the history and achievements of their own country. For Scottish history is not given adequate study in Scottish schools. The books most frequently used were both written more than fifty years ago, entirely from an English angle (even to the point of deliberate misrepresentation), and in language carefully chosen to make sure that nothing in the way of patriotic emotion could possibly be stirred up by any perusal of their stolid pages. Not that there could be much danger of engendering nationalism in any case, since Scottish history, even in this diluted form, is fed only to primary-school children. Scottish history ended officially with the wholesome defeat of Prince Charles Edward Stewart in 1746. Thereafter, it is "British" history that is studied; and "British" history, as everyone knows, is the history of England.

Nor is it in history alone that Scottish children are denied a knowledge of their birthright. Scotland enjoys the distinction of being the only European country whose schools give no systematic instruction in the native literature. A few enterprising teachers do, no doubt, occasionally depart from the rigid pre-examination curricula imposed on them from above, to share their delight in a favourite Scots author with their pupils; and the Burns Federation tries, in its rather limited and sentimental way, to stimulate an interest, among children at least, in the work of the National Bard. Nevertheless, it is quite possible for a child to leave school in, say, Glasgow, having heard only a little about Burns, rather less about Scott, and absolutely nothing about even the mere existence of Dunbar or Henryson, Ramsay or Fergusson, or, in our own day, MacDiarmid and the Lallans Makars.

Kirkegaard had a favourite saying: "Life can only be understood backwards. But it must be lived forward." None of these basic educational deficiencies was apparent in such detail as I sat thinking alone that foggy night over my hissing coin-in-the-slot gas-fire. One thing, however, *was* clear to me. I must embark on a progress to search out and discover my own land for myself— its history, its religion, its politics, its literature, its lore and its legend, its agricultural and industrial development, and what gave its people their peculiar local characteristics and native personality.

This book, and its companion volume, *Edinburgh and the South*, make up a record of that part of my Progress which concerns the Lowlands: a decade's Progress through many spheres of Scottish activity and thought. I hope that my account will enable not only visitors to our country, but many of my compatriots, to enjoy a richer and fuller appreciation of Scotland than can otherwise be gained without undertaking a considerable amount of arduous research.

Since my aim has been to convey as much as possible of the atmosphere of each of the Lowland counties, my manner of doing so has varied from chapter to chapter, in accordance with my impressions of the character of the individual counties. Dates indubitably look ugly things upon a page. But I have included a liberal sprinkling of them because the indication of the extremities of a man's life mightily helps the unhistorical reader to understand the nature of an achievement in its proper setting. The better-informed Scottish reader may feel that I have not taken enough for granted. Let him but remember how irritating it is to pick up a book about a country with which he is unfamiliar, only to discover that the author assumes his reader to possess an historical knowledge equal to his own. I have therefore tried to eschew half-explained historical allusions, wherever possible relating, or at least interpreting, the significance of such references.

Finally, a word about the disputable boundary between fact and fancy. Legends which have obtained a strong hold on local imagination, though perhaps scarce a fingerhold on authenticated history, are presented purely and simply as legends. I have tried always to distinguish between fact and opinion, and to state both sides of even those problems about which I happen to feel strongly. But we Scots are by nature a contentious people, and doubtless there will be found within these pages abundant " evidence " which will enable readers of almost any political or religious persuasion to accuse me of bias! However, " bias " in favour of one view at the expense of another has characterized every history of Scotland ever written, and is indeed concomitant with the ordinary process of intelligent personal judgment.

## II

The possibilities of perpetuating old and accepted errors, to say nothing of producing new ones, are almost limitless in a book of this sort. I have gone to considerable pains to make sure that my facts are accurate. I have also trespassed upon the patience of my father, Mr. Matthew Lindsay, and of my friends, Mr. J. M. Reid, Mr. George Emslie of the Mitchell Library, Glasgow, and Mr. G. D. McLeman in particular, who advised me on various points. To them, I owe a debt of gratitude. If, however, any errors have remained, the fault, of course, is entirely mine.

I have been indebted to a large number of books—too many to acknowledge individually. Instead of any such acknowledgment, the second volume of *The Lowlands of Scotland* will contain a bibliography which should be of assistance to those who may want to take up further individual aspects of my subject.

I am also grateful to the Editors of *The Bulletin* and the *Scottish Field*, who opened their portfolios of photographs to me and allowed me to choose what I wanted; to Mr. D. M. Cowie, of the Scottish Tourist Board, for a similar service; and to my friend, Dr. William Scott, who climbed to the top of Duncryne on a warm summer's day to take a picture specially for me.

Mr. George Bruce and the proprietors of the *Scots Review* gave me permission to reprint his poem *Gateway to the Sea*. Mr. Sydney Goodsir Smith kindly allowed me use *Largo,* from his collection *Skail Wind*. The New Alliance Press have my thanks for allowing me to use *The Salmon Loup at Gartness* and *Alone by a Tarn* from my own book *Ode For Saint Andrew's Night and Other Poems,* while similar thanks are due to Serif Books for *Ruins on a Cowal Hill* from *At the Wood's Edge*.

Finally, I am grateful to Mrs. Nigel Young and to my wife, who laboured with the intractabilities of my hand-writing to prepare the manuscript of this book for the press. The assistance of my wife did not end there, but she would not wish to be otherwise thanked.

Gartocharn,  MAURICE LINDSAY.
Dunbartonshire.
August, 1952.

# IN SCOTLAND NOW

The last sour petrol-puff of dust has settled,
whitening the moorland road; a westering sun
silvers beneath green leaves; the yellow-petalled
iris sends lustre signals; rabbits run
with a soft flurry of sand, and prick their ears
in feigned stone-stillness, hearing the faint sound
of menace tracking through their timid years;
and a lone curlew whushers from the ground,
wheeling aloft as if it had been spun.

It startles old ghosts up from history—
Fingal advancing with his cloudy host
over the moors, his mountain mystery
towering the years since Ossian's blind toast
rang through the halls of Selma: Tearlach's ranks
broken like bracken, dead crushed down on dead,
the wounded herded in deserted fanks
to wait cold English steel; the Cause unsaid
the Gaels' last gallant battle greatly lost!

Familiar things that keep old soldiers talking—
Hidallan's lust against young Fingal's bride:
how the old Fingal set his warriors stalking
Diarmid warm with Graunia at his side:
the talk of loot, the talk of strategy
that animated those whom Wallace led;
old women's voices hushed in tragedy,
conning the dire anatomy of dread,
uncertain when to flee or where to hide.

Knox with his rant of words forever hacking
the ancient roots of Scottish liberty;
those bleak, psalm-laden men whose souls in racking
cracked our quick joy and spilled our charity;
those gracious, gallant cellar-lords who sold
the birthright of our freedom for a bribe;
the men of smoke and steam whose lust for gold
reared slums to hide their damned, deluded tribe,
tamed by the cancerous ache of poverty.

*Cold, emptied passions; scraps of stranded chatter*
*worn flotsam of once ardent human pride—*
*what can it mean to us, or even matter*
*now that Time's restless and resistless tide*
*has rubbed away those creeds by which they stood,*
*altered mind's climate, tempered the heart's mood,*
*till most that once seemed honourably good*
*now lies dissected and discredited*
*with scarce a single gesture undenied?*

*So, sensing these heraldic figures tracing,*
*retracing their old steps, like folk turned blind,*
*I wonder if we met them suddenly, facing us*
*as man to man, could we together find*
*thoughts we'd all understand? Some common sign*
*to prove our kindred blood, each in his day*
*one living segment of an endless line?*
*Or should we learn that there no longer lay*
*a common frontier to a racial mind?*

*If words were all that mattered, we'd be staring*
*mutely across cold agonies of space;*
*for word was never made that could be tearing*
*those mists that blur each vague receding face.*
*And there's no ultimate tongue to strip the deed*
*of its accomplishment, reveal that ripped despair,*
*those running threads of doubt, which there was need*
*to bind up into action, then and there,*
*so long ago, in each relentless place.*

*But they'd all recognise the spring of heather,*
*the curlew chantering up his changeless fears,*
*those wet sea-winds that modulate our weather,*
*sheep nibbling through contented, grassy years.*
*So sight and sound and touch still intersect*
*to keep our grim, half-legendary land*
*a place of warm belonging, and protect*
*our brittle senses with a friendly hand*
*from dusty dreams of plunging, sterile spheres.*

# CHAPTER I

# GLASGOW

*"A city like Glasgow is a hateful place for a stranger, unless
he is reconciled to it by the comforts of hospitality and society."*
ROBERT SOUTHEY, 1819.

I

ONE Sunday afternoon in the spring of 1765, a youngish man
with a long, thoughtful face, strolled absent-mindedly over Glasgow Green.  He was running a risk, for, at that time, the fanatical
"high-flying" ministers of the City church disapproved of even
such moderate exhibitionism as a quiet walk on Glasgow's ancient
recreation ground; and they employed "bum-bailies" to augment
their "seizer's"—elders who paraded the town during the hours
of divine service to spy out and bring to kirk-justice as many
as possible of those who flagrantly offended the Lord by showing
themselves out of doors on the Sabbath.

The young man, amongst other things maker of mathematical
instruments to the University of Glasgow, was not, however,
molested; which was fortunate.  For just as he got to the herd's
house at the far side of the green, the answer to a problem that
had bothered him for months flashed into his mind.  The pedes-
trian thinker was James Watt; the idea which came to him, that
of the separate condenser necessary to harness steam as an efficient
motive force.  It is not too much to say that out of an illicit
Sunday afternoon walk, modern Glasgow grew.  The exploitation
of the new source of power brought about industrial development
on a scale never hitherto dreamed of in Scotland.  In one sense,
it caught the people of Glasgow unawares.  Their society had not
reached a stage at which the rights of the ordinary individual
assumed any importance, except in the minds of a few far-seeing
pioneers like David Dale (1739-1800), who combined wide-reaching
industrial enterprise with concern for the welfare of his workers,
and still found time to preach every week in his own sectarian
chapel.  But in general, as the last quarter of the eighteenth
century, with its long series of exciting revelations of promised
plenty and prosperity, wore greyly into the nineteenth, industrial
development unhappily became identified with grab and greed.

1

Glasgow rapidly multiplied and re-multiplied its population, attracting to its insanitary heart men and women from the surrounding countryside, and, particularly after 1846, huge hordes of Irish peasants starved out of their own country by the great potato famine. The old quarter of the City steadily deteriorated, becoming grossly overcrowded and disease-infested. The newer quarter, rising up towards the West, soon showed a decline in architectural standards as the spacious late-Georgian "classical" style gave place to the grosser Victorianism of innumerable self-contained and terraced family residences. The successful Glaswegian's sense of values, based firmly and finally on his own ability to make money, was reflected in the appearance of his new dwellings. Vulgarity and ostentation replaced poise, fair proportion and charm. Factories and yards sprang up with little regard for the common good, often even with insufficient forethought for the possibilities of long-range development. And round about them, in sordid rows packed tightly together at the expense of light to save the cost of "unnecessary" ground-feus, grew up the tenements, those grim, decadent descendants of the seventeenth-century Scots "lands". For the most part lacking even the most elementary domestic amenities of the age, these buildings were to house the workers on whom Glasgow's sudden prosperity so unevidently depended. Four walls, a roof and the minimum of insanitary air-space were good enough for "the working classes".

It is this nineteenth-century Glasgow, modified and adapted here and there to ease our more enlightened social consciences, that usually makes the strongest visual impression on visitors to the city. It occupies by far the greater part of the city's forty thousands acres. For the suburbs are made up of outer layers of those twentieth-century houses common to every industrial town, the majority of them jerry-built by municipal builders in the 'twenties and 'thirties, or hideously prefabricated in the name of Londonized planning, after the Second World War. There is practically nothing of the old town left to remind the citizens that their past does extend further back than the invention of the steam-engine.

Old Glasgow disappeared beneath the demolition hammer on the instructions of successive zealous nineteenth-century City Fathers, who, as ignorant of the possibilities of restoration as they were indifferent to the value of those cultural and historical ties which they so methodically severed, thought only in terms of utilitarian "improvement". When the famous and gracious-looking Buck's Head Inn, and the Tontine Hotel, with its celebrated coffee-room that housed all the best journals in Europe, both disappeared to make way for blocks of shop-tenements and offices notable "improvements" had been effected. The crowning "improvement" of all was the demolition in 1887 of the seventeenth-century Old College Buildings in the High Street. They had been replaced a few years before by the present University on Gilmorehill, built to the design of Sir Gilbert Scott—a monument of clashing styles and pointless embellishment, around which hardly a passing decade has failed to wrap some new oddity to the whole monstrous agglomeration.

Since the advent of comparatively cheap rail and road travel, Glaswegians have gradually become aware of the fatal mutilation which their ancestors wrought so energetically on the fabric of their city. Many of them have made the forty-five-mile journey across the neck of the Lowlands to the Capital of Scotland, where so much more of the past stands commemorated and preserved in stone. Some of them have even journeyed abroad where they have seen reflected in the proudly vaunted glories of other lands and cities the full extent of their own architectural impoverishment. They cannot any longer claim that their city is in any way outwardly distinguished or beautiful. So, as if to make up for this deficiency, they try to impress the stranger with its human qualities; the Celtic warmth of its hospitality; that strange, spontaneous kindness so often lurking unexpectedly behind the rugged countenance, or the brusque, forbidding manner.

Aware of the insistent domination of the money-making motive in the composition of his mental background, the Glaswegian is almost pathetically anxious to know what other people think of him and his city. "Is this your first visit to Glasgow?" is a regular conversational gambit which every stranger sooner or later encounters, perhaps in a railway compartment or over the forced intimacies of the tea-room table. If he answers in the negative, a suggestion of relief will seep into the voice of the questioner as he says: "Well, you'll know what to expect"; or something of that sort. But if the stranger admits that he has *not* been in Glasgow before, the next question will almost certainly be, "And . . . er . . . what d'you think of it?" Unless the stranger is blind to matters of architecture, hails from Sheffield, Birmingham or Manchester, or is of an unnaturally kind and gentle disposition, his answer must necessarily be such as to stir a gentle sigh in his inquisitor's bosom, a sigh that will be the prelude to a casual apology for the city's obvious shortcomings. Next, there may be a remark about the traditional warm-heartedness of its people; then the conversation will be diverted into less unpromising channels.

## II

Appropriately, the Cathedral Kirk is the oldest surviving Glasgow building. It incorporates the shrine of its patron Saint Kentigern (Ceann Tighearn), or, as he is more commonly known, Mungo (his Pictish "pet" name, *Munghu*, meaning "Dearest Friend"), who was buried there in A.D. 603. When the bishopric was refounded by King David the First, there rose over his bones in 1126 the first medieval cathedral; and the second in 1196. Both were burnt down. The third building, that which still survives, was begun early in the thirteenth century by Bishop William de Bondington, with the construction of the crypt. Ronald G. Cant and Ian G. Lindsay, in their pamphlet *Old Glasgow*, say of it:

"In plan, the building consists of a nave and eight bays, a central tower and transepts, and a choir of five bays with eastern chapels beyond. Under the choir is the lower church, and at its north-east angle is the chapter-house. The transepts extend no farther than the line of the nave and choir aisles, save on the crypt level, where the Fergus aisle forms a prolongation of the South transept. The west front of the nave was for long flanked by two towers, but these were removed in 1846-8. In its present form the Cathedral has a total internal length of 285 feet. The central spire, by far the most ambitious of its kind in medieval Scottish architecture, rises to a height of about 220 feet above the crossing.

"The style employed throughout most of the Cathedral is the form of early Gothic known in Scotland as First Pointed. . . ."

The learned authors display admirable restraint in describing the misguided mutilations whereby the Cathedral, docked of its two towers, was left with a "shilpit" appearance which greatly detracts from its impressive dignity. It lacks the size of the ruined Cathedral of St. Andrews; the refinement suggested by the delicate remains of Elgin Cathedral; and that triumphant northern surge of cool, adoring passion which is Kirkwall's magnificent red sandstone Cathedral. Yet, even minus its western towers, Glasgow Cathedral has its own definite quality—a balance of proportion of rare Gothic distinction.

However, the important points about it are: that it survived the Reformation at all (it was reprieved only until "ane new kirk be biggit ", the "new kirk" fortunately remaining unbiggit long enough to allow hot heads to cool); and that it still houses undisturbed the bones of the City's " official " founder.

Naturally, a City which has tried to jettison most of its past, is not greatly interested in its patron saint's erstwhile ongoings. The name of St. Mungo, in the minds of most people, suggests either a tri-annual prize offered to the citizen deemed in the space of the preceding three years to have most improved or beautified his city; or else the wooden-looking, papistical figure that features in Glasgow's Coat-of-Arms. Mungo has not the warm, romantic qualities of his friend Columba. In any case, it is much more " poetic " to have founded an Abbey and an Order on a lonely island in the Hebrides, than to have converted the turbulent Britons of Strathclyde into Christians who were later to transfer their emotional intensity from the worship of God to the equally unrestrained worship of Mammon. Nevertheless, Mungo's is a kindly figure hovering behind the later years of smoke and spiritual desolation.

Born about A.D. 525, he probably came from St. Serf's School at Culross, in Fife, with an early reputation for the achievement of miracles. He served first of all under the venerable Abbot St. Fergus at Carnoch, in Stirlingshire. When Fergus died, Mungo and his companions set off westwards, taking with them Fergus's body. In a cemetery close by the Molendinar Burn, once consecrated by St. Ninian, the first Christian apostle to the Picts of Scotland, they buried Fergus. And there, perhaps in the year 560, Mungo founded a community so ardent that it soon came to be known as Glasgu (Glasgow), the Happy Family. One of the most beautiful episodes in the whole vivid story of the Celtic Church is the meeting which tradition declares took place between St. Mungo and St. Columba. The two great teachers approached each other singing Latin psalms, and when they parted they exchanged pastoral staffs.

For many centuries after the founding of Mungo's community, Glasgow counted for little. Scotland did not become a single nation until the five predominant kingdoms that finally emerged out of the Dark Ages had slowly fused together, a process more or less achieved under King David the First. Dumbarton, farther down the Clyde, had been the old capital of Strathclyde. Both Rutherglen and Renfrew were made royal burghs, the former in 1189, the latter in 1396, long before a similar honour was conferred on Glasgow, which had to wait until 1611. Glasgow, twenty miles up from the sea, offered fewer natural advantages to shipping than its rival ports nearer the broad firth. But the existence of sandy fordable shallows in the Clyde had induced pre-historic tribesmen to settle near where the Cathedral now stands. Later, the Romans built a fort there. In 1345, Bishop Rae and Lady Lochow (Loch Awe), mother of Sir Duncan Campbell, the first Earl of Argyll, caused a fine stone bridge of eight arches to be thrown over the river at the Stockwell shallows, on the site of an earlier wooden bridge erected in 1285. That stone bridge, with minor modifications, did duty for more than 500 years. Since travellers had to come into Glasgow from near and far if they wanted to get across the river without wetting their feet, the place gradually became an important market, as well as the ecclesiastical capital of the South-West. Its importance was further increased in 1451 when another enlightened churchman, Bishop William Turnbull, founded the University.

Glasgow developed gently and naturally as a centre of learning and piety until the outbreak of those religio-political upheavals which preceded and accompanied the passage of the Reformation. It was a city in atmosphere perhaps not unlike St. Andrews, which also had a Cathedral and still has its University. Medieval Glasgow was built in a sort of double-cross pattern, with the *Highgait*, or High Street, as the centre-piece. Several of the old streets, under modern variants of their ancient names, still survive—the *Bridgegait*, for instance; and the *Fishergait* or *Stockwellgait*—so it is possible to visualize the pleasant lay-out that must have characterized the place when it was still a garden city.

The Cathedral nowadays sits in incongruous surroundings. The buildings of the Royal Infirmary tower above it, while behind, a statue of John Knox dominates a mighty hill of gravestones. Once, this mouldering mound was a fir-covered slope. An " improving " provost of the 1840's thought it would be a good idea to cut down the trees and turn the place into a cemetery which would bear the imposing name of Necropolis. There, Victorian Glaswegians who had achieved " position " made their last journey across the Molendinar to be laid to rest in pseudo-classical mausoleums. As a small boy, I used occasionally to wander about this place with a kindly relative, who regarded it as one of the more interesting showpieces of the city. I remember being distressed by the damp, musty smell that lurked behind the grills of those merchant princes' tombs—and astonished that so many, once thought so very remarkable, could now be so completely forgotten. But the Victorian Glaswegian laid great stress on the externalities, even in death.

To the south of Cathedral Square, the view is no less imposing, for there rises up an enormous stone wall, the ultimate defences

of Duke Street, Glasgow's prison for women. On the other side of
the road, one out-of-place little house unobtrusively keeps watch
over the busy street corner. By day, the road it shares with
the Infirmary opposite not infrequently carries hurrying ambu-
lances with one more unfortunate victim of the city streets
aboard. And far into the night, yellow lights that betoken pain
and suffering shine from layer upon layer of the Infirmary's square
windows.

But the windows of this little house have grown used to suffering since they were first erected in the pastoral days of the early
fifteenth century. Provand's Lordship is the only one to survive
of a group of manses which once surrounded the Cathedral.
The others were all connected with parishes, the respective incumbents living part of their time in these manses at the heart
of the See, and the remainder among their own people. The one
prebend ("Provand" is just the Scottish version of this Latin
word) maintained by a secular estate was that of Barlanark. And
it is this Barlanark manse that has come down to us. Needless
to say, its survival was due to happy accident, and not to any
foresight on the part of the City Fathers. The house came on
the market in 1906, the value of the ground as a site for development being its main attraction. Fortunately, a group of Glasgow
men came together to form a Club, securing tenancy in perpetuity
for an annual ground rent of £100. Then, in 1927, Sir William
Burrell, who later presented Glasgow with his magnificent art
collection and a handsome endowment to provide for its housing
outside the smoke-laden central area, gave the Club a large enough
sum of money to enable the house to be furnished in the manner
of the seventeenth century. As a result, Provand's Lordship is a
counterpart to Gladstone's Land, the headquarters of the Saltire
Society in the High Street of Edinburgh, but far richer in its
period furnishings.

Even the money-bitten Glaswegian likes to think himself a
Romantic at heart. (Indeed, in some ways he is, as I venture to
suggest later on.) So Provand's Lordship is credited not only with
having housed Mary, Queen of Scots, but with having been her
dwelling while she was writing some of the Casket Letters! On
the whole, modern scholarship confirms Andrew Lang's view that
the letters were, in fact, a forgery. But even if this hardy annual
amongst Scottish historiological problems was to be settled in
Lang's favour once and for all,[1] the legend about Mary would

---

[1] Possibly it has been so settled. See J. R. Black's *Andrew Lang and the
Casket Letters* (1951), which re-examines the Lang v. Henderson controversy
in the light of modern research.

probably persist; for, along with Prince Charles Edward Stewart, she provides an escape-valve for quite a deal of Celtic emotionalism. The contemplation of the beautiful Queen's sad fate, or of Prince Charles' unhappy defeat at Culloden, arouse gentle anti-English feelings in many Scottish bosoms. Of course, these feelings are quickly rationalized—after all, the offending houses of Tudor and Hanover have long since passed away; and what can ancient history have to do with present politics or economic fact? Thus, a process of sublimation occurs, and your Glaswegian retains his illusion that he is a fine patriotic fellow.

It was in the Cathedral of Glasgow that an important early chapter of the modern Scottish story was enacted in 1638. A still earlier chapter had been produced elsewhere, in 1560, when the Catholic Regent, Mary of Guise, mother of Mary, Queen of Scots, died after eighteen widowed years of struggle to hold back the threatening English from without and the gathering forces of the pro-English and anti-French Reformers within. No sooner was she dead than these two forces, hostile to the Scottish Crown, combined in an illegal Assembly which hatched the *Confessions of Fayth*, the first document to lay down the basic principles of Scottish Protestantism. It was followed up by the *Book of Discipline*, an even less liberal pronouncement which condemned the celebration of Christmas and Easter. (To this day, those religious festivals are less observed in Scotland than in England; especially Christmas, which gives place to the pagan festival of Hogmanay, held on the last evening of the year, and still generally observed in the Lowlands.) With the ranting rhetoric of John Knox to inspire them, the rabble mass found strength to destroy most of our early Scottish Cathedrals and churches, religious ornaments and polyphonic music. Aided by Mary of Scots' own misjudgment of the forces against her—and by her gentle, cultured nature and her generous share of human weaknesses—the Protestants gained the upper hand. Scottish Catholics became objects of general hatred, being abused in the most offensive and extravagant terms as if they were personally responsible for the evils which had crept into the hierarchy of their Church over the previous two centuries. Even to this day, religious intolerance is by no means dead, and it can flare up with equal suddenness at a Celtic versus Rangers football match, or at a middle-class drawing-room tea party.

Just under eighty years after the Reformation had been established by a rather irregular session of the Scots Parliament, a new revolution boiled up. James I and VI, though a Protestant, favoured Episcopacy; and so did his son Charles I, who, perhaps because he was the first King of Scotland to have no personal knowledge of the country, went so far as to try to enforce his will in the matter.

So, in February 1638, the first Scottish Covenant was launched at an open-air meeting in Greyfriars' Kirkyard, Edinburgh, amidst scenes of mass emotion. An orator of power and eloquence, the Reverend Alexander Henderson, headed a self-appointed purging committee known as the Tables. And in the following November, the Tables, in the guise of the General Assembly, met in Glasgow Cathedral to ensure that all the Episcopal archbishops and bishops and similarly minded ministers were "tried" and deposed. The sort of "trials" which followed have become horribly familiar to us in the twentieth century in other parts of Europe. The trumped-up charges ranged from playing cards, curling on the Sabbath day, carding and dicing in times of divine service, to incest. No evidence was produced that would stand up to the slightest examination in a modern court. The offenders were declared "deposed", and, although the Assembly voted its loyalty to the king, it thought it had demonstrated effectively that the reformed Church in Scotland was not within any earthly king's temporal jurisdiction. There it was wrong. For it took the Covenanters, the burnings, and the "killing times" to achieve religious "liberty", if what so one-sidedly followed could be given that much abused name. But this famous Assembly had revealed a number of curious traits which thereafter seemed to become confirmed in the Lowland character for many centuries.[1]

The most consistent was an upsurge of excessive Scottish individualism, of which Knox and Henderson were the fiery prophets. No doubt it was rugged individualism of a kind that once enabled the Kingdom of Scotland to rally round its leaders during the long years of struggle with the Plantagenets and the Tudors. But the idea of the common good must ultimately have triumphed in the majority of cases, or Wallace and Bruce would have had no armies.

The individualism which flowed unstemmed out of the flood of the Reformation certainly had some parallel elsewhere in Europe. The spread of learning resulting from the Renaissance and the development of the printed word, tended to give thinking

---

[1] Calvinism cannot be blamed for all our shortcomings, however. Undoubtedly, it confirmed existing urges and tendencies, such as a suspicion of pleasure for its own sake, no undue regard for the opinions of others, and a belief that excess, whether of virtue or of vice, is in some way commendable. There is little of balanced graciousness in the Lowland character. When it is met with, how unScottish it suddenly seems!

men everywhere more confidence in themselves, strengthening their belief in their individual rights. But in Scotland, this belief in "self" became, firstly, overweening and, in the end, well-nigh fatal.

The insistence of the Reformers that they and they alone were right; the pernicious doctrine of the "elect"; and the precedence created by their act of breaking violently away from the Mother Church—instead of reforming her from within, as moderates like the wise Bishop Elphinstone of Aberdeen advocated—divided the Lowland character against itself.

It has never really recovered from this violent operation. The countless minor denominations of the eighteenth and nineteenth centuries, all resulting from subsequent "secessions" from the Church of Scotland and its offshoots,[1] bear witness to that fact. If secular evidence is required, it is only necessary to attend a contemporary gathering of almost any group of Scots met together to try to get something practical done. One man disagrees with his fellows. Discussion leads to argument, and bitter words are tossed down. Even if a democratic vote is taken, more likely than not the leader of the defeated "opposition" will huffily withdraw his counsel. This lamentable inability to compromise and present a united front is, no doubt, ultimately a Gaelic heritage going back thousands of years. But the affairs of 1560 and 1638 gave it, so to speak, "modern" sanction. Perhaps we may also trace our "Here's tae us; wha's like us" attitude to the cultivated self-righteousness of the early Protestants. On the whole, the toast is painfully belied by our history. We are really a race of failures, we Lowland Scots, for our quarrelsomeness has enabled our English partners to "resolve" our controversies in England's best interests. True, we have not yet fallen into such a sad state of apathetic decline as our Highland brothers. But we have worshipped false gods so often and so fiercely, dissipating our heritage and our strength to so little ultimate purpose, that we are now left irresolute and weak, counting for little, except in a numerical military sense, in the affairs of these islands, and still less in the wider spheres of Europe. Collective impotence is, perhaps, the full price we have had to pay for the debatable benefits of our Reformation.

Throughout the whole of the seventeenth century, Glasgow was involved in these religio-political disturbances which laid waste the country and contributed much to bring about that state of poverty which, we are so often told, was the prevailing condition of Scotland at the time of the Union of the Parliaments. One of

[1] Some of them are dealt with in Chapter V, pp. 157-60.

the most picturesque Glasgow incidents in these depressing times is that which occurred, also in the Cathedral, when Cromwell attended divine service there in 1650. The preacher was the Reverend Zachary Boyd of the Barony, an ardent divine who, although he wrote voluminously, singularly failed to infuse his ardency into his verse. Mr. Boyd treated Cromwell to such a frank discourse on the demerits of "Noll" and his Roundheads that Cromwell's private secretary, Thurloe, who was sitting next to his master, asked whispering permission to "pistol the scoundrel". It says much for Cromwell's sense of humour that he chose another way of getting his own back. He invited Boyd to sup with him at his lodging in the Saltmarket, then led the divine in prayer until three o'clock in the morning. Thereafter, the humourless Zachary thought Cromwell a mighty fine fellow. Zachary left his not inconsiderable fortune to Glasgow University, a condition of acceptance being that the University had to publish a collected edition of his works. The University took the money, but put off publishing the verse for so long that in the end they were able to get by with the erection of a small bust of the poet instead. Similar verbal fire was possessed by many Scots divines and professors during the next three centuries, giving us the reputation of being brilliant metaphysicians. Unfortunately, Scots metaphysics is too often really little more than opinionative verbosity, generated at the white heat of intolerance.

Appropriately, Glasgow's only other pre-Union relics, all of which were erected in the seventeenth century, are now preserved in fragmentary form. The Tolbooth steeple went up in 1626, and has been part of two civic headquarters, both pulled down. The Tron steeple, which abuts defiantly across the pavement of congested Argyle Street, had assumed its present shape by 1636. (The original steeple went up between 1593-5, the kirk in 1592.[1]) Towards the end of the eighteenth century, the steeple was used as a guardroom for the gentlemen of the watch and ward service, the predecessors of the modern police force. One night in 1793, an amiable bunch of Glasgow hooligans, members of the Hellfire Club, decided to beat up the guard, and, in doing so, set fire to the church. A graceful Adam church was then built behind the steeple; but, true to tradition, the City Fathers, despite appeals from several cultural bodies, turned the whole building into the civic plumbers' store a few years ago. Finally, in the Bridgegait, rising absurdly through the roof of Glasgow's fish market, is the

[1] Remodelled on the fabric of the medieval Collegiate Church of St. Mary and St. Anne.

sole surviving fragment of the Guild Hall and Hospital built by the merchants of Glasgow in 1659.

One of the best of Scotland's Latin poets, Arthur Johnston, Doctor of Medicine (1587-1641), produced a series of " epigrams " upon some of the Scottish burghs. In 1685, one I.B. published a translation of some of them. The Glasgow " epigram ", though of no great literary merit, is not without picturesque interest:

" *Glasgow to Thee thy neighbouring Towns give place,*
*'Bove them thou lifts thine head with comely grace.*
*Scarce in the spacious earth can any see*
*A City that's more beautiful than Thee.*
*Towards the setting Sun thou'rt built, and finds*
*The temperate breathing of the Western Winds. . . .*

*More pure than Amber is the River Clyde,*
*Whose gentle Streams do by thy Borders glyde;*
*And here a thousand Sail receive commands*
*To Traffic for thee unto Foreign Lands. . . .*

*Thy Buildings high and glorious are; yet be*
*More fair within than they are outwardly.*
*Thy Houses by thy Temples are outdone,*
*Thy glittering Temples of the fairest Stone:*
*And yet the Stones of them however fair*
*Thy Workmanship exceed which is more rair.*

*That Neptune and Apollo did (it's said)*
*Troy's fam'd Walls rear and their foundation laid.*
*But thee O Glasgow! we may justly deem*
*That all the Gods who have been in esteem,*
*Which in the Earth and Air and Ocean are,*
*Have joyn'd to build with a Propitious Star.*"

Cynics and citizens of Edinburgh will no doubt feel that a good deal has to be set against the exercise of poetic licence. But the Yorkshire antiquary, Ralph Thoresby, having made the comparison in 1681, describes Glasgow as " . . . a very pleasant city, far exceeding Edinburgh itself in situation and cleanness ", while, a few years earlier, another Englishman had declared that " . . . for pleasantness of site, sweetness of air, and delightfulness of its gardens and orchards . . . Glasgow surpasseth all other places of this tract ".

Whatever the City's arboreal virtues—and so numerous are the

travellers' praises that they must surely have been considerable—
the references in Johnston's poem to the "thousand sail" trafficking in foreign lands is probably more poetic than accurate. For
Henry Grey Graham, in the chapter on Glasgow in his *Social Life
of Scotland in the 18th Century*, maintains that at the time of the
Union ". . . the trade was mean, and the commerce was insignificant, for the citizens owned no more than fifteen vessels, whose
aggregate tonnage was 1,182 tons, the largest ship having a burden
of only 160 tons. . . .

"The shallow channel of the Clyde, with its many sand-banks,
could not admit any vessels farther up the river than fourteen
miles from the Broomielaw . . . and up and down stream only
small boats could ply."

Thus, heavy cargoes had to be shipped to and from Dumbarton,
or Port Glasgow—since 1685 designed, as its name suggests, to
fulfil this rôle—by small boat or pack-horse.

The Act of Union changed all this. Whatever its effect on the
rest of the country, the Union set Glasgow on its course as a major
industrial city, and helped it to maintain this position for many
rich years. In 1707, the population of Glasgow was just over
12,500. By 1800, it had grown to 80,000. Such rapid transformation affected not only the outward appearance of the
City, but also the way of life and the character of the citizens
themselves.

### III

Scottish trade before 1707 flourished most vigorously on the
east coast, for the obvious reason that ports like Berwick, Leith
and Dundee were much more accessible to Holland or Norway
than difficult up-river ports on the far side of Scotland like
Glasgow. And the Continent of Europe was almost the only field
open to Scottish traders, since English laws, enforced by English
men-o'-war, barred Scots traders from America and the Indies.
This naturally occasioned some bitterness, especially since it was
generally felt that the English had contributed to the Scots
disaster at Darien by making it plain that molestation of the
settlers by the Spaniards would not incur the disfavour of
England, far less any counter-action.

Two centuries and a half after the event, it is now surely
apparent that Federated Union, as urged by the patriot Andrew
Fletcher of Saltoun (1655-1716), would have been a much more

satisfactory arrangement from Scotland's point of view. Commercial advantages would still have been secured, under conditions which would not have led to the sapping of native industrial enterprise, and the seducing of Scotland's fierce national energy in the interests of British colonization. Had Fletcher and his friends carried the day against the recipients of the Earl of Seafield's English bribes, Scotland might have offered a more favourable field for the labours of some of her most gifted sons. She might also have been spared such agonies as the Clearances; the long drain on the best of her manhood which whole-scale emigration caused throughout the nineteenth and twentieth centuries; the tragic over-concentration and unbalance of her economy which allowed the depression of 1929 to wreak such severe havoc in the industrial belt; and that gradual loss of vigour in her intellectual life resulting from her growing enforced dependence on the ways and decrees of London. That some sort of Union was inevitable, even desirable, not many Scots to-day would dispute. But even now, when the progress of science has at last made it plainly apparent that we are all of one world, and that our only hope of survival is by co-operation and compromise in the settlement of national differences, few would be foolhardy enough to deny the basic right of even the smallest nation to conduct its own domestic affairs in accordance with its beliefs and traditions.

The manipulated passage of the Act of Union caused anger in the hearts of most Scots, and riots in the streets of Edinburgh and Glasgow. A handful of Glasgow citizens, however, saw only opportunity in it. They came together, amalgamated their capital, collected a cargo of goods for barter, chartered a little ship from Whitehaven, and sent her off to Virginia, making use of the repeal of the law against Scots-American trade which the Act of Union included in its provisions. In due course, the captain brought back his ship laden with rum and tobacco; and also, according to tradition, some money in a stocking! Much of this tobacco was then resold to France at a goodly profit, and the basis was laid for a trade which steadily grew from year to year.

At first, however, the Glasgow tobacco traders had to cope with endless lawsuits instigated by their English rivals, designed as much as for any other purpose to thwart the Glaswegians and hamper their business. But by 1735, the Glasgow trade was thoroughly established, and great fortunes were in the making. Adam Smith's friend, Andrew Cochrane, is said to have been the wisest and most cultured of Glasgow's eighteenth-century

14

provosts. He it was who had to deal with Prince Charles during that gentleman's sojourn in the town in 1745; and he also it was who later squeezed out of an unwilling British Government substantial indemnification for the cost of refitting and victualling the Prince's Highland host. Cochrane attributed the spectacular rise of Glasgow to the acumen of four business men—Alexander Spiers of Elderslie; James Ritchie of Busby; William Cuninghame of Lainshaw; and John Glassford of Dougalston. The descendants of Spiers still own the family lands in Renfrewshire, purchased with his tobacco fortune. Cuninghame is remembered because he built the most magnificent of all the tobacco mansions; which, with pillars and façade added to it by David Hamilton (1768-1843), still stands off Buchanan Street where, after having been used for more than a century as the Royal Exchange, it is now to house the oldest of the City's libraries, Stirling's. Glassford, though he lost his fortune by gambling and unsound speculation, has a street named after him, perhaps out of gratitude for the persistent efforts he made to found other industries in the City.

Yet, however much these men and their kind achieved in the commercial way, socially they were regarded as upstarts. They did their best to marry their families with " the right sort ", and often they succeeded. But the scarlet cloak and gold-headed cane they adopted as their " uniform ", and their habit of dominating " the causey ", which was then the only paved section of the street, to the discomfort of lesser pedestrians, earned them a reputation for arrogance. Doubtless, many humble hearts secretly rejoiced at their fall, when, in 1775, the American War of Independence brought the structure of their virtual tobacco monopoly crashing to the ground.

The needs of the colonists who supplied the tobacco in exchange for the ordinary necessities of life led to the establishment of numerous manufacturing industries in Glasgow. The largest tannery and boot-making factory in Europe was set up in Glasgow during the first half of the eighteenth century. A glassworks, a pottery and a factory for making crystal were also established, while both the heavy industries and the textile industries staked their claims before the century was over. The pace of industrial expansion quickened enormously after 1775, when James Watt was first able to supply steam-engines in quantity.

The manufacture of inkles, or tapes, was added to the list, the secret having been wrested from the Dutch. Bleach-fields and print-works for the making of linen expanded from a small beginning at Pollokshaws in 1742, up and down the nearby valleys of the Clyde, the Leven and the Endrick. This was a particularly important development, because it prepared the way for the manufacture of cotton, which largely replaced tobacco in the trade with America. Printing established itself in 1770 in Glasgow; 1780 saw the Tennant Brothers' Welfare Brewery in production; in 1786, the first Glasgow distillery (the fourth in Scotland) was set up; in 1789, the Clyde Ironworks was founded; and in 1783, Provost Patrick Colquhoun and his friends set up the Glasgow Chamber of Commerce, the first of its kind in Britain.

Banks were established, among them "The Ship" and "The Thistle". The first shops, in the modern sense, were opened beneath the piazzas of the Trongate in 1750. There, the citizens could buy boots, jewellery, fabrics and, soon afterwards, stationery and beautifully printed books when the brothers Foulis opened up the City's first bookshop. They also ran for eighteen precarious years an Art Academy which, before it failed, gave instruction to David Allan, the "Scottish Hogarth",[1] and James Tassie (1735-1799), whose charming medallions brought him wide fame.

Golf began to be played on Glasgow Green. A student attending the University in 1721, James Arbuckle, smitten already with the post-Union Scottish literary disease of being more English than the English, left us an unintentionally comic description of the game. From his absurd heroics, we can at least learn that the human side of golf has not changed much with the centuries:

> " In Winter, too, when hoary frosts o'er spread
> The verdant turf, and naked lay the mead,
> The vig'rous youth commence the sportive war,
> And, arm'd with lead, their jointed clubs prepare;
> The timber curve to leathern orbs apply,
> Compact, elastic, to pervade the sky:
> These to the distant hole direct they drive;
> They claim the stakes who hither first arrive.
>
> Intent his ball the eager gamester eyes,
> His muscles strains, and various postures tries
> Th' impelling blow to strike with greater force,
> And shape the motive orb's projective course.
> If with due strength the weighty engine fall,
> Discharged obliquely, and impinge the ball,
> It winding mounts aloft, and sings in air;
> And wondering crowds the gamester's skill declare.

[1] See Chapter V, p. 143.

16

*But when some luckless wayward stroke descends,*
*Whose force the ball in running quickly spends,*
*The foes triumph, the club is cursed in vain;*
*Spectators scoff, and e'en allies complain.*

*Thus still success is followed with applause;*
*But ah! how few espouse a vanquished cause."*

As the influence of London's fashions started to impress both Edinburgh and Glasgow, families began to abandon their cramped "landings" in the older quarters of the city, moving into the new dwellings going up on the outskirts. Club life developed, as in Edinburgh; visiting players braved the wrath of the Kirk, though it led to the burning of most early Glasgow theatres; and gentlemen's subscription concerts were regularly organized, the programmes containing a nice blend of the latest Italian music and good Scots airs. The hour of the dinner meal was put forward to two or three o'clock in the afternoon, and hostesses no longer brought all their dishes to the table at the same time. Thus, although that trade upon which its prosperity had originally been built and sustained throughout the greater part of the century had largely vanished, Glasgow still contrived to flourish.

At the end of the century, it must still have been quite a pleasant place, in spite of the smoke-clouds gathering above the old town around the Cathedral, and smutting even the "classical" new town spreading out towards the West. John Mayne, who served his apprenticeship in the famous printing works of the Foulis brothers, set down in verse his keenly observed personal impressions of Glasgow's development toward the close of the eighteenth century:

" *In ilka house, frae man to boy,*
*Aa hands in Glasgow find employ;*
*Even little maids, wi' meikle joy,*
   *Flower lawn and gauze,*
*Or clip wi' care the silken soy*
   *For ladies's braws.*

*Their faithers weave, their mothers spin*
*The muslin robe, so fine and thin*
*That frae the ankle to the chin,*
   *It aft discloses*
*The beauteous symmetry within—*
   *Limbs, necks and bosies.*

17

*Look through the town! The houses here*
*Like noble palaces appear;*
*Aa things the face o' gladness wear—*
 *The market's thrang,*
*Business is brisk, and aa's asteer*
 *The streets alang.*

*Clean-keepit streets! so lang and braid,*
*The distant objects seem to fade;*
*And then, for shelter or for shade*
 *Frae sun or shower,*
*Piazzas lend their friendly aid*
 *At ony hour. . . .*

*Wondering, we see new streets extending,*
*New squares wi' public buildings blending,*
*Brigs, stately brigs, in arches bending*
 *Across the Clyde,*
*And turrets, kirks, and spires ascending*
 *In lofty pride. . . .*

*Wow, sirs! it's wonderfu' to trace*
*How commerce has improved the place,*
*Changing bare house-room's narrow space,*
 *And want o' money,*
*To seats of elegance and grace,*
 *And milk and honey."*

IV

In the century which followed, commerce ceased entirely to "improve" the place in any aesthetic sense. Certainly, it still further increased the milk and honey; but, for a long time, most of these symbolic commodities flowed only to the tables of the rich.

Industry, if not perhaps so beneficent a goddess as the apostrophising of eighteenth-century poets like James Thomson might suggest, is not inherently evil. Obviously, it can, and does confer great benefits on mankind. The Industrial Revolution had to come. To wish in its place a continuation of the primarily agrarian economy of pre-steam days is to indulge in false romanticism. In any case, although the politer poets of both England and Scotland regarded the countryside mainly as a suitable setting for idyllic summer pastorals about amorous aristocrats in the guise of shepherds and shepherdesses, we know, from less fanciful sources, as well as from the works of peasant poets like the English-man, Robert Bloomfield, and even Burns himself, that the life of an eighteenth-century agricultural labourer was often a grim and grinding struggle with only primitive instruments for aid; and, in the words of Sir Alexander Gray, with "Want an attendant not lightly outpaced". The matter for regret is not, indeed, the coming to Scotland of Industrialism, with all its great promise of wealth and plenty, but that its coming should have developed into a rout of the traditional decencies between man and man, because of the ruthless opportunism which mastered the souls of its captains.

The population of Glasgow doubled itself between 1801 and 1821. Within twenty years, it had doubled itself again, reaching a round total of 283,000 by 1841. By 1861, the doubling process had been repeated. Needless to say, it quickly became difficult for the civic authorities to cope with the steady inrush of immi-grants, a proportion of them of low mental standard and none too clean in their personal habits. The older parts of the city were allowed to become scandalously over-crowded and disease-infested, while crime and pestilence flourished. These problems have never wholly been solved in the heart of Glasgow, although, of course, the worst conditions prevailing to-day do not even invite comparison with the infinitely more squalid conditions of a hundred and fifty years ago. Nevertheless, Glasgow is still infamous for its over-crowded, tubercular-breeding slums;[1] and justly so, as anyone who cares to examine closely the housing conditions of the poorer parts of such districts as Anderston Cross or Gorbals can verify. Indeed, even under what is supposed to be a "sensible" planned economy, in the middle of the twen-tieth century Glasgow's housing problem, far from being solved, continues to get worse.

However, it is important to try to be fair to both sides. "Leftish" economists tell us that the rise of the capitalist system inevitably brought such major social problems into being, since much of the wealth acquired and spent on personal gratification,

[1] They have become an artistic theme! Gorbals has inspired Sir Arthur Bliss's ballet *Miracle in the Gorbals* and Robert McLeish's much more authentic dramatic indictment, *The Gorbals Story*. The novel, *No Mean City*, dealing with Glasgow's slums, attracted much attention between the wars. It was written by an ambitious man, MacArthur, with some very necessary assistance from a professional journalist. He tried to repeat his success with some short stories, mostly about Clydeside sluts seduced and/or raped by doss-house Indians, but failed to have any of them published. In despair, he finally threw himself into the Clyde.

or used for further development, depended upon the ready supply of cheap and submissive labour. On the other hand, we in our own day have seen the stifling effect of remote-control bureaucracy on human enterprise, even at quite humble levels. A compromise of sorts is gradually being arrived at, though now it is often the irresponsibility of "unofficial" collective labour which threatens to destroy the precarious balance.

However much some folk may contrive to restrain a justifiable bitterness when considering the bad side of the industrial evolution of the Lowlands, surely not even those who seek to whitewash it can restrain a certain sadness that man's inhumanity to man should have allowed things so to develop.

How did it come about? The comparative stability which followed the Act of Union allowed men, for the first time in two centuries, to devote themselves whole-heartedly to the arts and crafts of peace. The draining flow of the nation's virility London-wards was, as yet, a relatively harmless trickle; so the nation gathered itself together for a mighty gesture of self-assertion. Scotland had certainly lost her Parliament, and with it the power of controlling her own affairs; but, at least, she would show the world that in art and industry, she could still make herself felt in Europe. Country lairds experimented with new methods of farming, and new crops. The turnip was an eighteenth-century importation to Scotland. In Edinburgh, the movement in literature known as the Eighteenth-Century Revival arose, flourished, and achieved European significance. In Glasgow, the newly canalized energy built up Scottish industry at a truly incredible rate.

Local conditions were favourable. The city straddled a river potentially capable of carrying goods to the four corners of the earth.[1] In areas just outside the City boundaries, vast deposits of coal and iron lay waiting to be drawn upon. Over unthinkably large tracts of Time, nature had conveniently secreted these new resources for the benefit of enterprising Glaswegians. The harvesting of them has been fast, furious and wasteful.

Glasgow's dependence on the Clyde was further emphasized when Henry Bell's steamship *Comet* made its first dangerous and noisy voyage from Port Glasgow to the Broomielaw Quay on August 12th, 1812. Although most of the shipbuilding yards which sprang up along the river banks during the nineteenth century were not originally situated in Glasgow, the near-presence

[1] The first serious move to deepen the Clyde was made as far back as 1566. But it was not until 1775 that jetties in any number were built at the Broomie-law, and not until 1780 that Glasgow officially became a Port of Entry.

of this new industry, with its demands for a wide range of associated goods and machinery, stimulated the setting-up of new factories in and around the city; and the presence of so many ships in the making encouraged overseas trade.

Reading the life-stories of many of the eighteenth- and early nineteenth-century industrialists, it is impossible to avoid the conclusion that they looked upon the creating of their great commercial enterprises in a romantic light. Of course, they drew the traditional Lowland line where hard-headed calculation inevitably took over from romanticism. But men like Henry Bell, whose pleadings for the merits and possibilities of his best invention have about them a sort of disinterested ardency; or Robert Napier, the greatest of the early shipbuilders, who once excitedly got out of his bed in the middle of the night and woke up his foreman so that they could work out an idea that had suddenly come to him; or Kirkman Finlay, who organized a mighty export business and carried it on with defiance and daring under the very noses of Napoleon's soldiers; or David Dale who, with Robert Owen, set up the "model" welfare village of New Lanark for his spinners and weavers—these men do not seem to have been actuated solely by the urge for personal gain.

But with many of their successors it was a different story. The romantic urge for discovery and the overcoming of intellectual or technical obstacles soon began to be coated with the ulterior motive of plain and simple profit-making. Early Victorian industrialists made a great show of piety and benevolence, when these virtues did not affect their interests. But often, the piety evaporated as soon as it came into contact with such unsavoury realities as the appalling living conditions of their workers; the benevolence hardened whenever it conflicted with the gathering of increased profits. In fact, personal greed became tacitly legalized, and a putrid rottenness, confirmed behind a veil of religious hypocrisy, was the accepted middle-class norm.

A clear instance of this process in operation is provided by the history of Glasgow's cotton trade. Before the Industrial Revolution, osnaburgh[1] rough linen was the traditional fabric. It was made by weavers who carried through the process of wool preparation from start to finish, as a few crofters in the Outer Hebrides still do in connection with hand-made tweed. After the failure of the tobacco trade, the manufacture of imitation Indian muslin became a profitable business. From this, the textile men's interest

[1] So named because it originally came from Osnabrück in Germany.

spread to the preparation of cotton yarn. For a while, they were content to leave the actual weaving to the individual weavers, who increased in number when such men as Kirkman Finlay opened up fresh overseas markets for the finished goods.[1] But as Arkwright's spinning-frame was improved upon, notably by Archibald Buchanan's power-loom, which women could operate, machine-weaving became cheaper than hand-loom weaving. The yarn manufacturers then began to set up their own weaving factories, laying the emphasis on quality goods. This had the effect of gradually squeezing out many of the hand craftsmen. The working conditions of many of those employed in the factories was deplorable, and it is significant that most of the leaders of the Chartist and Radical risings which, under various names, began to erupt in Glasgow early in the nineteenth century, were weavers.

However, the trade flourished in and around Glasgow, reaching its peak, according to C. A. Oakley, in 1861. Thereafter, during the American war, the imports of raw cotton fell sharply away. But when they were resumed after the war had ended, Glasgow made little attempt to win back her old position, and Lancashire confirmed that supremacy which it still holds to-day.[2] The younger Glasgow business men coming to manhood in the worst age of mid-Victorian complacency, were concerned mainly with making money. At that time, a lot of money could be made more easily and quickly in the rapidly expanding shipbuilding industry. So the cotton trade was allowed to slip away, regardless of the difficulties its abandonment put on large numbers of skilled Glasgow weavers. It is worth remembering these facts concerning the cotton trade when one considers not only the apparently inexplicable abandonment of many other once-flourishing Scottish industries like boot-making, but also the unenterprising state of Scotland's industrial affairs in our own time.

By mid-century, the arrival of the railway in Scotland had opened up fresh possibilities to industrialists as well as to passengers. It was not long before the "pale toiling millions" created a demand for Sunday travel, and the first running of Sunday trains on the North British railway was amusingly commemorated by a Lanarkshire woman, Janet Hamilton (1795-1873), who came of Covenanting stock, and who did not learn to write until she was over fifty:

[1] America, of course, was the chief market until the civil war of the 1860's. It is curious to note that even as long ago as 1775 and 1865, the state of affairs in the New World could vitally influence our Scottish economy!
[2] But is in process of losing to India and Japan!

*" Now range up the carriages, feed up the fires!*
 *To the rail, to the rail, now the pent-up desires*
 *Of the pale toiling millions find gracious reply,*
 *On the pinions of steam they shall fly, they shall fly,*
 *The beauties of nature and art to explore,*
 *To ramble the woodlands and roam by the shore.*
 *The city spark here with his smart smirking lass,*
 *All peg-topped and crinolined, squat on the grass,*
 *While with quips and with cranks and soft-wreathed smiles,*
 *Each nymph with her swain the dull Sabbath beguiles.*
 *Here mater and paterfamilias will come*
 *With their rollicking brood from their close city home.*
 *How they scramble and scream, how they scamper and run,*
 *While pa and mamma are enjoying the fun!*
 *And the urchins bawl out, ' Oh, how funny and jolly,*
 *Dear ma, it is thus to keep Sabbath-day holy.'". . . .*

But to provide such delights, railway-engines and rolling stock
had to be made. Where better for their making than the Clyde
valley? Beneath the earth, more and more miners delved for coal;
certainly no longer heritable serfs with collars round their necks
bearing their master's names, but still wretched and under-fed.
As the sluggish social conscience stirred a little, women and
children were banned from the pits by Lord Shaftesbury's Act of
1842. But for the rest of the century, most miners and their
families continued to be housed in sordid rows of damp and insanitary single-ends, knocked together as cheaply as possible under the
shadow of the steaming bings that scar so much of the central
Lowlands. Glasgow grew still bigger: grew, in fact, to be the
second "white" city of the British Empire and the sixth in
Europe.

Ornate mansions went up over the pleasant rolling green fields
of Kelvinside and Pollokshields. The wealthy industrialists—and
there were many—salved their consciences by a rigorous attention
to narrow religious duties; by the execution of "good works",
sometimes carried out with a passionate sentimentalism suggesting
the existence of a secret guilt complex; and—occasionally—by
purchasing pictures of Highland cattle standing in the middle
of purple-girt burns, or of misty crofts and lone shielings; pictures
which perhaps went some way towards "squaring" that never
quite extinguished Celtic romanticism.

The old fervour of the South-West can be traced not only in
the frequency of the labour agitations which troubled Clydeside
throughout the century, but in the almost diabolical intensity

with which industrialists threw themselves into their single-minded task of making money. The sturdy Scots creed of individualism chimed happily with the Victorian conception of business ethics—the inviolable right of a middle-class man to "improve" his position and "get on in the world"; to work hard, and to send the hindmost—represented by what used to be called "the submerged tenth" of the population—without a single thought to the De'il, for whose tender mercies God had probably designed them anyway. Those who, three centuries before, would have devoted their passion to supporting their religion and, earlier still, to defending the freedom of their land, now found a more "civilized" outlet for their life's-blood.

Mid-Victorian industrial Glasgow had the vices and the virtues of many another major industrial city of Europe. But it contrived to retain its own dour, dark quality, a subtle blend of the dominating Celticism of its people, and that Knoxian Calvinism which the Reformed Church had stamped upon the native temperament. The dourness and the darkness tended to make the vices and the virtues more determined and more terrible in their respective intensities.

Horrible as is the contemplation of the social conditions of the majority of Glasgow's citizens before the 1860's, we should not overlook the extent of later Scottish Victorian achievement. For, during the last forty years of the nineteenth century, the modern civic conscience began to evolve. The scheme whereby Glasgow citizens receive their water from Loch Katrine—so pure that it does not even require to be filtered—was completed in 1855, after several years of Parliamentary opposition. Previously, Glasgow had drawn its water from the Clyde; and, although the Clyde was a salmon river up till the middle of the eighteenth century, a hundred years later it had become a stinking open sewer. (People still alive, and not so very old either, can remember the aroma which came off the river until the erection of the sewage farm in 1894.) In 1863, the City's first Free Hospital was built. A Medical Officer responsible for the Public Health was appointed in 1865, and the first Sanitary Inspector in 1870. Twenty years later, it became an offence to fail to report infectious diseases. At least, these were energetic steps in the right direction.

In marked contrast to the dandified gaiety of the later eighteenth century, the climate of the City's recreational and intellectual life throughout the earlier part of the nineteenth century had been cold and austere, at least among the better-off. The poorer people

24

took to drink—what we now call "hooch", or doctored spirits, being the favourite health-ruining bree—and fornication. The illegitimacy rate for the South-West of Scotland became the highest in the country. Who can blame them? Drinking and fornication are still the poor man's most accessible solaces. In any case, the pleasures of the bed were also widely enjoyed by the "upper classes", sanctified by the terrifying Bible-weighted bonds of Scottish Victorian matrimony. In an age when the bearing of a child had to be accomplished without the help of pain-relieving aids—labour pains were intended by God for the just chastisement of the female sex, according to the Knoxian Calvinist creed—and each confinement held the very real shadow of death over the mother, the Glasgow paterfamilias begat himself from ten to twenty children, most of whom died before maturity.

In the realms of culture, painting fared best. There are a number of possible reasons why this should have been so. The Scot is, I think, in the psychologist's jargon, predominantly a visile. On the whole, it is probably true to say that visual stimulants have affected his attitude to the arts more than any other. The epic grandeur of his Highland scenery, the kaleidoscopic colour-chording of the northern light effects, and the tempered roundness of the Lowland vistas all combine to make him so. Traditionally, the Celts have always been fascinated by colour and the interplay of pattern. In the arts of the Lowlander, this visual concentration has shown itself in the prominence given to nature by even the earliest recorded Scottish poets; in the passion for description which has affected most Lowland novelists; and in the strong appeal to the visual behind so much of the fulminating seventeenth- and eighteenth-century verbiage which passes for Scottish theology.

During the latter part of the nineteenth century, the wealthier industrialists could afford to sit back and take stock—perhaps even cultivate the accepted graces. After all, two or three dozen wealthy regular picture-buyers can provide quite a steady market for a group of artists. That market grew up and was nourished on the romantic landscapes of Horatio McCulloch (1805-67), John Milne Donald (1819-66), James Docharty (1829-78) and others. Later, the products of the more famous Glasgow School, who specialized in light effects, found their way into many a heavy brown parlour, and many an ornamented drawing-room.

Why, then, is so much of Glasgow's Victorian architecture tasteless and vulgar? Partly because the expanding rate of building left folk with little enough time to reflect before they turned first thoughts into permanent shape; partly also because the industrialists' architects confused grandeur, to which they thought their patrons were entitled, with mere ostentation. There was also a strong desire to recapture in stone the glory that was Greece, the grandeur that was Rome. So banks were built to look like Grecian temples, their creators overlooking the fact that the Greeks put up their buildings with a keen sense of their fitness for the function they were to perform.

In literature, Glasgow could not claim much distinction. The bookshop of David Robertson, at the foot of Glassford Street, snuggered the "Whistlebinkie" school into existence. A "whistle-binkie" was one who attended a penny wedding—Sir David Wilkie recorded on a famous canvas one of these weddings where the guests paid for their own entertainment—without contributing anything. He had therefore no right to a share in the festivities, although he could have a "bink" or "bench" by himself, and whistle for his own amusement. The name became attached to Robertson's group of writers because of the small-beer topics about which they usually wrote, and the fireside nature of their sentimentality. Its most famous representative, William Miller (1810-72), introduced to the world "Wee Willie Winkie". The Radical poet, Alexander Rodger (1784-1846), made at least one strange (and highly successful) bid to find favour with "upper class" sentiment in the matter of sex-relationship when he advised his fellows, through the mouth of a rather prudish maid, to "Behave yoursel' before folk".

Glasgow was for a time the home of John Gibson Lockhart and of Joanna Baillie (1762-1851), whose romantic verse-plays in English won her the friendship of Scott, though we now prefer to remember her for such lyrics as "Saw ye Johnnie Comin'?" As the century wore on, there were a number of writers like Robert Buchanan (1841-1901)[1] who associated themselves with English literature, moving to London to sink beneath the native English surge without leaving behind anything even half so creditable as "The Ballad of Judas Iscariot". Thomas Campbell (1777-1844), son of one of the Virginian tobacco lords, was a Glasgow man who twice became Lord Rector of Glasgow University, though his reputation rests mainly on "Ye Mariners of England". "The Pleasures of Hope", the long poem which first won him fame, is now forgotten, although we still remember that "'tis distance lends enchantment to the view". William Motherwell (1797-

---

[1] His famous attacks on Rossetti—*The Fleshly School of Poetry*, 1871—and Kipling—*The Voice of the Hooligan*, 1899—show up the blustering shallowness of his nature. He repented of them both before he died.

*Glasgow: The University, with the River Kelvin in the foreground*

1835) achieved some fame with his touching ballad "Jeannie Morrison", though, unfortunately, its pathos is just over-ripe enough to cause the modern reader embarrassment.

The true nineteenth-century laureate of Glasgow, however, was Alexander Smith (1829-67), the son of a Kilmarnock pattern-designer. In 1857, *A Life Drama and Other Poems* was published; its appearance resulted in the young poet being lionized and hailed as the greatest literary genius of the age. This he quite certainly was not. But neither did he deserve the subsequent revulsion of feeling which set in against him, stimulated by the gibes and parodies of that historical ballad-pasticher, Professor William Aytoun. His critics found his style "spasmodical", which indeed it was. But their horror of his "sensuous" imagery encouraged the poet to purge his later verse of all true sap. After holding the then poorly paid appointment of Secretary to the University of Edinburgh, Smith died, at the age of 37, of typhoid and diphtheria contracted as a result of overwork. He left us one of the most touching of Victorian elegies on lost love, "Barbara" (he himself had married Flora Macdonald, who outlived him, a descendant of the Jacobite heroine); the most vivid poem on Glasgow yet written; and *A Summer in Skye*, which ranks with Boswell's *Tour of the Hebrides* and Moray McLaren's *Return to Scotland* as one of the three best Scottish travel books ever published.[1] Smith's luminous descriptions of the contrast provided by the old and new towns of Edinburgh, his pages on Loch Coruisk so admirably captivating the pre-human atmosphere of that gloomy place, and his account of his voyage in the MacBrayne paddle-steamer *Chevalier* from Skye to Greenock in the autumn of 1853, are amongst the best things in a piece of word-painting which has become a frequently reprinted minor Scottish classic.

Smith knew intimately "the tragic heart of towns", especially the heart of mid-Victorian Glasgow:

> "City! I am true son of thine;
> Ne'er dwelt I where great mornings shine
> Around the bleating pens;
> Ne'er by the rivulets I strayed
> And ne'er upon my childhood weighed
> The silence of the glens.
> Instead of shores where ocean beats,
> I hear the ebb and flow of streets.

[1] Since writing this, Ivor Brown's *Summer in Scotland* has appeared, and deserves to rank as a fourth.

*Glasgow: The Cathedral, with the Royal Infirmary in the background*

Black Labour draws his weary waves,
Into their secret-moaning caves;
    But with the morning light,
That sea again will overflow
With a long weary sound of woe,
    Again to faint in night.
Wave am I in that sea of woes,
Which, night and morning, ebbs and flows. . . .

Draw thy fierce streams of blinding ore,
Smite on a thousand anvils, roar
    Down to the harbour-bars;
Smoulder in smoky sunsets, flare
On rainy nights, when street and square
    Lie empty to the stars.
From terrace proud to alley base
I know thee as my mother's face.

When sunset bathes thee in his gold,
In wreaths of bronze thy sides are rolled,
    Thy smoke is dusky fire;
And, from the glory round thee poured,
A sunbeam like an angel's sword
    Shivers upon a spire.
Thus have I watched thee, Terror! Dream!
While the blue night crept the stream.

The wild train plunges in the hills,
He shrieks across the midnight rills;
    Streams through the shifting glare,
The roar and flap of foundry fires,
That shake with light the sleeping shires;
    And on the moorlands bare,
He sees afar a crown of light
Hang o'er thee in the hollow night.

At midnight, when thy suburbs lie
As silent as a noonday sky,
    When larks with heat are mute,
I love to linger on thy bridge,
All lonely as a mountain ridge,
    Disturbed but by my foot;
While the black lazy stream beneath
Steals from its far-off wilds of heath.

*And through thy heart, as through a dream,*
*Flows on that black disdainful stream;*
*All scornfully it flows,*
*Between the huddled gloom of masts,*
*Silent as pines unvexed by blasts—*
*'Tween lamps in streaming rows.*
*O wondrous sight! O stream of dread!*
*O long dark river of the dead! . . ."*

V

So far, I have been mainly concerned with Glasgow down the changing centuries—Glasgow seen through the eyes of long-dead contemporaries. But I was born and brought up in Glasgow, and, although I no longer live there, I cannot regard it entirely objectively.

Two clear picture-sequences of Glasgow, no doubt photographed by my mind in childhood or adolescence, as all our strongest images and impressions are, come back to me whenever I let loose my feelings about the place.• One shows a cruel scene set in the runt-end of a squalid street, beside the shut gates of a yard. Overhead loom the rusting ribs of a ship upon which work has been suspended; a macabre, skeleton presence dominating the grey, late-afternoon atmosphere.

Suddenly a clamour breaks out behind the closed outer-door of a public-house. It jerks open, spewing out two youths battering at each other's face. A sickening blow, a gasp and one of them crumples on the muddy pavement, a red streak trickling over the shabby glaze of his jacket. The other youth looks contemptuously at the inert body, spits on its face, glances furtively about him, then disappears at a loutish slouch down an evil-smelling close mouth.

The second scene has about it the suffused texture of a Corot landscape, though the features are those of a cityscape seen from the crest of a granite bridge, the blurring caused not by country mists but by the hanging fog of a hundred smoky stacks. The muddy waters of the Clyde catch the last thin glow of a weakened late-autumn sun, so that the rippling, scum-coated surface looks as if it carries a gigantic strip of orange peel amongst the oily, floating garbage. A smart-looking modern ship towers above the parapet, making bridge and quayside seem brittle, toy-like restrictions holding back its swift sea-lapping liberty. Idly it nods its sturdy bow and dips its squat and powerful stern. Alongside the opposite quay, an older, blacker ship lists heavily to starboard as a scooping crane swings out over a waiting lorry. Farther down the river, two chugging ferries fuss past each other in mid-stream, carrying tired and dirty workers from the silent shipyards to the trams and buses which wait to take them on the last lap of their nightly journey home. Beyond, like a vast wood stripped bare for winter, spires and funnels stretch close-shouldered as far as the eye can follow. Across the bridge, tramcars rock and squeal on their rails, and a heavy lorry sends a deep throb pulsing to the bridge's very foundations. Steady lines of well-sprung cars swish away the better-off folk to the genteel suburbs of the west and south. Horse-drawn lorries and snub-nosed mechanical horses shunt backwards down narrow, iron-tracked warehouse lanes, amidst a mixture of hoof-clops, guttural oaths and whirring engine sounds. All the huge strength of a great city, a strength that has gone on expanding for more than two hundred years, is coming slowly to rest. The mysterious power turns to a standstill; the rich production ceases.

It has been a consistent feature of the Capitalist system that, since the advent of the Industrial Revolution, industry has been subjected to cyclic fits of trade depression every ten years or so. Economists have their blueprints nowadays for curing this disastrous phenomenon, which makes a hellish drawn-out uncertainty the lot of the poor folk solely dependent on the weekly pay-packets: so it may well be that Glasgow need never again experience these slumps in all their appalling severity.

The world slump of the early 1930's struck Glasgow and Clydeside with savage ferocity. The sturdy Victorian crescent in which I lived looked out upon a pleasant garden fringed by cherry-trees, laburnums and one pink chestnut. At each full shout of spring, the cherry-trees became flecked with sour-sweet foam; the laburnums dripped their glory of gold in a bright ecstasy of growing; and the single chestnut lit up its pale pink candles in breath-taking profusion. Behind our house ran the reversed curve of another lower-lying terrace. And over the back gardens and roofs of these lower houses, the great beaks of the riverside cranes could be seen dipping and straightening, dipping and straightening, as they picked up iron beams like bits of straw. Then one day the great beaks ceased to dip.

I was too young to understand the full implications of those troubled ten years, and, by good fortune none of my doing, I was spared the least touch of their cruel privations. But you cannot live in a city which shelters in its bug-infested, airless slums, more than 126,000 unemployed, rotting away their hopeless days on a level far below that of decent minimum subsistence, and be unaware that something unspeakably horrible is happening about you. You cannot keep up a polite pretence; not, at any rate unless your sensibilities have been singularly blunted.

The curious thing was that the sensibilities of many Glasgow people did become blunt at that time—extra blunt, perhaps I should say, for Glasgow perceptions have never been noticeably sharp—as a means of protection from the indignity of it all. I remember hearing people say, in connection with the long, straggling hunger marches that motorists sometimes encountered when returning from a Sunday afternoon "spin", "After all, they needn't starve. They've got the dole," or "What's the use of marching about like that? Far better go and *do* something." Do what?, I sometimes wondered. Do *what* with a permanently empty stomach, and a deadened, hopeless heart? A little Foreign Mission collecting perhaps? Or an extra-mural course on the glories of English literature?

In such a climate of bleak despair, is it surprising that so many of the ardent people of Glasgow and Clydeside should have gone "Red"; should have fallen an easy prey to the promise of work and plenty which the Communist creed holds out, masking those clauses that make the suppression of the workers' liberties essential if the "great end" allegedly in view is to be reached?

Since the Second World War, it has at least become clear to our rulers that Communism thrives on physical misery and despair, since these things experienced in extreme, as they were in Glasgow during the slump years, make personal liberty seem a worthless bauble, a small price to pay for the satisfaction of life's elementary physical needs.

In these post Second World War years, the heavy industries around Glasgow have been working more or less to capacity repairing war-time destruction, and fulfilling Scotland's share of that rearmament which should raise the price of war to a level at which no would-be aggressor should in future be willing to contemplate paying. But many of the nations which once bought heavy machinery and locomotives from Glasgow now make and build their own. Glasgow has still a dangerous unbalance, in favour of her heavy industries, for either her own well-being or the economy of Scotland to be sound and stable under more normal conditions. The "Red" spectre of the '30's has certainly been appeased for the time being; but it is by no means finally laid.

The second mind-picture of mine, of the corporate life of the City as a huge impersonal machine transcending even the greatest, of its citizens, is not really capitulation to facile romanticism. For there *is* a kind of glory about the enormous industrial achievements of this place. Its ships are amongst the finest and the loveliest that do business in any waters, and its men and women have justifiable pride in the skill and cunning of the craftsmen who for so many generations have fashioned them.

For a stranger to discover that there are other more particular aspects of Glasgow, it is only necessary for him to walk about its streets. Since the late eighteenth century, Argyle Street has been metamorphosed from one of the finest streets in Europe, to one of the ugliest and most populous. At· its East end, those bits and pieces of the past like the Tron steeple, lend it a brief pretence of dignity. But, as it makes its way westward, all such pretence vanishes. The plate-glassed multiple stores and the densely packed shops with their bargain offers and their garish window-lighting, make it a magnet for the crowds, especially on Saturday afternoons, when a broad throng jostles along its pavements, spilling over the road and slowing up the harassed crawl of the traffic. In the early years of this century, Argyle Street earned itself a reputation for drunken rowdiness, especially round about "closing time". On a Friday night, it is still impossible to go down a central Glasgow street without coming upon little knots of roaring drunks staggering round corners in unsteady twos and threes. Glaswegians bring their Celtic fervour to bear even on their drinking. I do not mean to suggest, with those so-called Temperance bodies whose intolerant and inaccurate self-righteousness reveals a fundamental immaturity of character and belies their name, that more people get drunk in Glasgow than in any other city of comparable size. It is the quality of the drunkenness rather than its quantity that is so remarkable; and the quality results in no small degree from the Scots practice of following a pint of beer with a "chaser", or "wee hauf" of whisky.

In the warm, steady glow of Glasgow's pubs, Will Fyfe's "common auld workin' man" may be found at week-ends drowning the sorrows of his team or celebrating their triumph in the weekly process of proving that Glasgow belongs to him—as indeed it properly does! But Buchanan Street, with its expensive shops; bustling Renfield Street and Sauchiehall Street; these three main shopping haunts of the middle classes, have to be seen between Monday and Friday for their characteristic atmosphere to be savoured.

Buchanan Street, which had its origin in the 1770's, and still looks faintly pseudo-classical above street level, attracts many of the wealthier shoppers; and, although it does not carry tramcars, is frequently the scene of some of the City's worst traffic jams. Glasgow is notoriously ill-equipped with car-parks, and the unfortunate motorist from outside the city often finds that he has no alternative but to brave the wrath of the police and leave his car wherever he can find a few vacant kerbside feet. On the whole, the Glasgow police are fairly tolerant over this issue, but, unlike the Edinburgh police, who paste several warnings on an offender's windscreen before they finally prosecute him, the Glasgow police ignore such little civilities and prosecute without delay whoever may be caught up in their periodic swoops. The good folk of Edinburgh allege sometimes that the fines of motorists add so substantially to the civic revenue of the rival city that, true to commercial tradition, the Glasgow police would regard the Capital's system of warning tags as just plain bad business!

The population of Glasgow is made up of what our ancestors used to call, and what the West-end *rentier* still do call, "the working classes" and the "middle classes". There are no "upperclass" Glaswegians. It has long been unfashionable to be "upper class" in Glasgow, and those who feel they belong to such a select category buy mansions or estates outwith the city boundary, and view the busy scene from a respectable, countrified distance.

I have never been able to understand the precise intricacies of this Victorian business of class distinction, which in Glasgow at any rate has persisted with extraordinary force. But in the big warehouses and in the olde-worlde whimsical tea-shops (so out of keeping with the homely traditions of Miss Cranston, who commissioned no less an architect than Charles Rennie Mackintosh to design some of them for her; or James Craig, who covered the walls of his premises with the pictures of contemporary Scottish artists), the "upper middle classes" may loudly be seen and heard.

They are, in their own view at any rate, these wives of Glasgow's many successful business and professional men, the bastions of civilization. They are also the unconscious heritors of a lively series of national prejudices which they were taught by their mothers and grandmothers never to question. Thus, one frequently hears dark whispers about the "Catholic" menace (whatever that may be): or uncharitable remarks about the Irish "element" (without whose labour much of the City's dirtiest work would probably have remained undone): or snappy little squirts of anti-Jewish venom that would do credit to the ghost of Hitler. Terrible stories of "working-class" women recklessly buying expensive delicacies which they, the virtuous tellers, could never dream of affording, are exchanged over prim cakestands; and bitter complaint is made that good, middle-class rate-money is being recklessly spent by the Corporation in providing city school-children with their daily health-giving pint of milk.

Yet one must not be too hard on these people. They may occasionally be found a little wanting when there is some question of the milk of human kindness being shared outwith their own little family groups. But rancours of an equally blind and stupid breed penetrate the aroma of "thick black", stale booze and human sweat in many a swing-doored pub. And do not brutish gang-fights and razor-slashings still break out, often ostensibly over matters of religion? Were it not for the support of the more enlightened "middle-class" minority, Glasgow could not even boast the culture she does, since, so far, every attempt to elevate the majority of the "working classes" to an appreciation of the finer arts has merely resulted in the reduction of the artist's vision to the spit-and-sawdust, workers-break-your-bonds level of Communistic propaganda. The arts, of course, are by no means the only, or even the principal ingredients of full living. One can still be a tolerable artist, and yet a poorish human specimen. And there are many Glasgow folk of all "classes" who have an abundance of those kindly qualities which once led a very young poet to call the city, rather Apocalyptically, "warm heart of Scotland with the generous hand"!

There may, indeed, be some who will think that I have over-stressed the sootier and snootier aspects of Glasgow's story at the expense of her virtues and achievements. Did she not organize in 1888, 1901, 1911 and in 1938, four great exhibitions which drew people from Europe and even the Americas? What about the art collection in her, admittedly architecturally comic though singularly well-conducted, Art Galleries? Is not that innate cultural zeal which, twice in the nineteenth century, led her to organize Music Festivals, gave her thereafter a host of flourishing choral societies of which the Glasgow Orpheus Choir was the most famous,[1] and has enabled her since to sustain a major part in supporting the Scottish National Orchestra, worthy of mention? Did she not give Charles Rennie Mackintosh his first major British opportunity when she invited him to build the Glasgow School of Art? Since Glasgow, with its Gaelic-speaking population of over 20,000, houses a larger concentration of Gaels than any-

[1] The Orpheus Choir, founded in 1901 and disbanded in 1951 by Sir Hugh Roberton, specialized in small-scale precision, and in the practice of pure "choralism". At first, it did something to improve standards of choral singing in Scotland. However, as it became more and more an instrument for the performance of the sentimentalized folk-arrangements and sugary tusheries of its conductor, its influence changed for the worse. At the finish, it could be said to have brought a blight on Scottish choral singing which it may take many vigorous years to throw off.

where else in Scotland, is nothing to be said about her position as *de facto* capital of the Highlands? And are her tramcars not the best in the world?

All these things, very possibly, are true. But, after all, other places have better orchestras, and finer collections of pictures; one major commission to the finest Scottish architect of the twentieth century does not make up for long years of subsequent neglect; many of Glasgow's Gaels now live reluctantly in the megalopolis as the only alternative to starving in the Highlands; and tramcars do not constitute an important part of civilization.

Glasgow's achievement is this: through the vision, the greed, and the sheer determination of her leading citizens, she overcame the powerful lethargic element of her Celtic make-up; and, blending her Celtic ardour with her Southern practicality, she made herself into one of the greatest centres of industry in the world of the nineteenth century. Her tragedy lies in the fact that the old imperialistic world of under-developed colonies, on whose markets she depended, has gone for ever, leaving her heavy industries inevitably doomed to slow contraction and decline; and that the unscrupulous pace of her industrial ascendancy has left behind a track of spiritual and physical desolation which it will take many future generations to repair.

I have written at some length about Glasgow because, although it is not by any means representative of Scotland as a whole, it is still the most vigorous and vital part of it. If I have seemed over-critical about this city of my birth, my severity has sprung from a desire not to allow natural love betray me into sentimental leniency. Whatever may have been its past failings and its aesthetic shortcomings, Glasgow in the middle of the twentieth century is colourfully, pulsatingly alive. Whatever the future may hold for Scotland in the way of domestic self-government, Glasgow will certainly have a major rôle to play. For while Edinburgh may legally be the capital of Scotland, and the seat of its present London-delegated administration, Glasgow for all practical purposes is still the nation's purse. And, as every true Glaswegian knows, money talks.

CHAPTER II

THE FIRTH OF CLYDE
AND ITS ISLANDS

*" My blood, sweet Clyde, claims interest in thy works,*
*Thou in my birth, I in thy vap'rous beams:*
*Thy breadth surmounts the Tweed, the Tay, the Forth;*
*In pleasure thou excell'st, in glistening streams. . . ."*
WILLIAM LITHGOW, 1617.

I

GLASGOW has one great advantage over every other major
industrial city in the British Isles. It lies within an hour's journey
of one of the loveliest natural " playgrounds " in the world—the
Firth of Clyde. An ancient mapmaker, Gordon of Straloch, gave
the open reaches of the river this pleasant-sounding name in 1653,
preferring it to the older nomenclature, Dunbryton (Dumbarton)
Fyrth, and thus early removing any parochial claims on its loveliness. Within the last century and a half, Glaswegians have
" appropriated " the coastlines and islands of the estuary, totally
changing their character. It seems proper, therefore, to treat this
holiday " extension " of Glasgow on its own, rather than with
those counties to which the various stretches belong.

Since the *Comet* made its first voyage, watched with curiosity
by orthodox sailors who prophesied its doom and praised the Lord
that they were propelled by the " Almighty's ain wind and no by
the deevil's sunfire and brimstone ", the Clyde has nurtured a long
succession of steamboat experiments and discoveries that have
made her name famous wherever there is talk of ships. Quite
rightly, her shipbuilders have lavished a minor part of their
talents in providing a fleet of river-steamers which, until British
Railways took it over, was one of the finest of its kind in the
world.

The development of the lower reaches of the Firth was a direct
result of the foresight of the *Comet*'s owner, Henry Bell (1767-
1830), who had been trained in a Bo'ness shipyard and a London
engineering firm, before, in 1807, he settled at Helensburgh to
study mechanics and look after a hotel. Within a year of the
*Comet*'s voyage, and her subsequent passenger voyages between

Glasgow and Greenock and Helensburgh ("the terms are for the present fixed at 4/- for the best cabin and 3/- for the second . . .") a rival, the *Elizabeth*, had taken the waters. By the summer of 1814, no fewer than nine steamers were competing for custom.

Holidays at the coast had occasionally been undertaken before the days of steam by wealthier folk who would now, perhaps, tour Europe by car. A Glasgow business man, Robert Reid (1773-1865), who wrote under the pen-name of "Senex", has left an account of three such trips to the coast which he made as a boy between 1778 and 1782. His voyage to Dunoon was undertaken in 1779. The family hired a wherry, having first made elaborate arrangements to keep themselves in food throughout the summer, since they could put "no dependance on getting provisions, not even fish, in such an out of the way place".

Dunoon, "Senex" tells us, was then considered by Glasgow folk to be "a Highland wilderness", though it was, in fact, a pleasant little Gaelic-speaking clachan built round the remains of its ancient castle. When the great day of departure came, the Reid family "had a pretty fair passage down the river till the tide met us at Dunglass; our progress now became slow, and a little below Dumbarton Castle, we fairly stuck fast upon a sandbank. Here we remained for several hours till the tide flowed, when we again got under sail. We did not touch at Gourock, but bore right on to Dunoon, where we arrived the same evening."

The Reids were at least luckier than another Glasgow gentleman who, as late as 1817, eschewing the dangerous, new-fangled steamboats, hired a "fly" (a fast, shallow-draught sailing-wherry) to take his family and himself to Gourock for summer quarters. With them, "all the first day was occupied in making the passage to Bowling Bay, where we cast anchor for the night: weighing anchor next morning, we proceeded down the Clyde, but were so buffeted by wind and waves that, after spending the whole day at sea, we were compelled to return to Bowling Bay. The third day, we succeeded in making Port Glasgow in the afternoon"; suffering, no doubt, from *mal de mer*, for they "abandoned the fly, hired post-horses, and so reached Gourock", the whole affair having cost the gentleman ("wet, sick and exhausted") seven pounds fourteen shillings and threepence. He really would have been much wiser to trust himself and his family to the excellent new steamer *Marion*, which would only have taken about four hours to do the journey, and cost him a matter of shillings.

While the Reids and a few other intrepid Glasgow families were

37

venturing thus far abroad, the poorer folk were holiday-making nearer home.   Some, indeed, never got farther than the jollities of the Glasgow Fair, held during the second fortnight of July; jollities which finally became so hearty, it seems, that the Fair had to be suppressed.   Some went inland to Cambuslang, or Strathaven.   Others, content perhaps with occasional day trips, favoured Partick, a former episcopal residence, though at the end of the eighteenth century more famous for its "crumpie cake and cheese"; or Govan, another pleasant village celebrated for its Sunday salmon suppers.   Both these villages were swept away in the expansion of the shipbuilding industry which followed the successful development of the steamship, and, like so many other once proud separate communities—Gorbals, Calton, Hillhead, Pollokshields, Maryhill, to name only a few—they were caught up in the expanding meshes of the Glasgow megalopolis.

So Victorian Glasgow developed a taste for holidays "doon the watter", the more so since the Cowal coast and the islands of Bute and Cumbrae were being opened up by builders.   In 1822, for instance, a Glasgow merchant prince took the first large feu at Dunoon, on the west side of the Castle.   There he built himself a mansion.[1]   Other merchants followed his example, and the High-land clachan soon became a little township of "villas" occupied mainly during the summer months.   Strone, Blairmore, Kirn and Innellan all grew suddenly from clachans to sizeable villages dotted about the shores of the Firth.   At the height of their glory, these stucco "villas", many of them large houses with coachman's quarters attached, must have looked quite impressive, invested as they were with the slow and prosperous air of Victorian suburbia.   Now, their leisured dignity has long since departed. Many of them are panelled off into rooms or flatlets.   Others are in a damp and peeling state of disrepair.

The merchant princes, having established their "places" at the coast, created a demand for faster and more comfortable steamers.   Until the second half of the century, so rapid was the development of the steamship, and so keen the competition between owners, many of them skippers of the "paddlers" them-selves, that within a very few years a fine new ship could be rendered obsolete, and therefore unpopular, by a new rival vessel.

During the 1850's, the issue became one of speed versus com-fort.   For a time, speed won.   The Clyde steamers of Alexander Smith's day were mostly lean, rakish affairs, designed to paddle themselves over the Firth with the minimum water resistance,

---

[1] It is now a Public Library.

their decks as free as possible of any luxury structures which might act as impediments in the face of a wind. And, of course, this interest in speed led inevitably to the practice of steamer racing.

The most famous of all the Clyde races took place on the 27th of May 1861. Two new vessels, the *Ruby* and the *Rothesay Castle*, owned by rival companies, were both scheduled to leave Glasgow at 4 p.m., bound for Greenock and Rothesay. The new and serious challenge of the railways, which, by leading railheads to Greenock and, later, Craigendoran, Gourock and Wemyss Bay, shortened the journey to the coast for the busy gentry who travelled daily to and from the city, was being met with one final fling by the " all the way" steamers.

Andrew MacQueen, one of the historians of the Clyde fleet, has given us this account of the contest. " It had been arranged that the steamers were to change berths at the Broomielaw on alternative days, and on Monday, 27th May, the advantage fell to the *Rothesay Castle*. Right well she availed herself of it, for, having the lead, she kept it, travelling as never steamer had travelled on the river before. At twenty minutes past five, the spectators on the Custom House Quay at Greenock saw her race past, with the *Ruby* in close attendance. Keeping up the pace, the *Rothesay Castle* finished at Rothesay Quay two and a half minutes ahead of her rival, having covered the distance in two hours twenty-eight minutes. The feat was suitably recognized, the awards being made the following Monday by Bailie Raeburn at the River-Bailie Court, where Captain Brown of the *Rothesay Castle* was fined a guinea for reckless navigation and Captain Price of the *Ruby*, in view of the reputation he had acquired for similar exploits, double the amount!

Price of the *Ruby* was not so easily cured of his passion for speed, however. A few months later, he ran a neck-and-neck race with another steamer, the *Neptune*, colliding with her twice, and missing out Gourock, where he should have called, in order to maintain his lead. The *Glasgow Herald* of the day asked in sententious tones: " What right has this man, Price, to entrap people into his vessel for a safe summer-day sail and then subject them to the terror of a violent death by explosion or collision? "

No right at all, of course. Shortly afterwards, Price lost his command, and racing, as it was known in the bad, dangerous days, gradually came to an end. Until the beginning of the Second World War, however, it was still not uncommon to find two steamers belonging to rival companies racing, with genteel regard for safety and river decorum, for the same pier. Now, alas, there are hardly enough steamers left in the Clyde fleet for two ever to be sailing in the same direction at once! [1]

However, the loveliness of the Firth of Clyde is not affected by the manner in which people cross its surface. On the north bank, the scenery is unmistakably Highland. The hills of "dreaming Cowal" sweep back in a blue haze to the rugged peaks of Argyll. Yet the curves and contours of the south bank are just as markedly Lowland, so rich are the fertile fringes of Renfrewshire and Ayrshire rolling gently away from the river.

To get properly acquainted with the Firth of Clyde, it is necessary to sail down to it from the Broomielaw. It is not enough to arrive at Greenock or Glasgow on an incoming liner or on the Irish boat. For one thing, these deep-water vessels hold too far out from the coast in the lower reaches; for another, they usually arrange to arrive, in obedience either to the state of the tide, or to some mystic ritual which I have never been able to fathom, in the "wee sma' hours", when hardly as much as a glimmering shore-light is visible.

No matter how often the voyage "doon the watter" is made, it retains its power to delight both eye and mind; first, with the variety of the spectacle sliding back along the river banks; second, with that sudden exhilaration which the sight and smell of the opening Firth raises up in most normal hearts. Here, scarcely twenty miles from busy, commercial Glasgow, the land of the Gaels with all its romance and ancient history, comes sweeping down to front the doucer Lowlands across the dancing waters of the Clyde.

Just over a hundred years ago, Alexander Smith described the journey in verse:

> " *The steamer left the black and oozy wharves,*
> *And floated down between dank ranks of masts.*
> *We heard the swarming streets, the noisy mills;*
> *Saw sooty founderies full of glare and gloom,*
> *Great bellied chimneys tipped by tongues of flame,*
> *Quiver in smoky heat. We slowly passed*
> *Loud building-yards, where every slip contained*
> *A mighty vessel with a hundred men*
> *Battering its iron sides. . . .*

[1] One must not be too hard on British Railways, though their autocratic methods and bad publicity cause much resentment among Clyde folk, who take a great interest in their steamers. Since the Second World War, costs have so increased that sailing has become a dear pastime. Many Glasgow workers, getting longer holidays with more pay, now seem to prefer Dublin or London to their former haunts on the Clyde.

> *. . . At length the stream*
> *Broadened 'tween banks of daisies, and afar*
> *The shadows flew upon the sunny hills;*
> *And down the river, 'gainst the pale blue sky*
> *A town sat in its smoke. . . .*
>
> *. . . We reached the pier*
> *Where girls in fluttering dresses, shady hats,*
> *Smiled rosy welcome. An impatient roar*
> *Of hasty steam; from the broad paddle rushed*
> *A flood of pale grey foam, that hissed and wreathed*
> *Ere it subsided in the quiet sea.*
> *With a glad foot I leapt upon the shore,*
> *And, as I went, the frank and lavish winds*
> *Told me about the lilac's mass of bloom,*
> *The slim laburnum showering golden tears,*
> *The roses of the garden where they played. . . ."*

That is still a fairly accurate piece of reportage, even down to the floral description, for the climate at the coast is relatively frost-free and mild, and such foreign exotics as yuccas can be seen in many a garden, rather self-consciously absurd in their Scots surroundings, and perhaps a little less luxuriant than nature originally intended.

The finest vessel of the river fleet was undoubtedly David Mac-Brayne's Royal Mail paddle-steamer *Columba.* Built in 1878 by J. and G. Thomson of Clydebank, she made the journey between Glasgow and Ardrishaig—called the Royal Route, not out of tribute to its scenic magnificence, but because Queen Victoria once went over it—daily during the summer months, with very few interruptions, for fifty-eight years. For her period, she was a model of spacious comfort below deck; outwardly, she was remarkable for her pleasing combination of size and grace. Seven o'clock in the morning, and later, eleven minutes past seven, was the traditional hour for her to cast off her ropes at the Broomielaw. I made my first trip "doon the watter" in her a few years before she went the sad way of all old ships, and I can still vividly recall the excitement of that first experience.

We were to set out, I think, on the first day of July; mother and father, nurse, four children, dog, cat and goldfish. Although we could depend on being able to purchase rather more than could the Reids, nevertheless a great deal of luggage had to be taken. The packing was done systematically during the last days of June. I do not think I slept much on the night before the day of our departure.

It began early. We got up at five in the morning, and had breakfast half an hour later. For some reason, that breakfast had a special quality of its own. Its ingredients were those of many another breakfast eaten since—porridge, bread and butter, and a boiled egg—but I can still remember the extra flavour those comestibles seemed to acquire that morning. (No doubt it was in a similar mood of anticipation that the poet Southey generously praised the excellence of Scottish breakfasts while staying at Old Meldrum.)

After breakfast, we children were expected to keep out of the way of our elders, for a horse-drawn lorry arrived outside the house at six o'clock to cart the luggage down to the quay. I was given the job of guarding the cat while the luggage was being grunted and manœuvred round the bends of the staircase. The cat, a venerable beast who lived to be eighteen and would then be about twelve, had the idea that if he managed to escape while the front door stood open to let the carters move freely in and out, he would not have to undergo his annual holiday ordeal of transportation by basket; hence the need for one of the family to stand guard.

At last, the luggage had rumbled away, the cat had been safely basketed, and it was time to prepare ourselves for the arrival of the taxi. That taxi-drive itself was something of a novelty. Usually, I went to children's parties in a cab: a musty affair, upholstered in faded green, and driven by a red-nosed, mufflered coachman, whose characteristic smell was almost as strong as that of the horse that pulled the contraption.

Ordinary mortals who go about their affairs during the hours of daylight would do well to take an occasional ride through an industrial city at half-past six in the morning, if only to remind themselves how large a section of the community has to do "day labour, light denied" in order to keep essential public services running. The new sun shone out from a clean sky this July morning, glistening the roof-tops of the tenements, and lighting up even the drabbest side-street with the promise of a fair day.

The *Columba* lay on the south side of the river, her two red and black funnels setting off nobly her huge, gilded paddle-boxes. The moment you climbed up her gangway, your nostrils were assailed by a peculiar aroma that was all her own. After some years, I discovered that it was a mixture of heated engine oil, good galley cooking, and well-scrubbed cleanliness, to which, down the river, the scudding tang of salty spray was added. But, at that time, analysis did not matter. The smell was wholly entrancing.

*Glasgow: "Greek" Thomson's Great Western Terrace*

We were to establish ourselves in the cabin, or the "saloon" as it was more grandly called. The "saloon" consisted of a number of seated bays lined with dark red velvet plush, and richly draped with similar hangings. It gave an impression of well-established opulence and time-saturated sea-going. All went well at first. I carried the cat's basket down the companionway, and the cat remained obligingly silent. But at the entrance to the "saloon", a liveried steward looked at me and my burden with an unmistakable air of hostility.

"What's in that basket?" he demanded.

"Provisions," I answered, with a happier promptitude than I have displayed on many a more important occasion since. He grunted and let us past. We chose an empty bay, and comfortably dispersed our bits and pieces.

Those final moments of waiting seemed the most interminable of all. Above our heads, busy feet tapped out their walking patterns on the deck. In the orange glow of the engine-room, the great gleaming monsters hissed and sizzled quietly to themselves, as if anticipating the moment when the flicker of a dial and the loosening of a lever would send them plunging backward and forward in all their pride of power.

Seven o'clock! Five minutes past! And then the mishanter occurred. A long, thin stream of clear liquid suddenly raced down the floor. Its place of origin was unmistakably the basket at my feet.

In a moment the steward was at my side.

"Your provisions seem to be leaking, sir," he observed acidly. (That "sir", to one of my tender years, seemed an additional humiliation.) "You'd better take them on deck."

I was delighted. I certainly had no desire to spend my first voyage in the feminine confines of the cabin. Now, someone would *have* to stay on deck to see that the cat was not shipped prematurely ashore.

Up there, things were happening. The Captain, an impressive and recognizably Highland figure even beneath the disguising weight of his gold braid, was pacing his bridge, which straddled the ship from one paddle-box to the other between the two funnels. (It has always seemed strange to me that, until about 1920, it apparently never occurred to the designers of paddle-steamers that the funnel was a fairly major obstacle in the way of the helmsman's vision.) The Captain took one final look at his watch; then he pulled the clanging brass levers at his side. The paddles began to thresh the water, nosing the ship's bow out towards the centre of the river: with a couple of dirty splashes, the

*Glasgow: The New Skyscape*

ropes were tossed into the water, to be retrieved fussily by puffing steam capstans at bow and stern; and then the long, lean hull, shuddering a little at first, began to slide slowly forward.

Past close miles of shipyards, resounding with the racket of the riveters welding together the rusty hulks of the ships that would sail to-morrow's seas; past docks, full of towering ocean-going liners, and queer-looking tramp ships with foreign characters scrawled across their sterns; past grumphed-up, dirty old dredgers, squatting in the middle of the river, digging away the mud that forever strives to slip back into its ancient bed; past low-built hoppers carrying the mud far down the Firth to be dumped in the deeps around Ailsa Craig; past the chain-drawn car ferries at Renfrew and Erskine; past Bowling, with its stone-pencil monument to Henry Bell, and its huge oil port and depot cut back into the hills; past Greenock and Gourock, and over the broad Firth to Dunoon and Innellan.

The salt of the open sea blows in upon Innellan, and the mountainy freshness of the Highland hills creeps down on it from the North. These things I have noticed many times since. Twenty years ago, my joy was all at landing on a pier which stuck far out into the water. As I walked up that pier for the first time, I wondered what lay beyond the gates: Glasgow's Highland fringe to be sure. But it has come to mean so much to me that I must claim the luxury of a more lingering description.

II

The Clyde begins to open its arms as it stretches past Craigendoran and Port Glasgow. These two places really mark the point at which river becomes firth. The south side of the upper Firth has little enough to commend it scenically, except that its inhabitants look out on the north side, and so enjoy one of the finest vistas imaginable.

Port Glasgow is nowadays a sordid, down-at-heel little town. It was not always so. When the Glasgow merchants purchased twenty-two acres of land from Sir Patrick Maxwell in 1688 to build their port, it must have been a pleasant spot. Indeed, the fertile strip on the shore containing Newark Castle—still preserved as a shell, though now tightly hemmed in by industrial buildings and a shipyard—and its neat row of attendant cottages, aroused favourable comment from several eighteenth-century travellers. Port Glasgow got a good share of the American tobacco trade. It became the principal Customs-house port for the Clyde, an honour it retained until 1812; and, in 1762, it built the first graving-dock the river possessed.

But in due course, the inevitable happened. As soon as steam-driven, floating machinery made the dredging of the Clyde up to Glasgow feasible, Port Glasgow's importance declined. It did, however, retain for the first few decades of the nineteenth century a fairly extensive timber trade with America. The rotted stumps of the old timber ponds may still be seen sticking forlornly out of the mud at low tide, for some distance to the east of the town. Port Glasgow regained economic stability by taking to ship-building. Once Port Glasgow began to be industrialized, its visual ruin was assured. At the back of the narrow strip of coast-land, steep braes climb to the heights of Kilmacolm. So, there being no room for expansion outwards, the town developed upwards, and "lands" or tenements went up cheek by jowl. Whatever their virtues when spaciously laid out in larger towns, tenements are everywhere a disfigurement in places where nature unkindly heightens the contrast between her architecture and man's. From the Craigendoran shore, Port Glasgow, now joined to Greenock in fact, though not in administration, seems a sooty blur staining a pleasant stretch of the river.

Still, it can claim at least one intellectual distinction: for, on the 23rd of November 1824, it became the birthplace of James Thomson (" B.V.")—1834-82—author of that paean of pessimism, *The City of Dreadful Night*.

Greenock, which occupies the southern shore of the Firth for a further four miles or so from the boundary of Port Glasgow, has over-shadowed its rival neighbour. The surviving remains of Newark Castle, with charity and some little stretching of the imagination, could perhaps be said to preserve for Port Glasgow at least some outward semblance of a historical pedigree. Greenock has no such visual reminder of feud and foray to take the mind of her citizens further back than the middle years of the eighteenth century, when she suddenly became a busy port specializing in the herring trade. But Greenock's roots go deep none the less.

The son of the first Sir John Shaw, himself Sir John, and ancestor of the present family of Shaw Stewarts, founded the town's modern prosperity by beginning to build its first harbour just after 1707. (Part of that harbour survived, incidentally, until the present century.) The existence of the harbour led naturally to the development of a good fishing fleet, and this, in turn, resulted in the growth of a flourishing herring-curing and exporting business. Throughout the latter part of the century, indeed, the herring industry made its odoriferous presence known over stretches of the surrounding countryside. This was perhaps not quite such an unpleasant distinction as it would be to-day, when the herring trade usually has as its adjunct an offal factory for turning superfluous herring into such by-products as fish-manure.

Greenock also handled a considerable share of the Glasgow merchants' tobacco trade and, from about 1765, it became associated with the refining of West Indian sugar. But these trades declined (or died out altogether, as in the case of the herring industry, although a herring still features in the town's ancient motto) and shipbuilding and its associated concerns gradually absorbed the major attention of the Greenockians. They, too, had a bad time during the 'twenties and 'thirties of the present century and, economically, their position to-day is dangerous and insecure.

Attempts are being made to attract light industries to the towns and a promising beginning has been made. But grave perils attend all such industry-baiting schemes. If they were to result in young Scottish industrialists being encouraged to set up new concerns or in older Scottish firms being induced to expand Greenockwards, the benefits might be considerable. Unfortunately, that drive and initiative commonly supposed to be the distinguishing characteristic of Scottish business men since the eighteenth century, seems largely to have deserted them. Now-adays, they are constantly being outwitted and out-manœuvred by their English competitors. Far too many Scottish firms are content to " sell out " to rival English companies. Even if the Scottish " branches ", as such bought-over concerns often become, continue to operate for a time in much the same way as before, at the first hint of depression, the English parent firm naturally inflicts its cuts and curtailments on its more remote subsidiary company, rather than upon its own headquarters. This process used to be called " rationalization " in the between-the-wars period. One can see the rationale behind it, of course, but it only makes sense from a purely English viewpoint! The same threat of insecurity hangs over the heads of workers in branch factories of American concerns, though to a lesser degree, since American industrialists are usually reluctant to abandon their hard-won British footholds. Scotland can never become safely balanced economically merely by declining on a national scale the responsibilities of the founder-employer in favour of those of the casual hired employee.

It was from the wharf at Cartsdyke, a neighbouring hamlet now engulfed in the greater town, that several vessels concerned in the ill-fated Darien Expedition slipped their ropes one pleasant spring morning in 1696. Nineteen years later, an unwelcome visitor descended on the district while Sir John Shaw and his local warriors were absent attending to matters concerned with the first Jacobite rising. This visitor's object was the lifting of good fat Lowland cattle, and his name was Rob Roy. It was what we nowadays might call a combined operation, for "the cateran bold", having secured a goodly number of suitable beasts, ferried them across the Clyde and up the River Leven to Loch Lomond, in boats "borrowed" from the inhabitants of the Dumbarton shore; thereafter, he drove his capture north to Balquhidder on foot. It so happened that a small naval ship was lying off Greenock at this time; so, with a stiffening of her "regulars" to assist them, a band of Greenock citizens set out in pursuit. They recovered the boats.

Greenock's most illustrious citizen is, without a doubt, James Watt (1736-1819). The inventor of the steam-engine has given his name to all sorts of constructions in his native town, but the bield in which he first saw the light has long since been pulled down. This sad failure on the part of Greenockians to preserve the birthplace of their most famous son was discovered by none other than Samuel ("Self Help") Smiles, when he came north in search of information and "atmosphere" for his *Lives of Boulton and Watt*.[1]

Besides his inventions to improve the steam-engine, Watt's other achievements included the independent discovery of the composition of water, and the invention of copying ink.

Hamish MacCunn (1868-1916), the Scottish composer, was also a native of Greenock, the son of a local ship-owner. During his career, he conducted the Carl Rosa Opera Company (who commissioned and produced his best work, the opera *Jeanie Deans*, in 1894), and finally became Professor of Composition at the Guildhall School of Music in London. Unfortunately, his musical style alternated rather unhappily between a genuine Scottish lyricism and the Germanic influence strong in his day. He is still remembered by some of his racy and vigorous cantatas, like "Bonnie Kilmeny" and "The Lay of the Last Minstrel", which retain some of their old popularity amongst Scotland's amateur choral societies. The wider musical world knows him for his overture, "The Land of the Mountain and the Flood", composed when he was nineteen; and Greenock remembers that his boyhood and

---

[1] Boulton of Soho, eventually of New Birmingham, became Watt's English partner.

adolescence were spent there, and that he never quite forgot his home town, even in the days of his London success.

Greenock has been particularly prolific in literary men. The novelist John Galt (1779-1839), though actually born at Irvine, farther down the coast, made periodic trips to Greenock with his mother to meet his father's ship. In 1788, the family transferred to a new house at the north-west corner of West Blackhall Street and Westhouse Street, which still stands, bearing a commemorative plaque to remind us of its distinction. After the years of travel abroad, of trading and colonizing in Canada, of meeting the famous folk of his day, and of writing upwards of twenty books, four or five of which have become Scottish classics perpetuating vernacular speech and behaviour in the west before English influence made itself felt, he came back to Greenock, a broken man, to die.

Curious, is it not, that the two late nineteenth-century poets who stand out in British literature of the age as being most at war with themselves—James Thomson and John Davidson—both came out of the same airt? John Davidson (1857-1909) was actually born at Barrhead in Renfrewshire, the son of a severely sectarian Free Church minister. But his most impressionable years were spent at Greenock. He has left us a verse-picture of the town in his " Ballad of the Making of a Poet ":

> " . . . this grey town
> That pipes the morning up before the lark
> With shrieking steam, and from a hundred stalks
> Lacquers the sooty sky; where hammers clang
> On iron hulls, and cranes in harbours creak,
> Rattle and swing, whole cargoes on their necks;
> Where men sweat gold that others hoard or spend,
> And lurk like vermin in their narrow streets;
> This old grey town, this firth, this further strand
> Spangled with hamlets, and the wooded steeps,
> Whose rocky tops behind each other press,
> Fantastically carved like antique he!ms
> High-hung in heaven's cloudy armoury,
> Is world enough for me."

The village of Cartsdyke, now part of Greenock, had perforce to be " world enough " for that poor school-mistress and itinerant pedlar Jean Adams (d. 1765), sometimes credited, on somewhat slender evidence and against the superior claims of William Julius Mickle, with the authorship of that fine song, " There's nae Luck

Aboot the House". She died, poor thing, in a Glasgow Poorhouse from an all too prevalent nineteenth-century combination of extreme poverty and religious mania.

Another poet who found that he could only earn his living as a school-teacher in Greenock's Grammar School by undertaking to abjure "the profane and unprofitable art of poem-making" (the phrase, rather surprisingly, is Galt's!) was John Wilson (1720-89). Nobody reads "The Clyde" nowadays. But within its pages is to be found this effective description of Greenock before it came under the influence of steam:

> "Where the broad marsh, a shuddering surface lies,
> Fair Greenock's spires in new-born beauty rise;
> And many an infant city rises round,
> Emerging swiftly from the teeming ground;
> .     .     .     . .     .     .     .
> While groves of masts aloft in ether rise,
> And cordage warping wide obscures the skies.
> As in the film-winged bee's industrious hive,
> Some stretch their wings for flight, and some arrive,
> Some treasure in their cells the golden store,
> And some, adventurous, sail in quest of more;
> So fleets arriving here with every gale,
> Within the port shall drop the flying sail;
> While some departing shall their wings display,
> To greet the rising, or the falling day. . . ."

One other literary connection distinguishes Greenock. Burns' Highland Mary, a servant girl from Auchamore Farm, Dunoon, now lies re-buried in the new Greenock Cemetery. Neil Munro once opined that, of all Burns' heroines, she it was who appealed to him most, because of her virginal, unattainable elusiveness. However, in a recent biography of the poet, Hilton Brown has marshalled the facts concerning the discovery of the remains of an infant's coffin in the poor lassie's grave. The evidence is not complete enough to prove that Munro's "virginal unattainable" may neither have been so elusive nor so virginal as the novelist fancied. But, in Hilton Brown's own words, while ". . . no jury on earth would convict on the existing evidence, few juries would be left without a strong suspicion of guilt". Virgin or mistress, her statue stands on the Castle Hill at Dunoon, gazing perpetually across the water towards "the auld clay biggin" at Alloway where her poet was born.

Important as Port Glasgow and Greenock are industrially, and

49

inescapable as the smoky sight of them is to anyone who sails on the Firth, they are not in any sense holiday resorts. But they have a " new " neighbour (in reality, much older than themselves); a kind of dormitory suburb which, besides being the principal railhead for the Clyde steamer service, has virtually no industries of its own, and goes out of its way to make itself attractive to visitors. Gourock is separated from the hinter-world by a rocky ridge called the Drum, which slopes down almost to shore level, and through which runs what is said to be the longest railway tunnel in Scotland. The Drum probably saved Gourock from the fate of becoming an industrial port. Not even its safe and sheltered bay could compensate for such an isolating landward barrier.

But, in spite of the fact that the name "Nae-Place", once belonging to a house in the old part of the town, is sometimes applied to the town itself by cynics who mean to imply that the burgh lacks character—in spite, too, of an unkind Glasgow habit of referring to squint things as "all to the one side like Gourock", in allusion to the villas which climb up from its water front—Gourock has had its moments. That great Scottish Admiral of King James the Fifth's navy, Sir Andrew Wood, embarked on an island-taming trip from "Goraik on the west border" in 1494. It is also credited with the invention of herring curing in 1688, while, in 1777, the Gourock rope-works, though now no longer operating in the burgh, set up an association which has become famous. In the days when yachting was still a feasible pursuit, Gourock had several flourishing yards, and many were the famous yachts that rode at anchor in the quiet shelter of her bay between salty dashes after racing cups and honours. Possessing both a supposedly Druidical stone, "Granny Kempoch", to which ancient mariners performed passing obeisance, and the Cloch, one of the most important lighthouses on the upper reaches of the Firth, to aid more modern mariners, Gourock retains its claims on the attention of seamen.

Thereafter, the southern coastline of the Firth changes in character. From Inverkip—an enclosed, old-world-looking village, once famous for the tenacity of its witches, and now more familiar to the motorist than the mariner—to Fairlie, the landscape takes on a curious reddish tinge. This is due partly to the prevalence of red sandstone rocks, and to the fact that the stately, though rather ugly, castellated mansions which ornate the coast around Wemyss Bay, are built of this material. From the Cowal shores, too, this opposite coastline often seems to bask in the lingering rays of suns that have already sunk behind the foothills of Argyll.

Not many of the holiday-makers who throng the streets of Largs
during the summer season are much interested in anything which
happened as long ago as 1263. Yet it was at the Battle of Largs
that King Alexander the Third effectively cracked the last fingerhold of the Norsemen on Scottish soil. King Haakon the Old of
Norway set out with over sixty ships—the finest fleet ever to leave
his shores—in a final bid to subdue Scotland. For a time he raided
inland, reaching as far north-east as Stirling. But a storm scattered and wrecked his fleet, driving several ships ashore near
Largs, and his own flagship to the Cumbraes. On the plain of
Haylee, Alexander the Steward came down upon the remains
of the Norse host. It was a skirmish rather than a battle. But it
finished the Norse war that had festered for four and a half
centuries. The older parts of Kelburne, the seat of Lord Glasgow
and the most interesting house of its kind thereabouts, may well
have looked down from its woody seclusion on this curious
conflict.

Largs has another warlike association, for it houses in the
vault of the Montgomerie family the dust of that Sir Hugh Montgomerie who captured Hotspur at Otterburn. But its prevailing
associations have been peaceful. Since the eighteenth century, it
seems deliberately to have set itself out to be a holiday resort.
Indeed, "Senex" relates that it was already a fashionable watering-place when he was there in the summer of 1782. With long
hours of sunshine, its pastoral-coloured outlook across the narrow
water which separates it from Greater Cumbrae, and its views of
Bute and the Cowal shore, it certainly has much to make it
attractive. I, for my part, have sought its pleasures only in
winter. From the once hectic June holiday of St. Colm's Fair—
now revived in genteelly purged form—to the autumn holiday in
September, the up-to-date hotels, the nickel-plated cafés, and the
chromium ballrooms along the esplanade become mere trans-
plantations of Glasgow life, obliterating the place's quiet natural
character. The Gogo Burn and the hills behind, with their splendid panorama of the opening Firth, are, to my mind, vastly more
rewarding than the town itself. Fairlie, its smaller neighbour, is
one of the railheads for the Arran steamer traffic. Thereafter, the
coastline slopes away through the hydropathical resort of Seamill
and West Kilbride, to the fringe of the Land of Burns.

It is, however, the northern coastline of the Firth, whose lochs
are fingers holding back the sweep of the Highland hills, that
gives the Clyde its beauty and its rich variety.

Craigendoran, the "otter's rock", marks the beginning of the
northern arm. Once the North British Railway Company's

steamer terminus, and later that of the L.N.E.R., it is still maintained by British Railways, apparently rather grudgingly. The old idea that certain piers and railway stations must be served, regardless of whether or not their receipts showed a profit, because they provided a useful public service, no longer finds official favour. A word from London repeated through an Edinburgh sub-office, and a whole community may find itself deprived of its pier or station, because its winter receipts show a paper deficit.

Like most of the piers once served by the gaily coloured paddle-steamers of the L.N.E.R named after characters from the Waverley Novels Craigendoran Pier has itself now come under sentence. The "otter's rock"—the threshing of the first paddle-wheels there a century ago no doubt scared off the last of these timid creatures—has, however, one other topographical distinction. It is the point at which the West Highland Railway takes to the hills, and begins its long, steam-exacting ascent towards Mallaig, a railhead for the Western Isles. The doomed pier and the station at Craigendoran provided the sole purpose for the place's existence. But some opulent-looking houses grew up around them, one the last home of "James Bridie", the Scottish dramatist—and more recently a private housing estate.

They stretch, these houses, almost to Helensburgh, the most easily accessible of the Clyde's watering-places. This town was built on the site of the village of Milligs in 1777 by Sir James Colquhoun of Luss, in honour of his wife. His idea was, it seems, to attract " bonnet-makers, stocking, linen and woollen weavers " to his town, which he planned with admirable care at the foot of the stey brae above the Firth. However, no "rude mechanicals" came to spoil the Helensburgh air, so, in 1802, when the place became a burgh of barony, the plan was adapted to make Helensburgh a residential town, its spacious lay-out modelled on the New Town of Edinburgh.

Helensburgh's nearest direct contact with industry was the attraction it had for Henry Bell, builder of the *Comet,* in 1807. Bell lived in and ran for some years an establishment called the Baths Hotel, which modern visitors now know as the Queen's.

Since the days of Sir James, Helensburgh has developed along schizophrenic lines. Her sea-front is now a row of glittering plate-glass windows, overlooking an esplanade, a beach, and a pier that has only a sufficient depth of water to accommodate a paddle-steamer at high tide. Since a bus can carry the cloth-capped worker and his family from Glasgow in the space of an hour, beach and shopping centre—lower Helensburgh, as the more aloof residents sometimes call them—are thronged with daily trippers throughout the "season". But the upper Helensburghites—the folk who live in those ornate, ascending rows of stately mansions —stay within their hillside strongholds during the daylight invasion of the town's lower reaches. Many Glasgow business men retire into upper Helensburgh's socially rigid seclusion, while others travel daily to and from the city.

Helensburgh, leisured and pleasure-providing, looks over the Firth at Port Glasgow and Greenock. Often it is not a particularly pleasant outlook; but on a fine winter evening, the sinking sun can sometimes daub the smoke-heavy clouds with its low, oblique rays, and invest these sorry monuments of unplanned industrialism with a transient black-and-golden glory.

The Gareloch, the uppermost of the Clyde lochs, has been at various times the scene of clan stirrings and clashes; a resting harbour for the yachts of the wealthier merchant princes whose mansions have sprung up around its genial villages; a dumping ground for rusty derelict tonnage in time of slump; and the concealed site of a huge war-time port.

Glen Fruin, the "glen of sorrow", about three miles above Garelochhead, was the scene of the famous ambush of the Colquhouns by the MacGregors on a winter's day in 1603. The Colquhouns found themselves trapped between two MacGregor forces, led respectively by Allistair, and John his brother, who fell in the battle. The unfortunate Colquhouns lost over a hundred of their best men, and their lands were plundered and pillaged. The MacGregors are also supposed to have massacred a band of students from Dumbarton Grammar School, who were so indiscreet as to follow in the tracks of the Colquhoun force, presumably to watch the fun.[1]

After this affair, the chief of the Colquhouns appeared before King James the Sixth at Stirling, accompanied by the widows of the slain men, all clad in black, and carrying the bloody garments of their late husbands. The King, who was highly susceptible to such displays of organized stagecraft, flew into a royal rage, and ordered the MacGregors to be outlawed.

It became a crime punishable with death to bear the Mac-Gregors' name, and the clan were thereupon hunted and slain like beasts by the forces of the Earl of Argyll, who was entrusted with the task of exterminating them. Greatly to his discredit, this same Earl of Argyll, who had a personal quarrel with Colquhoun of Luss, had previously been urging the MacGregors

[1] See Chapter III, p. 73.

to commit the very offences for which he was now punishing them.

Allistair MacGregor managed to elude his pursuers for nearly a year. In the end, he was lured out of his hiding-place by Argyll's promise that he would either get him the King's pardon, or convey him safely out of Scotland. Argyll then solemnly marched his "guest" across the Border to Berwick, where he promptly re-arrested him and brought him back to Edinburgh. Two days later, after writing his "confession", MacGregor was tried and found guilty. His request that his scaffold should stand a foot or two above those of his confederates was granted. His head was in due course publicly exhibited in Dumbarton, where, besides providing food for the sea-maws, it no doubt proved a suitable warning to other potential law-breakers.

Years later, another Colquhoun laird was involved in a different sort of fracas. When the paddle-steamer *Emperor* arrived at Garelochhead pier on Sunday the 22nd of August 1853, her passengers and crew found a force of local police and game-keepers waiting to preserve the sanctity of the Sabbath by refusing to allow them to land. The Captain of the ship, stout fellow, was in no mood to put up with this sort of feudal nonsense, so he manœuvred the *Emperor* alongside the pier while some of the younger passengers leapt ashore and gave battle to the Colquhoun force, finally routing it. What upset the newspaper chroniclers of the time was not so much the engagement itself, though bottles and sticks were freely used, as the fact that the inhabitants of the neighbouring village lined the shore, cheering in an unseemly manner! Sir James Colquhoun then had recourse to the law courts to get his way. For a time, Clyde steamers did not call at private piers on Sundays, but eventually Sunday sailing became as acceptable a pastime as Sunday golf—which, however, is still resisted with antique heat in Arran to this day!

The heather-clad hills to the west, and the gentle slopes of Ros-neath promontory—called by Scott an island in *The Heart of Midlothian*—contain pleasant little villages with unusual-sound-ing Gaelic names like Mambeg (named after the breast-shaped hill behind it); Shandon (perhaps a corruption of Shantoun, a hill between Glen Finglas and Glen Fruin), once the home of Robert Napier and now possessed of a large hydropathic;[1] and Clynder, the meadow of the water.

[1] Hydropathic hotels were nineteenth-century institutions where guests could undergo "the water cure", and where, originally, nothing stronger than water might be drunk. They now make no pretensions towards moral improvement, and are, indeed, simply large hotels. This one has since been demolished to make way for a caravan park.

Faslane, once one of the sleepiest of the Gareloch villages and a former home of the Earls of Lennox, was suddenly transformed into a large port equipped to handle the heaviest of traffic, during the Second World War. Thick clusters of railway sidings knot together alongside the quays in astonishing profusion. Now, the port is run by Metal Industries Limited as a shipbreaking yard. Amongst other famous ships to meet their doom there have been the Cunard liner *Aquitania*, and the little *Lucy Ashton*, whose paddles in happier days so frequently echoed across the waters of the loch as she nosed her way round anchored steam yachts and "tramps".

I never drive past Faslane without experiencing an acute sense of depression. For there, lurching against the quay, or beached in the sandy mud, are the twisted remains of some ship decomposing beneath the relentless prying of blow-lamp and crowbar. It takes so much longer to build a fine ship than to destroy one; and, although I am well aware that such feelings are mere sentimentalism, the sight of this necessary triumph of the destructive element saddens me!

On the outer shore of the Rosneath promontory stand Kilcreggan and Cove, looking across the Firth to Gourock. Their villas are favourite places for retired Glasgow men who do not wish to become too inaccessible to their city friends. From Cove, the coastline takes a sharp curve into the narrow hill-pressed fiord waters of Loch Long, the lake of ships. Some of King Haakon the Old's galleys sheltered here before going out to their storm-scattered defeat at Largs. During the summer season, a paddle-steamer (by kind permission of Whitehall officials, who have turned these deep waters into a torpedo-testing station, and who, a few years ago, tried to have them closed to the public altogether) makes its way up to Arrochar. Like Loch Goil, the arm which sweeps round the peninsula of Ardgoil to the north, Loch Long is a decidedly unfriendly looking stretch of water. The high hills which close in on it shut out much of the sun. The few surviving monuments of the ancient clan life, which must once have enlivened its shores, like Carrick Castle, stand legendless and deserted.

Ardentinny (made famous by Sir Harry Lauder's often-sung wish to go "Owre the hills to Ardentinny", there to see his "bonnie Jeannie"), Blairmore, Strone and Kilmun (where, in 1829, the enterprising Robert Napier built a row of villas known as "the cannisters", giving abundant proof, as Neil Munro puts it, "that engineering and architecture are very different arts") lead round into the Holy Loch, which is not so much a loch as a big tidal bay. Various theories have been advanced to explain the name of this loch. One is that a vessel carrying sand from the Holy Land for the building of Glasgow Cathedral was wrecked on these shores; another suggests that the loch was the site of the cell of St. Mun, a sixth-century Irish saint. In any case, piety has had long associations there, for the first Earl of Argyll, Sir Duncan Campbell, founded a collegiate church at Kilmun in 1442, and the place has been the family burying-ground ever since. Only a few broken-down stones of the original church tower still survive.

Although the head of the Holy Loch is unprepossessing at low tide, the receding sea uncovering a wide belt of sludgy mud, it is an attractive by-water when the tide is full, and the breaking waves whiten the grass fringe of the fields with a coating of salt. The River Echaig jabbles down the valley of the lovely little inland Lock Eck,[1] before it moves majestically on to lose itself in the Holy Loch. Glen Massan and Glen Lean also toss down their brawling Highland burns into the " big" Echaig and its tributary, the "wee" Echaig, just above Ardanadam. Through the valley of the Eck, the road runs across to Glen Branter, site of a Forestry Commission training camp, then over to Strachur, on Loch Fyne. Through Glen Lean, another road climbs, by devious twists and braes, to Loch Striven, Loch Ridden and the Kyles of Bute. This road also passes through Glendaruel, " the fold of sleep", where, according to legend (which, in one rhymed version, goes to the air preserved and made famous by Mrs. Kennedy-Fraser), Deirdre, " loveliest of women born ", having fled with her lover Naoise from the lust of old King Conchubar of Ulster, made her bridal bed.

These three noble glens hold out a magnificent Highland prospect, if you approach the Holy Loch from the seaward end. But if you drive down upon the Loch through the mountain passes, the ·view is very different in character. Gourock lies distantly across the water. Ardanadam—or Sandbank, as it sometimes calls itself, partly for obvious physical reasons, and partly because its pier, now out of passenger use, had to be made the longest in the Clyde—is a centre of the yacht-building industry. Even in our hard-pressed mid-twentieth-century days, one may still see the hulls of big yachts stilted for the winter, their prows leaning high above the road, their decks covered with slate roofs.

Hunter's Quay, so named because it was built on the estate of the Hunters of Hafton, one of whom erected Dunoon pier (in which operation, it is said, the father of Robert Louis Stevenson,

[1] About 1820, David Napier put in it his *Aglaia*, the first iron steamer in the world.

then a young engineer, was employed), is the administrative centre of Clyde yachting. None who saw her could readily forget the sight of the last *Shamrock* of Sir Thomas Lipton riding anchor off Hunter's Quay before it set out to cross the Atlantic. During the Clyde Fortnight, early in July, regattas are still held, when the waters are flaked with the leaning sails of the smaller classes. But the great days of yachting have gone. It is inconceivable that men will ever again possess enough money to build and sail the extravagant white-winged glories of Lipton's day.

Hunter's Quay, with its yachting connection, pretends to a social distinction, after which its more plebeian neighbours, Kirn and Dunoon, do not ettle. Dunoon shares with Rothesay, in the Island of Bute, the distinction of being the most popular of those Clyde holiday resorts to reach which it is necessary—unless you wish to make a long roundabout road journey through Glen Croe and over Rest-and-be-Thankful—to cross the water. During July, particularly during the second fortnight of the month when Glasgow is enjoying its "Fair", Maws and Paws frae the wynds and close-mous of St. Mungo's City, bring their weans (children) to Dunoon. The place is a thronging bustle of townsfolk anxious to make the most of the West of Scotland's not over-generous allowance of sunny, rain-free hours; and yet, at the same time, equally anxious not to forego the transferred delights of picture-house, dance-hall or fish and chip shop. During the last week-end in August, when Dunoon holds its annual Cowal Games, crowded steamers come lurching hourly towards the pier, water dripping through the fretwork of their canted paddle-boxes, while pipers on the shore enliven the air with desultory skirling in preparation for the day's contests.

The pipes have sounded at Dunoon on less peaceful occasions than the Cowal Games. Stormings, battles and massacres have all centred around the Castle hill.

The Old Castle itself, now a laroch, is supposed to have been a stronghold of the Dalriadic Scots. Later, Somerled of the Isles, progenitor of the MacDonalds, had possession of it. It was also used sporadically by the Norse raiders as an outpost. The Norsemen were fought and finally driven out by the High Stewards of Scotland, one of whom married the Princess Marjory, daughter of King Robert the Bruce. Their son, Robert, the young High Steward (hence the royal name of Stewart), made a spectacular descent from Bute, and stormed Dunoon Castle, which was then held by an English garrison. Nearly forty years later, he became King Robert the Second, and as a reward for the help he had received from his friend Sir Colin Campbell, he made that knight hereditary keeper of the Castle. This gave the Campbells of Argyll their first substantial footing in Cowal. During the centuries that followed, they extended their hold over it at the expense of the native Lamonts, culminating in that disgraceful act, the Massacre of Dunoon. In 1643, that Covenanting Earl of Argyll, whose leering eyes wavered as he met the gaze of the gallant Montrose on the way to his execution, set out to destroy the Royalist-minded MacDonalds and MacDougals. The opportunity which his position as head of the Government offered to rid himself of the Lamonts at the same time seemed too good to be missed. So he ordered his own followers to besiege the Lamont strongholds at Ascog and Toward. At Toward, however, the Lamonts held fast, until the Campbells suggested a parley to settle their differences. As soon as the defences were withdrawn, the Campbells seized the Lamonts and locked them up in the courtyard of the castle, while they plundered their victims' lands.

Then the Campbells carried their captives off to Dunoon, where thirty-six Lamont gentlemen were hanged on a convenient ash-tree. About two hundred lesser Lamonts and their womenfolk were shot or dirked, the dead and the half-dead being thrown into a hastily dug pit, where their bones were discovered half a century ago during the making of a road. Not only on account of the later Massacre of Glencoe did the name of Campbell become synonymous with treachery and deceit amongst all decent High-landers! In due course, however, retribution overtook the Glied Earl, for after the Restoration he met the same death as his old enemy, Montrose.

Long after the douce bodies of Greenock had taken to occupy-ing their days with the intricacies of civilized business, murder and rapine went on in the Highland fringe across the narrow water. How dark, how threatening the Cowal hills must often have looked to those anxious Lowland traders! And how differ-ent the wild Gaelic-spoken Highlanders must have seemed when they occasionally crossed the Firth at the Cloch to trade or buy supplies!

The Cloch-Dunoon ferry was first officially operated in 1658 by the Campbells of Ballochyle, under charter from Archibald, Mar-quis of Argyll, who insisted on an eight-oared galley being kept ready at all times to carry him across the narrow waters. Probably this link with the Lowlands was commonly used by traders and cattle-drovers. The Cloch lighthouse went up in 1791.

Dunoon's rise as a holiday resort has been recent and rapid. When "Senex" made his summer stay in 1779—goat's whey was the attraction that brought the occasional eighteenth-century holiday-maker so far afoot—his family was unable to hold any conversation with the inhabitants of the village because none of them spoke English. Even in 1822, Dunoon consisted only of a church and its manse, three or four slated cottages and a few thatched huts. Gaelic was commonly spoken until the century had reached its turn. Now, you may hear the braid vernacular of Glasgow, and the nicely varied drawls of Northern England; but not a single word of the old tongue.

Yet about Dunoon there still hangs an aura of the past, which is the only memorial to the Gaels and their songs. The names of feature, hill and sea are Gaelic; so are the names of some of the streets and houses. And there are still any number of Campbells and Lamonts in the place, living peacefully side by side, their ancient scars and wrongs forgotten. This muffled, historical aspect of Dunoon can best be experienced on a winter's day, when the grey town is lit by the thin rays of a December sun slanting across the eternal Gaelic hills.

Those of us with Celtic blood in our veins are said to be traditionally predisposed towards melancholy reflection upon vanished glories. It has often struck me as strange that the Scottish remnants of a race which once mastered half the world, should be unable to shake themselves out of this individualistic remembering, in order to band together to combat the decay which so energetically threatens their future. Yet, from time to time, I have found that this mood of hopeless melancholy triumphs even over the strong admixture of Lowland blood in my own veins. Once, standing by the levelled ruins of a cluster of cottages on a hill above Innellan, and looking over the emptied glens around Loch Striven, where in Napoleonic times a thousand men were raised for the defence of the realm, it came over me so strongly that I made a lament of it:

*A salt wind that had gashed the crags of Kilda*
*and Islay with its whipped Atlantic tang*
*curled wearily up the brae, stirred weeds and grasses*
*as bluebells on the ruins nodded and rang*
*their Grecian perfume over lichened stones*
*scattered like braxied sheep's half-rotten bones.*

*Two centuries ago these clachans breathed*
*odour of peat-reek onto Gaelic air.*
*Men yoked their wooden ploughs; tilled, harrowed, reaped;*
*knew sweat and wind and rain, the flesh's bare*
*brief ecstasy, begetting future men*
*to bend new seasons under the hand again.*

*Theirs was a meaningful rhythm of movements, growing*
*each into each; the curve from birth to death*
*as bounded as the rarely noticed rainbow;*
*oh, they were Scotland, a way of life, a faith!*
*Pipes wait no longer on a listening wall,*
*their coronach the screeching seagulls' brawl.*


*They were my folk, these vanished, vanquished people*
*who now sleep barren on this childless moor*
*where straggled whin still flints the sun's bright shining,*
*though the shallow soil knows only rabbit-spoor,*
*and knuckles of bracken push in greedy haste,*
*to sinew and confirm the dead fields' waste.*


*And I, in whom their pointless pride still lingers,*
*lean from my times to sense their shattered past*
*as if the sightless air still hid their talking*
*in folds of wind. The illusion doesn't last.*
*The shore road echoes up a drone of cars;*
*two submarines incise the Clyde with scars.*


Mere romanticism, you may say. These Innellan clachans must
have been draughty and damp, the diet of their folk unbalanced
and ill-varied. Yet in the more than thirty years that have passed
since these youthful verses were written, the adequacy of the
underlying values of our materialistic society have been called
deeply in question.

Certainly there could no more be a return to a crofting economy
than a new evangelical revival: and there would be little enough
hope for the economic life of Highlands or Lowlands if they had
to rely upon their own resources.

However, the Highlands and Islands Development Board
has done much to stimulate small-scale enterprise, and the
thought of oil exploitation sets a glint in Highland as well as
in Lowland eyes, even if the prospects are alarmingly short-
term. Odd it would be if oil were to unite Highland and Lowlands, as nothing else has ever quite succeeded in doing!
Yet then there could be real hope for Scotland the nation, provided her people can sink their alarmingly disruptive individualism long enough to make sustained co-operative action
possible. This thought, too, has often come to me as I have

climbed the hills behind Innellan: hills that cut off the late evening sunlight. They have no real Lowland summit; for each smaller peak stands dwarfed by one higher and more rugged, as the ascending ridges of the mist-swept mountains of Argyll stab at the torn clouds.

On a good day, the view from the lower hills is panoramic. First, there is the fertile belt around Toward, whose modern castle was built for Kirkman Finlay in 1832 by David Hamilton, the architect who put the pillared façade on Glasgow's Royal Exchange. Now, Castle Toward is the property of Glasgow Corporation, who use it as a country school where city children, many of whom have never been outside the tenement-shrouded half-light of a slum street before, are given short courses. Beyond the Toward shore, the deep waters of Loch Striven reach into the heart of the mountains. With that happy disregard for local amenities which the Admiralty so often shows, the wind-wrecked ruins of a large naval camp disfigure a stretch of the eastern shore of the Loch, while the abandoned hulks of discarded naval vessels lie stranded farther up the beach.

Opposite the mouth of the Loch, Rothesay, the principal town of Bute, curves round its peculiarly sheltered bay. That worthy Scottish littérateur, George Eyre-Todd, noted down his impressions of the place fifty years ago:

"The town and bay all summer long make up a brilliant scene. There are steamers constantly coming in from the outer world with crowds of gay and happy folk, then going off, with dusky plumes of smoke and dazzling tracks of foam, across the blue waters that wind into the far recesses of the hills. There are yachts that come sweeping with white wings silently round cape and inlet. And there are the little boats that dance everywhere merrily on the sparkling sea. At the same time, ashore, pier and esplanade are bright with the dresses of the holiday throng, and the strains of Strauss and Mendelssohn drift on the sunny air from the bandstand among the trees. . . ."

Since George Eyre-Todd wrote, Strauss and Mendelssohn have been replaced by "Honey, be Mine" or "You're askin' a mighty lot, baby", blared not from the bandstand—its odd-looking iron-work tracery would surely be incapable of embracing such vulgarity—but from loudspeakers hidden in the foliage of the flood-lit esplanade trees. Otherwise, the summer scene is much the same as it was fifty years ago; even, no doubt, a hundred years ago.

Three Rothesay characters impressed themselves strongly upon my boyhood memory. Two of them were old men with long, nicotine-stained beards, who faced each other on rainless mornings across a giant draught-board in the gardens behind the pier. Every now and then, after much thoughtful sucking of the broken clay pipes that hung from the corners of their mouths, one or other of the ancients would move his draughtsman with a long, hooked pole. Such moves were few and far between, and I never had the patience to watch a whole contest out. But once, attracted by the brittle sound of outdoor applause, I hurried over to join the little cluster of folk who made up a screen against the sea-breezes. An ancient had just beaten his opponent, making the score of the season's campaign sixteen-fifteen in the victor's favour.

The third character was a stout widowed fisherwoman who used to wheel her barrow of fresh herring aboard the early morning steamer, and hawk its cargo round the Innellan houses. She wore a man's soft hat and a pair of pin-striped flannel trousers beneath her scaly apron. "Aye, they're fine and fresh the morn, lass," she used to assure our decidedly unprepossessing spinster cook, long since turned a sour sixty. I used to suspect that the frequent appearance of herring at our table was not unconnected with this subtle form of greeting, especially as cookie's favourite wish, expressed to us children in moments of unguarded relaxation, was, "Goad! If only ah culd get a maan! "

Rothesay Castle is supposed to have been founded about 1098 by Norway's King Magnus Barefoot, who left traces of his ambition to subdue Scotland all over the western sea-board. It was probably because of this menace that King David the First settled at Renfrew the English knight Walter Fitz-Allan the first High Steward, whose descendants later came to the Scottish throne. The Castle changed hands several times, the Stewarts twice recovering it from the Norse, then temporarily losing it again to the English during the time of Edward Baliol's usurpation in 1334. Cromwell's troops, in their customary civilized manner, set it alight as a royalist stronghold in 1650. Just over a quarter of a century later, it was finally burned by the brother of that Earl of Argyll who was unsuccessfully engaged in rebellion against King James the Seventh and Second. In 1376, King Robert the Second made his natural son, John, Constable of the Castle, an honour that has remained in the family ever since. Old King Robert the Third died of grief within its walls when he learned that his son and heir, Prince David, Duke of Rothesay, had been starved to death at Falkland by his uncle, and that the Prince's brother, who later became the poet-king, James the First of Scotland, had been seized at sea by the English.

To-day, the Castle is surrounded by other tides than those of bitter battle, and few of the holiday-making throng who surge past its walls ever give a thought to the high dramas of the past enacted there, though guide-book legend draws their attention to the existence of the " Bluidy Stair ".  A barn-storming nineteenth-century " ballad " commemorates the scene of lust and murder which is supposed to have taken place in 1228, when Olaf, King of Man, and Husbae, a Norwegian chief, descended on the island with eighty ships, captured the castle, and slew the Steward himself against the wall.

" Oh, Rothesay's touer is roun about,
    And Rothesay's touer is strang,
And loud within the merry waas,
    The roar o wassail rang.

A skald o Norroway struck the harp,
    And a guid harper was he,
For herts beat wud and looks grew wild
    Wi his sang o victorie.

When the feast was owre, and aa was husht
    In midnicht and in mirk,
A lady was seen, like a sprite at e'en,
    To pass by the haly kirk.

She stude at the fuit o the chapel stair,
    And she heard a fuitstep's tread.
The wild Norse warrior was there,
    And thus to the lady said:

' I'm Ruari Mor, the island chief,
    I'm Roderic, Lord o Bute;
For the Raven o Norroway flies abune
    And the Lion o Scotland is mute.

Yet kiss me, lovely Isobel,
    And lay your cheek to mine;
Though ye bear the bluid o the High Steward,
    I'll woo nae hert but thine.'

' Awa! awa! ye rank butcher,'
    Cried the lady Isobel;
' Beneath your haun my faither dear
    And my three brave brithers fell.'

' *It's I hae conquered them,' he said,*
    ' *And I shall conquer thee;*
*For if in luve ye winna wed,*
    *A waur weird ye sall dree.'*

' *The stars'll dreep oot their beds o blue*
    *Er you in luve I'll wed;*
*I liefer wad flee to the grave and lie*
    *I' the mouldy embrace o the dead!'*

*An eye was seen wi revenge to gleam.*
    *Like a shot star in a storm,*
*And a hert was felt to writhe, as hit*
    *By the never-dying worm.*

*A struggle was heard on the chapel stair,*
    *And a smotherit shriek o pain,*
*A deidly grane, a faa on the stane,*
    *And aa was silent again.*

*May morning woke on the Lady's bouer,*
    *But nae Isobel was there;*
*May morning broke on Rothesay's touer,*
    *And bluid was on the stair.*

*And rain may faa, and Time may caa*
    *Its lazy wheels aboot;*
*But the steps are reid, and the stains o bluid*
    *Will never be washen oot."*

Until steam supplanted water-power, the weaving of cloth provided employment for quite a number of Rothesay's citizens. The remains of the mill which David Dale acquired and worked there are still to be seen.

The rest of Bute[1] bears little recorded history. At Dunagoil, the remains of a vitrified whinstone fort survive; there are ruins of towers at Kilmorie and Kilspoke, and ruins of chapels dedicated to the saints Ninian, Cormac, Mary and Blane. There are still older stone circles at Kingarth, near the red-sandstone village of Kilchattan; and at St. Colmac, by the sandy beaches of Ettrick Bay. Before their silent, mutilated majesty, one may speculate

---

[1] The name of the island is thought to derive from the Norse *bot*, the precise meaning of which is not known, though it may refer to the hut or bothy of St. Brendan.

and wonder at the effectiveness with which Time does, indeed, "caa its lazy wheels aboot", carrying so much away that must once have seemed enduring.

During the "season", it is possible to take a steamer from Rothesay or Kilchattan Bay which will carry you over the Firth to Millport, the main township on Greater Cumbrae, lying at the back of a deep bight that can nevertheless become dangerous water in a winter gale. Apart from being a popular watering-place and the site of a Marine Biology Station, where the hidden ongoings of the denizens of the deep are scientifically probed and analysed, the place has little historical interest, although its devotees are loud in their praises of its holiday charms. Not a trace remains of the camp which King Haakon set up in order to mount the Battle of Largs. And even the Reverend James Adam, that celebrated early nineteenth-century divine who asked the Lord to shower his favours on "the Great and Little Cumbrae and the adjacent islands of Great Britain and Ireland", is beginning to assume the qualities of legend. Lesser Cumbrae contains a tower built by Robert the Second and destroyed by Cromwell's soldiers, a single farm, and a lighthouse.

If, on the other hand, you take a steamer from Rothesay sailing in the opposite direction, you will be carried through the lovely Kyles of Bute, where a rocky point of the island eats deeply into the shores of the mainland, causing to be formed the channel known as "The Narrows"; past the mouth of wood-clad Loch Ridden; past Colintraive and Tighnabruaich, both of which look as if chunks of Pollokshields has been transplanted to a Highland setting; past Ardlamont Point, and the house in whose grounds a famous murder occurred in 1893; past the mouth of verdant Loch Fyne; and across to Arran, the largest island in the Clyde.

Arran is fifty-five miles in circumference, has an area of one hundred and sixty-five square miles, and is densely mountainous in the north. Goatfell[1] tops all the other mountains, with its 2,866 feet. Behind it stands Ben Tarsuinn. Cir Mhor, Caisteal Abhail and Ben Nuis. The southern half of the island, though also undulating in character, is flatter and less fearsome in its aspect.

Geologically, Arran is of the greatest interest. The huge granite mass of the northern mountains is surrounded by a band of slate into which it penetrates, an indication of its once molten condition. To the south and west, the slate is bounded by old red sandstone, while to the east and north, the sandstone is edged

---

[1] " Goat " means either " sacred " or " windy ", and has nothing to do with the stumble of a beast. " Fell ", from the Icelandic, means " hill ".

by carboniferous rock. The sandstone in Glen Dubh is said to be almost quartz, white and tinted, with crystals of amethyst. At the southern end of the island, the rocks are mostly of the trap order. From ten to twenty feet above the sea level, a terrace that was once the beach belts much of the island.

Botanists, archaeologists, mountaineers and anglers are all drawn to this island, which has managed to preserve to an astonishing degree its ancient Gaelic way of life. Gaelic is still widely spoken in three distinct dialects, and the careful policy of preservation which the present "Laird", the Duchess of Montrose, and her predecessors have enforced has done much to hold back the encroaching Lowland tide. There are no "holiday resorts", in the usual sense of that term, in Arran. Brodick, Lamlash and Whiting Bay do attract a fair number of young folk, whose white flannels and suburban accents may be flaunted on the tennis-courts during the week, or who may be found on boating expeditions to the Holy Isle which dominates the seashore off Lamlash. But, on the whole, those who go back to find refreshment on Arran year after year come from the limited group of people who derive their amusement from rest or the contemplation of Nature.

Donald MacKelvie (1867-1947), who ran a family grocery and bakery shop in Lamlash for many years, brought the island unusual fame: for it was to his researches that we owe the famous "Arran" potatoes.

History and pre-history have left marks and legends in the great silences of Glen Rosa and Glen Sannox. There are still deer in the mountains, passing before the eyes like climbers' casual thoughts, as they must so often have appeared to the real heroes of history; those

> ". . . forgotten farmers who sleep
> beneath their soil and the shining song of the plough;
> old fishermen beyond winds' roughest sweep,
> for whom the restless sea frets vainly now;
> lone keen-eyed shepherds on the quiet hills,
> watching their days go grazing down the skies. . . ."

And there are legends—legends that have come tumbling through the centuries like the waters of the Cluny Burn. Legends which keep their dark secrets inviolate against the battering of Time and the elements, like the Druid stone of Tormore, and those cists, cromlechs and chambered cairns of the "Clyde" type to be found at several places in the southern half of the island. To stand beneath the Tormore slabs and think of the shaggy, passionate people who must once have worshipped there, but who have now passed utterly away, as if they had never lived and loved, leaving behind them only the testimony of these stones, and their poor, cramped morturial remains—to think of these early primitives in this, their sacred place, is surely to remind oneself how vain is the complacency of our own scarcely less insecure age! Lewis Grassic Gibbon saw in the Druid Stone Circles a romantic symbol of a fairer, freer life in an age when the world was still young. Other folk, warm in the wishful assurances of Sectarian Christianity, see them merely as picturesque relics of heathenish blindness. To me, they are a terrifying monument to the hopeless plight of man, wandering lost and lonely down the indifferent ages; a reminder of the transience of the cooling universe birling its pointless course through immeasurable, inconceivable space!

Arran, however, also provides an antidote against the crushing influence of its antiquities. For it has given shelter to identifiable heroes: men famous in Scotland's story for the temper of their courage. Oscar and Ossian may or may not have lived in our world of flesh. If they did, then according to an ingenious nineteenth-century divine, Dr. Hately Waddell, many of the major happenings of their lives occurred on Arran. The great caverns in the basaltic cliff face at Drumadoon (which sounds like something out of a poem by Yeats) near Tormore, were, he maintains, where Fingal landed and sheltered on his way from Morven to the Irish wars. A " heathy space " marked by two boulders, nine paces above the road half-way between Blackwaterfoot and Sliddery, according to Dr. Waddell, traditionally marks the hero's grave. Similarly, he identifies the burying-place of Malvina, Oscar's betrothed, near Blackwaterfoot; that of Oscar on the Sliddery water, opposite Glenree; and that of blind Ossian himself " in a great mound close to Clachaig farmhouse ". Dr. Waddell's thesis can neither be proved nor disproved, and, in any case, Fingal and his fieres live on in the racial imagination.

A later being, of whose existence there is no doubt, also found shelter in the Drumadoon caves: King Robert the Bruce. There he had arrived with three hundred men from Rathlin Isle in February 1307, and there, too, he presumably saw the famous spider. Sir James Douglas and Sir Robert Boyd had re-won a foothold on Arran for Bruce from the English forces of Sir John Hastings. Bruce and his forces next took Brodick Castle by storm. Then the Bruce waited until a signal, indicating that his leal followers were once more ready to rally round the standard of freedom, should come to him from Carrick, his own earldom across the water. An anonymous eighteenth-century balladist re-created the scene:

> " *When day gaed doun owre Goatfell grim,*
> *And darkness mantled aa,*
> *A kingly form strode to and fro*
> *On Brodick's Castle waa.*
>
> *And aye he gazed ayont the Firth,*
> *Where blasts were roarin' snell,*
> *And oft he leaned upon his sword,*
> *Sad, muttering to himsel'.*
>
> *' In vain, in vain,' at length he cried,*
> *And hung his head in woe,*
> *When streaming far through storm and gloom,*
> *He saw the beacon glow. . . ."*

The King thereupon embarked at King's Cross Point, to the south of Lamlash. When he reached Turnberry, however, he learned that the beacons were but an accidental conflagration, and that the English forces were still apparently all-powerful. But there could be no turning back. The descent on Carrick did, in fact, mark the beginning of Bruce's ultimate victory over English Edward.

Brodick Castle, now in the care of the National Trust for Scotland, houses a table said to have been used by the Bruce. Part of this castle's ivy-covered walls date from the thirteenth century, and may well have seen the consternation of the English warden when he found his stronghold attacked by the forces of Douglas and Bruce, forces, the presence of which on the island he was, according to the poet, John Barbour, quite unaware. Certainly the remains of Loch Ranza Castle must have echoed to the Bruce's hunting-horn. In "The Lord of the Isles", Scott paints this pastoral water-colour of the place:

> " *On fair Loch Ranza streamed the early day;*
> *Thin wreathes of cottage smoke are upward curled*
> *From the lone hamlet which her inland bay*
> *And circling mountains sever from the world;*
> *And there the fisherman his sail unfurled,*
> *The goat-herd drove his kids to steep Ben Ghoil,*
> *Before the hut the dame her spindle twirled,*
> *Courting the sunbeam as she plied her toil.*"

The only other island in the Clyde of any size or character is
Ailsa Craig, a rock not dissimilar in appearance to the Holy Isle.
The Craig lies out from Girvan, on the Ayrshire coast, and is
known to sailors as " Paddy's Milestone ". Its columnar trap was
used for the making of curling-stones, and no doubt still is, if
the tools for the " roaring game " are being fashioned these days.
Apart from the lighthouse-keeper and his family, the only other
inhabitants of the Craig are the flocks of gulls who nest in its
flaky crevices. Ailsa Craig startled Keats, who came on it during
his walking tour of 1818, into a better sonnet than such occasions
usually produce from itinerant poets.

" *Hearken, thou craggy pyramid!*
  *Give answer from thy voice—the sea-fowls' scream!*
  *When were thy shoulders mantled in huge streams?*
*When, from the sun, was thy broad forehead hid?*
*How long is't since the mighty power bid*
  *Thee heave to airy sleep from fathom dreams?*
  *Sleep in the lap of thunder or sunbeams—*
*Or when grey clouds are thy cold coverlid!*
*Thou answers't not; for thou art dead asleep;*
  *Thy life is but two dead eternities—*
*The last in air, the former in the deep;*
  *First with the whales, last with the eagle-skies—*
*Drown'd wast thou till an earthquake made thee steep;*
  *Another cannot wake thy giant size.*"

There is a delightful story of the Craig's one military engagement. A Catholic Ayrshire laird of the sixteenth century, Hew
Barclay, had the idea of seizing the Craig and turning it into a
refuge for distressed Papists. In preparing this brilliant and
original scheme, it is possible that he had the support of the makar
Alexander Montgomerie—support which probably cost the bard
his royal pension, and earned him a spell in prison. However, a
nasty-minded Protestant parson of Paisley, who made a hobby of
persecuting Catholics, got to hear of the scheme, and managed to
reach the Craig first. In the skirmish which followed the landing
of Barclay and his party, the parson of Paisley succeeded in drowning the resourceful laird. A pity, I have always thought!

# Chapter III

# DUNBARTONSHIRE

*"I have seen the Lago di Garda, Albano di Vico, Bolsena and Geneva, and I prefer Loch Lomond to them all. . . . Everything here is romantic beyond imagination."*

Tobias Smollett, 1771.

I

So wrote Dunbartonshire's most famous literary figure in his last and greatest novel, *Humphry Clinker*. Loch Lomond is by no means all of the county: indeed, parts of the loch come within the boundaries of Stirlingshire. But the greater part of this majestic expanse of water does belong to Dunbartonshire, and forms its finest scenic glory.

By devoting a chapter to the Firth of Clyde, I have, to some extent, already anticipated this chapter. For the irregularly shaped county of Dunbarton takes into its two hundred and sixty-one square miles, much of it moorland, not only the Clyde's northern bank from Yoker to the Gareloch, and so round the coastline of Rosneath promontory and up the eastern shore of Loch Long, but also the Highland parish of Arrochar at the extreme northern corner of the shire, and the two detached parishes of Kirkintilloch and Cumbernauld forty-odd miles to the east. The physical basis of the modern county was set out in the granting of the old lands of Lennox.

When King Alexander the First's younger brother David (who eventually became King David the First of Scotland) was made Prince of the ancient kingdom of Strathclyde, he was faced with the serious problem of Norse expansionist aggression. He had been educated at the Normanized court of England's King Henry the First, whose Queen was David's sister. To help him defend his principality against this menace, he therefore imported Saxon and Norman knights, whom he probably thought he could trust better than the old Celtic families. One of them, Walter Fitz-Allan, the first High Steward of Scotland, played a leading rôle against the Norsemen, and his descendants eventually merged with the royal line of Stewart. Another, Arkil, son of a Northumbrian chieftain, settled at Dumbarton in 1069 or '70. (*Dun*, the

70

Gaelic prefix meaning hill or hill-foot, often became corrupted into "dum" when it was absorbed into Middle Scots, and both spellings are to be found applied to this shire and its county town. The accepted compromise is that the town shall be Dumbarton, the county Dunbartonshire.) In the middle part of the twelfth century, his son Alwyn MacArkil became the first Earl of Levenox or Lennox, in the Leven or Lomond district. Both these names are probably derived from *leamhanach*, "a place abounding in elm trees". Loch Lomond, according to the historian Nennius, who flourished about A.D. 796 and whose *Historia Brittonum* is an important source of King Arthur and Merlin stories, was once called Loch Leven. And the two names are still associated in Fife, where the Lomond Hills overlook Loch Leven. The Lennox family did not retain Dumbarton Castle when Maldwin (1217-70), the third Earl, received his charter of confirmation from King Alexander the Second in 1238. But they made their imprint on subsequent history none the less. Their chief seat was Balloch Castle, situated probably on the eastern bank of the Leven just as it leaves the loch. Two of Maldwin's brothers, Aulay and Gilchrist, founded those famous Lomondside clans, the Macaulays and the MacFarlanes.

The lands of the Lennox once included large tracts of Stirlingshire, as well as nearly the whole of Dunbarton county. Its lords, few of whom died with their boots off, reigned over it with the absolute feudal sway of monarchs, and on more than one occasion, challenged the authority of the King himself.

William Wallace, it is said, once found a safe retreat in the Castle at Balloch when pursued by his English enemies. Robert the Bruce, after his defeat by the men of Lorne, sheltered in a cave on Loch Lomondside, a mile or so beyond Inversnaid, which later became known as Rob Roy's Cave. The fifth Lennox Lord, Earl Malcolm (1292-1333), came to the Bruce's assistance, and no doubt enabled the future king to exchange the uncertain shelter of damp rock for the fastness of the formidable stronghold at Balloch, or of Lennox Castle, on the island of Inch Murrin.

Earl Duncan (1385-1425), the great-grandson of Earl Malcolm, married his daughter Isabella to Murdoch, son of the infamous Regent Albany, and cousin of the poet-king, James the First, who was then enduring his eighteen years' imprisonment in England. Although Murdoch himself became an equally unpopular Regent in due course, this proved an unfortunate match for the daughter of the house of Lennox. For when King James came out of captivity, he decided to avenge the death of his older brother Robert at Albany's hands, and to root out the Albany stock.

Consequently, Murdoch, his two sons and his aged father-in-law, Earl Duncan, were all put on trial for treason and duly executed on the Heading Hill at Stirling. One other son who escaped made use of the short remainder of his life to storm and burn Dumbarton Castle, killing the King's uncle in the doing.

Isabella had, meanwhile, been imprisoned in Tantallon Castle. But the Lennox earldom was not forfeited, so she was eventually allowed to return to Inch Murrin, where she devoted herself to pious works, amongst others, the founding of the Collegiate Church at Dumbarton in 1450.

Having thus lost husband and sons, she died without male issue, and the earldom was partitioned—not without family strife —between the descendants of Earl Duncan's daughters, Margaret and Elizabeth. Elizabeth's grandson, Sir John Stewart of Darnley, got half the lands and, after much legal wrangling, the title. The rest of the estate was divided between Napier of Merchiston and Haldane of Gleneagles, both of whom had married Margaret's daughters. Because of this partitioning, the inventor of logarithms was born at the Napier's country seat, Gartness on the Endrick. And a hamlet, now almost joined to Balloch, got the name of Haldane's Mill, a name it still retains, though the mill has long since disappeared.

A Lennox and a Haldane both featured amongst the slain in the Flodden casualty lists. Eventually, the son of a Lennox, Lord Darnley, married Mary, Queen of Scots, their son becoming James the Sixth and First. The earldom thus merged with the royal line; indeed, the later Stewarts are usually referred to as the Lennox Stewarts. Unfortunately, they lacked those brilliant if erratic qualities of kingship which enabled the earlier Stewarts to weather the storms and stresses of their rude and violent centuries with brave if usually tragic distinction.

The Lennox title, elevated to a dukedom, was recreated by James the Sixth and First; but the lands of the Lennox were finally sold by the sixth Duke of Lennox, illegitimate son of Charles the Second and the Duchess of Portsmouth, to the Marquis of Montrose, whose descendants still retain part of them to-day .

The family which to some extent took over the position of the Lennoxes when that powerful house fell—the Colquhouns of Luss —owed their initial advancement to their superiors. In the reign of Alexander the Second (1214-49), one, Humphrey of Kilpatrick, obtained from Maldwin, third Earl of Lennox—who seems to have been a powerful and influential character—a grant of the lands of Colquhoun. In accordance with the prevailing custom, Humphrey's descendants called themselves after their newest and most extensive territorial acquisition. The first stronghold of the family was the Castle of Dunglass, by Bowling, the ruins of which still stand, in spite of the thoughtlessness of eighteenth- and early nineteenth-century civic dignitaries who authorized its stones to be removed for the repairing of a quay. The Colquhouns, with their lands on the fringe of the Highlands, were, on the whole, a law-abiding clan much respected by their Lowland neighbours, who must often have been thankful for the presence of such reliable Highlanders between themselves and the wilder clans of the North.

Dunbartonshire, half Highland, half Lowland, was the scene of much bitter clan feuding. The Highlanders could keep watch down the glens and passes around Loch Lomondside as the Low-landers reared their crops and cattle. Plundering descents were relatively easy and profitable, and in these days of difficult and poor communications, retribution could not easily be executed against the caterans. The worst offenders were undoubtedly the MacGregors, aided from time to time by their friends the Macaulays and the MacFarlanes.

It is not easy to trace the origin of the lengthy feud between the MacGregors and the Colquhouns which culminated in the tragic rout of the Colquhouns in Glen Fruin, described in the previous chapter. Some blame the Colquhouns, who allegedly refused hospitality to two travelling MacGregors passing northwards after a visit to Glasgow. The hungry MacGregors, it is said, thereupon killed and ate a Colquhoun sheep, an offence for which they were pursued, caught and brought before the Colquhoun chief, who, under his feudal powers as "lord of pit and gallows", sentenced them both to be hanged. A series of reprisal raids for this affront (though it was legal enough under the laws of the day) began in 1527. Thereafter, the MacGregors became implicated more and more deeply in the business of rapine and raid, until they got themselves made a proscribed clan. Apologists for the Mac-Gregors allege that the Colquhouns were thus, in fact, the first aggressors, but, on the whole, the weight of available evidence seems to settle the main burden of blame on the MacGregors.

Some later Colquhoun chieftains made minor appearances in Scottish history. Sir John Colquhoun, the son of Sir Alexander, was made a Baronet of Nova Scotia by King Charles the First, and fought on the King's side throughout the Civil War. Cromwell saw to it that the laird's loyalty cost him the substantial fine of two thousand pounds. The seventeenth laird, Sir Humphrey Colquhoun, was a member of the last Scottish Parliament, where he stoutly opposed the incorporative Union with England. He died without male issue. So that his daughter's husband, a Grant, should inherit the estate and title, Sir Humphrey resigned his Baronetcy to the Crown, obtaining a new grant which made it possible for his son-in-law and his heirs to inherit the title, provided their name was changed to Colquhoun, and that the Grant and the Colquhoun lands should never be amalgamated. To-day, the Laird of Luss, the ninth baronet under the new grant, retains more of his ancestral territory than any other ancient family in the district.

## II

By our ordinary standards of measurement, the Lennoxes and the Colquhouns carry their pedigrees back to a highly venerable antiquity. But Dunbartonshire, and particularly Dumbarton, has seen the proud ceremonial of people more ancient still—people who have long since disappeared from the earth's surface, their story clouded by the variability of legend, their memorials pathetically fragmentary.

At Old Kilpatrick, legend has long had it that St. Patrick, the patron saint of Ireland, was born. Unfortunately, the Irish poet Oliver St. John Gogarty, in his witty and provocative study *I Follow Saint Patrick*, shows fairly conclusively that this could not have been so.

Kilpatrick was, however, the western terminal point of the thirty-six-mile-long Roman or Antonine Wall which Antoninus Pius, the adopted son and successor of the great, the genial, the poetical Hadrian, caused his subordinate Lollius Urbicus to erect across Scotland about the year A.D. 144, by way of containing the " barbaric " Caledonians of the North. Donald A. Mackenzie, in *Scotland the Ancient Kingdom*, gives us this reconstruction of the defences:

" This Scottish wall had a stone foundation fourteen feet broad and, here and there, stone culverts, and on the foundations, sods were laid in the western area, and masses of earth and clay in the eastern. It appears to have been about ten feet in height. The northern side was protected by a ditch about twelve feet deep and about twenty feet wide. . . . There was a military way on the south side of the wall."

The Wall, on its way towards Carriden-on-Forth, runs through Dunbartonshire's two detached parishes, Kirkintilloch (meaning, perhaps, " fort at the end of the hillock ") and Cumbernauld, so called after the confluence of the streams at Castlecary. They

*The Firth of Clyde from above Gourock before the disappearance of the pleasure steamers*

both boast of an erstwhile strong Covenanting tradition. And both carry through their territory, in a line almost parallel to that of the Roman wall, the Forth and Clyde canal, a structure much used for heavy traffic before the coming of the railways.

Kirkintilloch had its laureate in David Gray (1836-61), who was born in the neighbouring hamlet of Merkland, and educated at Glasgow with a view to "waggin' his pow in a pulpit". But the claims of literature proved too strong. Together with his friend, Robert Buchanan, he made a madcap descent upon London, which he hoped to take by literary storm. This, however, was not to be, for, although he was befriended by Monckton Milnes (later Lord Houghton) and Sydney Dobell, young Gray caught consumption, aggravated, no doubt, by his first night in the megalopolis, which he spent sleeping on a bench in Hyde Park. Shortly afterwards, he came home to his mother's cottage to die. As he lay awaiting the end, the page-proofs of his poem "The Luggie", celebrating his native river, gladdened his eye; and he poured his last energies into a sonnet-sequence, "In the Shadows", a deeply moving confession of faith, written literally in the face of Death. Had he lived longer, the original note detectable in his best work would doubtless have risen above the influences of Thomson and Wordsworth.

Kirkintilloch has one other distinction—a peculiar one. Under a privilege of the comic licensing laws of Scotland, Kirkintilloch regularly voted itself "dry"—a curiously uncivil gesture towards less ascetic travellers.

The Roman Wall, from which we made that diversion, was probably held, not without difficulty, for about fifty years, during which time it was twice penetrated and partially "turned" by the liberty-loving Celts. Indeed, it became known in Scotland as Graham's Dyke, after a legendary Highlander who was reputed to have first broken through it. In the end, the Romans abandoned it. But they did not abandon their attempts to subdue the future Scotland for another two centuries. The Scottish expedition of Severus probably reached the Moray Firth, which he took to be the limit of the land. Later still, the celebrated general, Theodosius, pursued the Picts right up to their naval bases in Orkney and Shetland. But the golden age of the Roman Empire was over. By the time the Romans finally withdrew, the Picts from the North and the Scots from Ireland had taken to acting in concert.

Meanwhile, Dumbarton changed names several times—Nemthur; Alcluid; Caer Bretain—before, in the sixth century, it became generally known as Dunbreatan (Fortress of the Britons),

*The Firth of Clyde: P.S. Waverley, the last seagoing paddle-steamer in service, at Arrochar*

the capital of the Cymric kingdom of Strathclyde, which stretched from Loch Lomond southwards to the Derwent in Cumberland. The Norse laid siege to it and took it in 877, ravaging the countryside and greatly weakening Strathclyde. But it was not until the first decade of the eleventh century that Strathclyde became part of the Gaelic Scotland of King Malcolm the Second; the last subking of Strathclyde—the childless Eogan or Owen the Bald, a vassal of Malcolm's—helping his overlord against the forces of King Canute at the Battle of Carham in 1018.

Since the possession of a fortified castle was an essential element of practical politics before the days of "modern" warfare, Dumbarton Castle has been something of a keystone in Scottish history. The rock itself, standing on the edge of the Clyde a little way apart from its more sylvan brother-eminence Dumbuck (which now has to suffer the indignity of being gradually quarried away), is basaltic with two peaks. No doubt it has been used as a fortification since men first learned to fight. Besides sheltering or imprisoning countless anonymous warriors, it has given "hospitality" to many distinguished visitors, often under tragic circumstances. When William Wallace was captured at Robroyston, after his betrayal by the false Menteith, he was interned at Dumbarton Castle before being carried to London to face his barbarous end. The boy king David the Second sailed in 1334 from beneath the castle walls to the safety of France; and in 1548, the six-year-old Mary, Queen of Scots, set out for the same destination.

Twenty-three years later, when her cause was all but lost, Dumbarton Castle was one of the two last Scottish strongholds which held out in her favour. Such, indeed, was the importance of castles in those days, that so long as Edinburgh and Dumbarton were in Marian hands, there was hope for her. That hope was dramatically shattered on the first of April 1571, by a force acting on the instructions of Mary's former father-in-law, Lennox, now Regent of Scotland. He chose for leader of the expedition Thomas Crawford of Jordanhill, who had been one of Darnley's gentlemen, and whose evidence of what took place at the Queen's last visit to Darnley in Kirk o' Field, later helped to send her to her long imprisonment and bravely met death at Fotheringay. Some months after the Castle was taken, Crawford sat down to write an account of the proceedings to John Knox. And here is what gladdened the gloating eyes of the great Reformer early in the New Year of 1572:

" . . . we depairted from Glasgow ane hour before the sun

setting, I haveand providit of before the ladders and cords and crawes of iron to put betwix craigs (rocks) to put cords to . . . and swa we passed forewart while we come to the hill of Dumbuck, within ane mile of the said castle; and there, about ane eftir midnicht, we lay doun our ladders and cords, and sortit all our business as it were long to write. . . . Now, we had mony fosses (bogs) to pass, and ane deep water, brigit with ane single tree, afore we came to the castle; and the formaist of us bure the ladders, and swa we passed forwart. And because they suspected nocht the highest pairt of the craig, there was not ane watch in that pairt of the wall abune, within six score of foots to the pairt whaur we entered. . . . When we had knit the ladders of threescore steps, we were yet twenty steps from ane tree that was abune us; to which tree the guide and myself won to without ladders with great difficulty, taking cords with us . . . and swa letting the cords hing doun to the tree. . . . Be (by the time) this was done, daylicht was come, because it was long of doing. . . . At the entry of the first man upon the top of the wall, the watch that sat beside saw him, and immediately he cried and wakened the place. And ane clud of mist fell about us which was little lichter than the nicht, and there comes out of sundry houses of the place men running naked . . . we won their artillery and their powder and their bullets, and turned the samen to themselves . . . because the mist was so done thick, some lap the walls and escapit, and other some we got, as ye have heard. . . ."[1]

One of those who escaped was Lord Fleming, the Governor of the Castle. But one of those whom they "got", clad in mail shirt and steel cap, was Archbishop Hamilton, the last Catholic Archbishop of St. Andrews, of whose execution thereafter at Stirling, Knox would certainly have heard.

What Crawford omitted to tell Knox was that the "guide" was one Robertson, a soldier of the castle whose wife had been whipped, on the orders of Lord Fleming, for thieving. Nor did Crawford recount the disaster which so nearly befell them when the leading man was half-way up the ladder. He was seized by an epileptic fit and could neither move up nor down. The resourceful Crawford thereupon bound him firmly to the ladder, then turned it round so that the rest of the force could pass over the poor wretch.

The news of Crawford's victory greatly elated Queen Elizabeth, who lost no time in sending a message of congratulation to Len-

[1] I have standardized and slightly modernized Crawford's spelling in the interests of intelligibility.

nox. Queen Mary, on being told of the loss her cause had sustained, showed little outward concern. There was still Edinburgh. Two years later, that last stronghold also fell.

During the seventeenth century, Dumbarton Castle was occupied in rather a desultory fashion by the troops of Cromwell; returned to the Crown at the Restoration; and retaken by the Covenanters, who failed to hold it, so that in turn it became a prison for themselves. Since Marian times, the place had not been properly maintained, and we learn the extent of the disrepair from several official surveys which had been preserved; but, like the reports of our numerous advisory committees to-day, little cognizance appears to have been taken of the alarming state of affairs related by the surveyors, and less action to implement their expert advice.

The castle made one last flourish in Scottish history. During the '45, it housed several eminent Jacobite prisoners. Dunbartonshire was almost solidly anti-Jacobite in sentiment; yet by means that have never been fully explained, several of these prisoners contrived to make a successful escape.

A myth grew up that under the terms of the 1707 Treaty of Union, Dumbarton Castle was one of four such establishments to be permanently garrisoned. The Treaty of Union, however, lays down no such commitment, and, in fact, the castle played no significant military rôle after the middle of the eighteenth century, although the military made some use of the place during the First World War when it became a barracks. Now, it is a museum, housing in stony coldness the casual, worn flotsam of history— old weapons, old armour, and those odd accoutrements of living to which not even antiquity can give that significance which we strive to make them possess.

From the top of the rock there is a view to be had which compensates for the effort of climbing. To the east, the Clyde winds round towards Glasgow, forming one boundary of the county; past Bowling, with its winter harbour for part of the Clyde fleet, and its huge oil installations burrowing deep into the hill; past Clydebank, a mid-nineteenth-century burgh which grew into an important ship-building centre with astonishing rapidity; and so to the landward edge of the county. Above the river and behind Old Kilpatrick, there rises the double-tracked arterial road to Glasgow, built during the depressions of the 'twenties and 'thirties, and grandly known as the "Boulevard". Westward, the Firth opens its arms towards the Cowal Hills. Northwards, the Vale of Leven leads the eye up to Loch Lomond, and frames the noble mountains beyond.

III

Visitors to Dumbarton, or indeed to any of the county's industrialized burghs, cannot possibly carry away very pleasant architectural memories. In Dumbarton's case, the story is much the same
as that of Glasgow. So sudden was the industrial expansion of
mid-Victorian days that the restoration of old property seemed a
foolish waste of time and money. Apart from the broken arch of
Isabella's Collegiate Church, which now stands in front of the
red sandstone town buildings like a dessicated, severed limb,
and " Glencairn's Great House ", the old town house of the Earls
of Glencairn, no memorial of the older phases of the town's
existence remains.

Generations of Dennys once made Dumbarton[1] famous as the
home of great ships; as famous as the more recent name of John
Brown has made Clydebank, cradling-place of the Cunarders
*Queen Mary* and *Queen Elizabeth*. But sprawling shipyards,
engineering shops, and one of the largest and ugliest red-brick
factories in the West of Scotland, have removed all graciousness
from the outward personality of Dumbarton.

Clydebank, which suffered severely during the between-the-wars
slump, and in two sharp air raids during World War Two,[2] is even
less prepossessing, with its closely ranged rows of tenements, and
its narrow, over-trafficked streets. This hard-working burgh
possesses the distinction of having in its Town Hall quite the
most absurdly hideous public building I have seen in all Scotland.
But the housing scheme growing up towards the Boulevard behind
the old town has at least made possible a healthier way of life for
the new generations than they could ever have hoped for in the
pre-war town. That part of it which is made up of so-called
"traditional" houses is also pleasing to the eye.

Dunbartonshire probably contains more contrasts than any
other Scottish county. Not only are there those contrasts of scenery
which result from the meeting of the Highlands and the Lowlands.
There is also the astonishing contrast in ways of living found
within the ten miles or so which take in Clydebank on the river,
and the inland residential agglomerations of Bearsden and Miln-

[1] From 1776 to 1850, Dumbarton was the site of a flourishing glass works
company which became famous for the quality of its products. The town's
other industries to-day include boiler tube making and whisky bonding.
During the Second World War, the Clyde's twenty-two shipyards built
one-third of all British naval tonnage. And by the end of the war, they had
built more ships for the Royal Navy than the total tonnage of the Navy in
mid-1938.
[2] Only five houses in the whole burgh went entirely skaithless.

gavie, in the parish of West Kilpatrick. Bearsden (*buran din,* "entrenchments of the fort", connected obviously with the nearby Roman Wall), until the latter part of the nineteenth century, was a pleasant little country village. As merchant after merchant built himself a pompous and ornate stone mansion, complete with coaching accommodation, its rustic character was gradually filched from it. Now, it has virtually no separate existence of its own, its close proximity to Glasgow having helped to turn it into a well-to-do dormitory suburb.

Much the same fate seems outwardly to have overtaken Milngavie (pronounced *Milguy,* and probably derived from *meall na gaoithe,* hill of the wind), a few miles farther to the northeast. Glasgow's tramcars once made their swaying way to the very outskirts of the old village. But the place has somehow contrived to retain a little of its former personality, and it boasts of quite a healthy communal life. It has the rare distinction of being an uncommonly musical township. Six times or so every year, the Parish Church Hall takes in three hundred people who have come to listen to chamber music performed by the leading ensembles of the day. Although the setting is by no means ideal— the chairs are as peculiarly uncomfortable as the seats of music-lovers, by Victorian tradition, ought to be; and the steeple clock has a habit of interrupting the sublimest utterances of the world's greatest musical minds with its mundane pronouncements of the hour—nevertheless, the achievement is astonishing. Glasgow, for all its millions, cannot raise an audience half that size for similar concerts, and I doubt if the position is very different in any English city furth of London. Since 1854, Milngavie has had a tame loch in the nearby Mugdock reservoir, an adjunct of Glasgow's main water-works at Loch Katrine, from which it is separated by twenty-six piped miles, thirteen of them encased by tunnelling. This stone-banked loch has a path round it, and is popular with week-end strollers who do not care to take their country exercise "neat".

The River Leven, which covers six winding miles between leaving Loch Lomond and flowing round Dumbarton Rock into the Clyde, runs through the centre of the parish of Bonhill (*boghn-uill,* foot of the rivulet). The parish has become famous as the birthplace of Tobias George Smollett (1721-71), who came into the world at the old house of Dalquhurn. Educated at Dumbarton and at Glasgow University, Smollett took the fashionable road to London in 1739, with a play in his pocket which was meant to take the metropolis by storm. All his life, Smollett had hankerings after success in the theatre, and the preface to his play *The Regicide*, published in 1749, is the outstanding example in Scottish literature of the lengths to which unsuccessful authors will go to account for their own lack of talent by the malicious intrigues of their supposed enemies. A glance through the stilted lines of Smollett's tragedy shows very clearly why Garrick would have none of it, and why it never found a producer. So great was his embitterment at this set-back that Smollet went to sea for several years as surgeon's mate.

In his own sphere, the then relatively untilled soil of the novel, Smollett was, of course, an extremely skilful and successful master. From the publication of his first picaresque novel, *Roderick Random*, to the appearance of *Humphry Clinker* in 1771, Smollett's abilities as a sketcher and caricaturist of the manners of his time became surer. English critics sometimes suggest that he had a coarser touch than Henry Fielding. It has always seemed to me that such a judgment is based to some extent on an absence of knowledge of the habits and characteristics of Scottish people in the eighteenth century.

As with most authors, the writing of masterpieces failed to keep the proverbial spectre of the wolf, so familiar to creative artists of any generation, from his door. So Smollett turned out an incredible quantity of " hack " work, the most important of which was his enormous *History of England*. It is said that a nobleman who met Smollett socially and took a liking to him, requested the novelist to send round copies of all his books for inclusion in the aristocratic library. To the nobleman's horror, the books arrived on a fully laden cart, followed by a correspondingly large bill.

To help him in this " hack " work, Smollett employed a team of hungry literary hangers-on. When Dr. Alexander Carlyle[1] visited London in 1758, he met Smollett, and recorded this glimpse of the great author's ways with his "assistants":

> " . . . By this time the Doctor had retired to Chelsea, and came seldom to town. Home and I, however, found that he came once a week to Forrest's Coffeehouse, and sometimes dined there; so we managed an appointment with him on his day, when he agreed to dine with us. He was now become a great man, and being much of a humourist, was not to be put out of his way. Home and Robertson and Smith and I met him

[1] The close friend of John Home the playwright, " Jupiter " Carlyle (1722-1805), so-called because of his imposing visage, which even impressed Scott, left one of the most vivid accounts of life in eighteenth-century Scotland in his racy *Autobiography*, which he began at the age of eighty and did not live to complete. His resistance to the Church of Scotland's ban on ministers attending the theatre led to the adoption of a more reasonable attitude by the Kirk authorities.

there, when he had several of his minions about him, to whom he prescribed tasks of translation, compilation or abridgement, which, after he had seen, he recommended to the booksellers. We dined together, and Smollett was very brilliant. Having to stay all night, that we might spend the evening together, he only begged leave to withdraw for an hour, that he might give audience to his myrmidons; we insisted that if his business permitted, it should be in the room where we sat. The Doctor agreed, and the authors were introduced, to the number of five, I think, most of whom were soon dismissed. He kept two however, to supper, whispering to us that he believed they would amuse us, which they certainly did, for they were curious characters.

"We passed a very pleasant and joyful evening. . . ."

The Doctor, however, had his weaknesses. He was vain, malicious and willing to lend his pen to the service of unsavoury political causes. He even spent a short term in prison as a result of a political libel, and the experience embittered him for the rest of his days.

A recent American biographer[1] remarks:

"The fact that Smollett may never, consciously or unconsciously, have forgotten his Scottish origins and that he never completely and consistently identified himself with English life or lost his sense of isolation and detachment, only enhance in one respect the value of his observations; for it means that Smollett wrote, as it were, from the vantage point of two cultures."

Proof of this lies in the emotional reaction which welled up in Smollett when the news was brought to him of Cumberland's butchery at Culloden. He was no Jacobite. Yet, he immediately sat down to write that vigorous lament, "The Tears of Scotland":

> "Mourn, hapless Caledonia, mourn
> Thy banish'd peace, thy laurels torn!
> Thy sons for valour long renown'd,
> Lie slaughter'd on their native ground;
> Thy hospitable roofs no more
> Invite the stranger to the door;
> In smoky ruins sunk they lie,
> The monuments of cruelty. . . ."

[1] *Tobias Smollett: Traveller-Novelist*, by George M. Krahl.

It was pointed out to him by his friends that such sentiments as those expressed in the poem's six original stanzas could be regarded as treasonable, and might get their author into trouble. Whereupon, Smollett added a defiant seventh stanza which, though on a lower literary level, made even more plain the nature of the author's sentiments:

> " While the warm blood bedews my veins,
> And unimpaired remembrance reigns,
> Resentment of my country's fate
> Within my filial breast shall beat;
> And, spite of her insulting foe,
> My sympathising verse shall flow:
> ' Mourn, hapless Caledonia, mourn
> Thy banish'd peace, thy laurels torn.' "

As he grew older, the business of organizing his " myrmidons " became wearisome. His health, too, began to suffer. Always a keen traveller, he tried through the good offices of his friend David Hume, the philosopher, to procure a consulship at Nice or Leghorn. Hume failed in his attempts, and after a last visit to Scotland, which he greatly enjoyed, Smollett set off for Italy, into final voluntary exile. Worn out and ill as he was during these last six years, he managed to produce his best travel book, as well as *Humphrey Clinker*. Had health been granted to him for another few years, he would have fallen heir to the Dalquhurn estates, and his monetary worries would have been relieved. But he died at Antigniano, near Leghorn, in September 1771.

The Victorians, with that arrogant prudery which allowed them to consider themselves more " refined " than any mortals who had hitherto coarsened God's earth, found Smollett wanting in taste. (Curious, was it not, that those generations whose own artistic taste was as poor as that of any other age in the history of our civilization, should have been so loudly censorious of their betters?) Nowadays, Smollett's astonishing vigour and humour need no defence, and most of his novels are available in modern editions.

In Smollett's day, the Vale of Leven was apparently an Arcadian paradise; for in his " Ode to Leven Water " he addressed it as:

> " Pure stream, in whose transparent wave
> My youthful limbs I wont to lave;
> No torrents stain thy limpid source,
> No rocks impede thy dimpling course,

*That sweetly warbles o'er its bed,*
*With white, round polished pebbles spread;*
*While, lightly poised, the scaly brood*
*In myriads cleave thy crystal flood;*
*The springing trout in speckled pride,*
*The salmon, monarch of the tide;*
*The ruthless pike, intent on war,*
*The silver eel and mottled par*
*Devolving from thy parent lake,*
*A charming maze thy waters make,*
*By bowers of birch and groves of pine,*
*And edges flowered with eglantine. . . ."*

An English traveller, Thomas Pennant, confirmed Smollett's view. "The vale between the end of the lake and Dunbarton," Pennant wrote in 1771, "is unspeakably beautiful. . . ."

But the edges of the Leven have long since lost their eglantine. During most of its course from Loch Lomond to the Clyde, the river flows past factories and industrial townships. Across the river-mouth from Dumbarton Castle, the ancient village of Cardross once stood, though the modern village lies a few miles to the west. Here, King Robert the Bruce had his palace; here he spent his last days with his beautiful young second wife, his lion, his falcon and his fool. And here, on a long day in 1329, he died of leprosy, all his proud courage flaring up in one last kingly gesture as he instructed the weeping Douglas to carry his heart to the Holy Land and hurl it amongst the Saracens. But Sir James Douglas died on his way to the Holy Land. His body was brought back to Douglas for interment, and Bruce's heart was buried in Melrose Abbey.

The Leven's steady strength, and its relative freedom from "mineral and organic ingredients", made it naturally suitable for harnessing to the business of bleaching, printing and dyeing cotton. The first successful move towards wresting away Holland's superiority in this industry was made about 1728, when bleach-fields were established at Pollokshields, in Renfrewshire, and at Dalquhurn. Workmen were brought over from Holland to instruct the natives. From this humble beginning, the industry spread over the country. But its greatest concentration remained in the Vale, where there were at one time in simultaneous operation six large print fields and five bleach-fields, as well as other related minor industries. In 1835, Turkey Red dyeing and printing was also established in the Vale at Croftengea.

To house the workers employed in these industries, Renton,

Jamestown and Alexandria were built along the banks of the river. They can never have been attractive places at any time, but the harrowing experience of prolonged and concentrated un-employment which struck the Vale when the bleaching industry collapsed in the years following the First World War, has left them with a permanently down-at-heel look. The Calico Printers Association, virtually an English monopoly, offered substantial sums to the Scottish Calico printers for their concerns. In a very short time the Calico Printers' Association became the owners of most of the bleaching fields and Calico printing works in Scot-land. During the depression, the redundant Scottish factories were closed down, a process which, when accomplished, com-pletely wrecked the economic basis of life in the Vale, and threw many thousands of Scots craftsmen out of work. The human legacy of their industrial tragedy[1] is reflected in the high sickness and unemployable figures for the district, and in the many ill-formed and under-nourished young people to be seen about the streets.

Many of the huge and gloomy factories used by these indus-tries are now divided into smaller units, or crumble, part-derelict. The handsome red sandstone factory on the outskirts of Alex-andria where once Argyll motors were made, and which later housed Clarence Hatry's artificial silks concern—its failure led to a sensational trial—is now also split up among smaller con-cerns, having for many years housed the manufacture of Royal Naval torpedoes.

New and well-landscaped housing in these Vale of Leven towns has done much to brighten their environment in recent years.

In Balloch, British Silk Dyes Limited has set up a factory where fine silks are coloured, the waters of Loch Lomond, now also used to supply drinking water, apparently being only second in suitability to the waters of certain Swiss lakes for this purpose.

IV

Balloch (probably derived from *beul loch*, the mouth of the loch) was, until the middle of the last century, a rural village. It

[1] Yet another illustration of the inept shortsightedness of Scottish business men when pitted against their English rivals?

has grown considerably in size, and rural cottages have given place to villas and bungalows. But, in spite of this, and the presence of the silk-works with its tall chimney stack, Balloch still manages to preserve a countrified air, particularly during the off-season.

As the Leven leaves the loch, it flows round a little wooded island before sweeping slowly under the Balloch bridges. Opposite the island, both banks of the river are lined with motor boats and dinghies. On a summer's day, the streets of Balloch throng with holidaymakers; some, perhaps, making their way down to the pier from which paddle-steamers cruise up to Ardlui, at the head of the loch: others may be filling up the motor-boats whose agents loudly advertise from the roadside the peculiar charms of the famous loch as seen from their own craft. It is always good to see people enjoying themselves, and, from April to September, Balloch is a centre of enjoyment. Hikers and climbers from Glasgow, bent under heavy packs, detrain at Balloch and set off on long tramps through the mountains. Buses draw up beside the jetties, allowing boys who make a hobby of listing their places of origin to learn the name of many a remote corner of England. Some of the buses, engaged perhaps on protracted tours from Midland industrial towns, announce their destination in rough detail—"The Three Lochs", or "The Five Lochs", or perhaps "The Trossachs". Others, more succinctly, merely carry the one word "Scotland"; which at least allows a certain latitude to the driver!

The tourist trade has now become a major Scottish industry. Venerable diehards lament this necessity—for necessity it is—and complain of the blow which Scottish pride has thereby to suffer, to say nothing of the vulgarization entailed. I cannot see that there is anything humiliating in making the most of your country's scenic glories, provided steps are taken to check vandalism. The blaring forth of distorted dance music on over-magnified amplifiers as a means of attracting visitors to sail on the loch, and the plastering of the river-banks with ill-contrived and vulgar slogans on hoardings seems to me to be vandalism of a most offensive and anti-social order.

A beauty-spot as accessible to a large industrial city as Loch Lomond is to Glasgow, inevitably attracts its week-end quota of vandals. The late Laird of Luss, Sir Ian Colquhoun, while welcoming all who came to enjoy without spoiling, took a commendably firm line with those who, either out of sheer ignorance, or thoughtlessness, or for calculated profit, sought in any way to lower the dignity of the countryside. Loch Lomondside is now to be a

National Park area, so its preservation in its natural condition seems to be assured.

The nineteenth-century Balloch Castle and its parks were bought by Glasgow Corporation in 1915 as a place of week-end recreation for the citizens of the Scottish wen. A bus service runs at five-minute intervals between Balloch and the City, augmented by a train service which, at any rate, during the summer, is fairly frequent.

The western side of the loch has always been the most popular with the tourists. This is partly because that winding, twisting road—by modern standards, absurdly narrow—which, in its twenty-four difficult miles, carries the traveller out of the rolling Lowlands into the heart of the Highlands, is also the main route to the north-west.

Along the first part of the journey, every other bend reveals an imposing tree-sheltered lodge gate. Most of these lochside mansions date only from the nineteenth century, although some of them stand on the sites of older castles or houses. First comes Cameron House, acquired towards the end of the seventeenth century by Smollett's grandfather, Commissary (Judge) James Smollett of Bonhill. Both this house and the Bonhill estate went to the novelist's sister, Mrs. Alexander Telfer, and it is still in the possession of her descendants, the Telfer-Smolletts. Auchendennan, on the site of one of King Robert the Bruce's hunting-lodges (how many fine lodges these old kings had to choose from!), is now the largest youth hostel in the world. Presumably, Auchenheglish, the Gaelic derivation of which means "field of the church", stands on the site of some ancient chapel. Arden, one of the newest mansions, was built by a Lord Provost of Glasgow, Sir James Lumsden, in 1860. Two and a half miles south of Luss, Rossdhu (*ros dubh,* the black promontory), seat of the Colquhouns, looks placidly over the waters of the loch. The old castle was replaced late in the eighteenth century by a square but gracefully proportioned mansion, to which several later additions have been made.

Luss itself, which gives its baffling name to the parish— etymologists have not solved its origin[1]—is the only village of any size on the loch-side. Its white-washed hotel, looking down the single street that runs from the main road to the pier, and the

[1] Legend suggests the French *luce,* a lily, because a certain Baroness Macauslan, whose husband distinguished himself at the siege of Tournay, died in France. Her body was brought to Luss for burial, and the coffin was strewn with *fleur-de-luce,* some of which took root and reached the surface. They became a cure for pestilence! More probably, Luss simply derives from the Gaelic *luss,* a plant.

flowering orderliness of its little cottage gardens, give it a primly picturesque appearance. Behind the village, the wooded hills rise steeply. After rain, white-flecked burns brattle and brawl through the bracken and the heather, gathering together first in the Edintaggart burn, then finally merging for the last stretch of their turbulent passage in the rich clear surge of Luss Water.

The present postcard appearance of Luss, however, is not a century old. An old guide book in my possession contains a drawing of the place which shows the present stone kirk, and a straggling row of mean-looking, thekit (thatched) cottages, not very different from Hebridean black houses. That, certainly, was the prospect which greeted the jaunting Lakers, William and Dorothy Wordsworth, accompanied by a rather morose and erratic Coleridge, when they arrived at the place in the summer of 1803. Dorothy kept a journal of their travels,[1] and she recorded that the houses in Luss had "not a single ornamented garden". Here, too, she "first saw houses without windows, the smoke coming out of the open window-places; the chimneys were like stools with four legs, a hole being left in the roof for the smoke, and over that a slate being placed upon four sticks".

On the evening of August the 24th, the party returned to Luss Inn to spend the night. It had been a sunless day, cold and raw. Coleridge had been feeling unwell, so had remained indoors. Dorothy and William had wandered up the lochside, admiring the islands, and the majesty of Ben Lomond, yet comparing all that they saw unfavourably with their own Lakes.[2]

Towards the end of August, Scottish evenings often become cold, and most families light their sitting-room fires at tea-time. When the Wordsworths asked for a fire to be lit in the sitting-room of the inn, Dorothy tells us that the girl hesitated, and when she brought in the tea-things explained that ". . . 'her mistress was not verra willing to gie fire'. At last, however, on our insisting upon it, the fire was lighted: we got tea by candle-light, and spent a comfortable evening. I had seen the landlady before we went out, for, as had been usual in all the country inns, there was a demur respecting beds, notwithstanding the house was empty, and there were at least half a dozen spare beds. Her countenance corresponded with the unkindness of denying us a fire on a cold night, for she was the most cruel and hateful-looking

---

[1] *Tour in Scotland: A.D. 1803*, by Dorothy Wordsworth.
[2] Wordsworth, accustomed to the pretty miniaturism of Cumberland, found that "the proportion of diffused water was too great" in the Loch Lomond countryside. Professor Wilson ("Christopher North"), more perceptive as regards Scottish scenery than his greater contemporary, later commented: "The diffusion of water is indeed great; but in what a world it floats!"

woman I ever saw. She was overgrown with fat, and was sitting with her feet and legs in a tub of water for the dropsy—probably brought on by whisky-drinking. The sympathy which I felt and expressed for her, on seeing her in this condition—for her legs were swollen as thick as mill-posts—seemed to produce no effect; and I was obliged after five minutes' conversation, to leave the affair of the beds undecided. . . . It came on a stormy night; the wind rattled every window in the house, and it rained heavily. William and Coleridge had bad beds, in a two-bedded room in the garret, though there were empty rooms on the first floor, and they were disturbed by a drunken man, who had come to the Inn when we were gone to sleep."

At least, the Lakers were luckier than the journalizing French geologist, Faujas St. Fond, who arrived at Luss on a wild night in 1784, also in search of a bed. The hostess, her dropsy no doubt then less far advanced, signed to him not to speak, and hustled him across the yard into a stable. There she explained to him that the Justiciary Lords did her the honour of lodging with her when they were on their circuit. One of them was asleep in the Inn now, and out of respect for the law, no one must disturb him. Whereupon St. Fond was bidden God-speed and forced to travel a further fifteen miles up to Tarbet.

This curious attitude towards tourists and travellers—it is at the bottom of the modern anti-tourist reaction—is, I think, a Gaelic characteristic. At least, I myself have certainly encountered it on several occasions when travelling in the Highlands. However, by 1819, Luss Inn had apparently come under new management. For another Laker, the poet Robert Southey, arrived at it on Sunday the 26th in the company of the engineer Thomas Telford, with whom he had just spent six weeks touring around Scotland. Southey records:

"The house at Luss is a tolerable Inn, not unlike Arrocher (Arrochar) which is far the best in the Highlands, but sufficiently good. From hence, the peculiar character of Loch Lomond is seen; it spreads to a width of nine miles and is interspersed with islands,[1] some so small as to be mere dots upon the surface; others of considerable extent . . ."

Several managers have come and gone since 1819, and a modern traveller, being anxious to view "the peculiar character" of Loch Lomond, from the vantage point of Luss, need have no fears about his reception at the inn. For it has grown into a comfortable little hotel which combines the highest standards of modern

[1] There are over thirty islands on the loch including the "mere dots".

comfort and cuisine with something of its old distinguished atmosphere. Beneath its genial rafters it is still possible to see again in the mind's eye the Wordsworths having tea beside that hard-won fire; or Southey and Telford relaxing after a hard day's coaching down the rough lochside road; or, earlier still, Boswell and Johnson, homeward bound from the Hebridean journey, jolting noisily past the windows on their way to spend the night with Sir James Colquhoun at Rossdhu.[1]

The learned Doctor also considered the islands, but the prevailing rain perhaps affected his judgment. "Had Loch Lomond been in a happier climate," he recorded, "it would have been the boast of wealth and vanity to own one of the little spots which it encloses, and to have employed upon it all the arts of embellishment. But as it is, the islets, which court the gazer at a distance, disgust him at his approach, when he finds, instead of soft lawns and shady thickets, nothing more than uncultivated ruggedness."

Round wooded bays and steep-cut rocky corners, the road winds up the loch; past Inverbeg, at the foot of Glen Douglas, where another hotel welcomes the traveller; past half-hidden roadside cottages, many of which offer, in shaky calligraphy, "Bed and Breakfast". (How refreshing a boiled country egg and bread and butter can be as the prelude to a good night's rest between cool, clean sheets in such a place, after a hard and happy day in the open country!) Round the tall shoulders of Ben Bhreac; and so up the narrowing lochside to Tarbet, in the parish of Arrochar. Tarbet gets its name from *tarrain bata*, a portage, from an incident alleged to have occurred during Haakon of Norway's final Scottish expedition. He is said to have drawn several of his vessels across the narrow neck of land which separates Tarbet from Arrochar, on Loch Long, and to have sailed them, harrying and plundering, down Loch Lomond, penetrating as far as the outskirts of Stirlingshire, where much coastal wealth had been carried for safety. A practically minded literary chaperon round these parts a hundred and fifty years ago, writing in the plural form favoured by those who think their words need such an aid to seem imposing, declaimed loftily: "We entertain some doubt, however, of the correctness of the tradition, as we apprehend that the Danes (sic) would rather have chosen to sail up the river Leven into Loch Lomond, even though the navigation be so difficult as to require horses to be used at present to drag vessels against the stream. It is easier to drag vessels against the ordinary current of a river than over dried ground."

[1] Presumably Burns also called at Luss on his second solitary Highland Tour of 1787, when he had his hectic horse-race with a saddle-less Highlander.

*The Firth of Clyde: Loch Fad, Bute, with the Arran hills behind*

Indisputably. But not when you have to sail under the ramparts of a castle manned by your enemies, before you can reach the mouth of your river!

St. Fond, refreshed no doubt by a good night's rest at Tarbet, did not allow his experiences at Luss to blind him to the charms of Loch Lomond when he looked at it next morning. "The superb Loch Lomond," he wrote, "the fine sunlight that gilded its waters, the silvery rocks that skirted its shores, the flowery and verdant mosses, the black oxen, the white sheep, the shepherds beneath the pines . . . make me cherish the desire not to die before again seeing Tarbet. I shall often dream of Tarbet, even in the midst of lovely Italy, with its oranges, its myrtles, its laurels, and its jessamines."

Nowadays, modern travellers no longer have to suffer the torments of jolting coaches and cold or flea-ridden inns; but so fast is the pace of their journeying that often they have little time to stand and stare. In summer, the lochside road carries an endless stream of cyclists and cars; and particularly on Sundays, it demands a high degree of concentration and skill to get from one end of the road to the other in safety. The walker is continually harried, not only by the noise and commotion of the traffic, but by acrid-smelling petrol-puffs of dust which forever assail his nostrils and throat on a dry day.

At Tarbet, a road forks left over a brae to Arrochar, on Loch Long. By Tarbet, the North of Scotland Hydro-Electric Board have built a pleasing stone village to house those who maintain the plant at Loch Sloy. In these centralized days, when buildings are going up all over the country in accordance with standardized London-passed plans, regardless of whether or not such houses fit into the countryside upon which they are being imposed, it is good to see at least one new village made of the native materials. For this pleasing bit of building, we have to thank Mr. Thomas Johnstone, the first chairman of the Board, whose insistence that stone should be used wherever possible in the Company's building operations, overcame the usual barriers of bureaucratic protest.

The descent on Loch Long from above Arrochar is perhaps a little disappointing. It was by this route that the Wordsworths came upon it. (Coleridge, having got tired of the jaunting car, had, in Neil Munro's words, "just left them in the feckless and impolite way the poets of the period seemed to cultivate") Although they were in rather a depressed mood, Dorothy, with that insight she so often showed for divining the atmosphere of a place, noticed that "the stillness of the mountains, the motion of

*Dunbartonshire: Tarbet, Loch Lomond*

the waves, the streaming torrents, the sea-birds, the fishing-boats, were all melancholy. . . . I thought of the long windings through which the waters of the sea had come to this inland retreat, visiting the inner solitudes of the mountains. . . . From the foot of these mountains, whither might not a little barque carry one away? "

Such womanly romanticism is surely permissible under the historic shadows of the Argyll foothills. For beyond the loch lie the jagged spears of Highland mountains, facetiously nicknamed " Argyll's Bowling-Green " by an unknown wit: Glen Croe, and the once-dreaded " Rest-and-be-Thankful " carrying one away into the delightful blend of ever-shifting light and colour that give the Western Highlands so much of their character. What really settles upon Arrochar, and, indeed, on Loch Goil and Loch Long, that air of melancholy is their relatively small quota of daily sunshine. Shut in by high mountains, a cold, grey atmosphere fills the glens, even when a bright sky above reveals that less sheltered places are enjoying the reality of sunshine.

Loch Long is best seen from the deck of the steamer, if the full weight of its mountain-brooding is to be experienced. But in order to see it at its most genial, it is necessary to climb the hills behind Whistlefield, on the Gareloch. From this eminence, distance not only lends enchantment but softens the severity of the view.

The parish of Arrochar, ancient home of the MacFarlanes, since the eighteenth century a clan without a chief, encases the northern tip of Loch Lomond. The depredations of the MacFarlanes, second only to those of the MacGregors, led to " MacFarlane's Lantern " becoming a local sobriquet for the moon. " Loch Sloy " was their battle-cry.

At Tarbet, a right fork carries the traveller up past Inveruglas; beneath Ben Vorlich; past Eilean Vhow; and so to Ardlui, at the head of the loch. Ardlui—no one is sure whether the name means " height of the creek " or " bend of the shore "!—has a pier, a hotel, a station on the West Highland Railway (which ribbons itself invisibly through the wooded slopes from Craigendoran), and a cottage which is also a tea-room. Highland cattle staring in shaggy immobility are often to be seen on the slopes of Glen Falloch, which carries the road past Inverarnan over the county border into Perthshire.

In summer, the daily steamer lies at the pier for several hours before making its unhurried way back to Balloch. In the late afternoon, it steers a leisurely zigzag course across the loch, calling first at Tarbet, then going over into Stirlingshire to pick up passengers at Rowardennan; across the water again to Luss;[1] back between the verdant, lily fringed islands to Balmaha; then finally into Balloch, where trains wait to carry tourists to Glasgow or Craigendoran.

## V

The main islands on the Dunbartonshire side are Inch Murrin (*Innis na Muirn*—island of hospitality), the largest and most thickly populated—there are about a dozen dwellings on it, some of them permanently occupied—where the ruins of the Lennox stronghold may still be seen; Inch Lonaig, yew island, so named because it is supposed to have been planted with yew trees for the use of King Robert the Bruce's archers during his rearmament campaign; Inch Connachan, Colquhoun's island; Inch Galbraith; Inch Moan, moss island; and Inch Tavannoch, the monk's island. With the exception of Inch Murrin, which lies off Kilmaronock parish, most of these islands are clustered around Luss Bay. The three main Stirlingshire islands are Inch Cailliach, the island of nuns, which once gave its name to a Lennox parish and contained the parish church; Inch Cruin, the round island; and Inch Fad, the long island. Inch Fad, Inch Tavannoch and Inch Lonaig all have a few houses or cottages on them, most of which are seasonally occupied. Mail and provisions are brought out twice a week by Alec MacFarlane of Balmaha, whose forefathers have sailed the loch for generations. Alec himself probably knows more about its dark and treacherous moods than anyone else. He has the unusual distinction of being the only postman in Britain who is not required to wear uniform.

The parish of Kilmaronock lies to the east of Balloch. On the shore of the loch, looking out over Inch Murrin, two famous houses stand. Boturich Castle, once the seat of the Haldanes who fell heir to part of the Lennox lands, was reputedly the scene of one of Squire Meldrum's adventures. Squire Meldrum was a gallant sixteenth-century warrior around whose undoubtedly real exploits legendary feats-of-arms were embroidered by Sir David Lyndsay of the Mount in his poem, "The History of Ane Noble and Valliand Squire William Meldrum, umquhyle Laird of Cleish and Binns".

This particular episode in the Squire's military career was certainly based on fact. In 1515, Marion Lawson, widow of John

---

[1] Since the above was written, Luss pier has, most unfortunately, been closed, because of a dispute between the laird and British Railways as to who is to pay for its upkeep.

Haldane of Gleneagles, while living peacefully in her castle at
Strathearn (enjoying, we learn from the poem, the pleasant atten-
tions of the gallant Squire), heard that her lands around Boturich
were being harried by the MacFarlanes. Squire Meldrum and his
men immediately set out for Loch Lomond. When they arrived,
the Squire rode up to the walls of Boturich where

> " He cryit and said ' Gif owre the house.'
> The Captain answerit heichly,
> And said ' Traitor, we thee defy.
> We sall remain this house within,
> In to despite of all thy kin!'
> With that, the archers bauld and wicht,
> Of braid arrows let flee ane flicht
> Amang the Squire's company. . . ."

Nothing daunted, the Squire's company laid ladders to the outer
walls, and during the hand-to-hand struggle in the courtyard which
followed, the MacFarlane was brought to his knees before the
Squire himself, who, however, made a practice of sparing the lives
of honourably defeated enemies. The poet goes on:

> " And sa this Squire amorous
> Seizit and wan the lady's house.
> And left therein a Capitane,
> Syne to Strathern returnit again;
> Where that he with his fair Lady
> Receivit was full pleasantly
> And to take rest did him convoy.
> Judge ye gif there was mirth and joy.
> Howbeit the chalmer door was closit,
> They did but kiss, as I supposit.
> Gif other thing was them between,
> Let them discover that luvvers been:
> For I am not in luve expert,
> And never studyit in that art. . . ."

However, a few lines later on, the poet tells us that in due course:

> " . . . this Lady fair
> Ane dochter to the Squire bare. . . ."

leaving us to draw our own conclusions!
Ross Priory was visited several times by Sir Walter Scott, when
it was owned by the Edinburgh advocate, Hector MacDonald, son
of MacDonald of Boisdale, who had married a Ross heiress and
who later added her name—Buchanan—to his own. While staying

here on various occasions, Scott gathered together a good deal of material for "The Lady of the Lake" and *Rob Roy*. An excursion he made in the autumn of 1817 to Rob Roy's cave, apparently caused a good deal of gossip amongst those literary people who had already identified "the Great Unknown", as the "Author of Waverley" was then still commonly styled.

The parish of Kilmaronock has no significant history. Gartocharn[1] (field of the cairn), the only village in the parish, lies at the foot of that strangely shaped landmark, Duncryne (hill of the cairn). Gartocharn village is only about a hundred years old. But the descriptive Gaelic-derived names of the surrounding farms, Blairlusk (the burnt field), Badshalloch (the clump of willows), Gallingad (the wood of the withies) and many another equally evocative, are a reminder both of the vividness of eye and the ancient, unbroken continuity of those who patiently till the unfailing soil.

Curiously little poetry has been written about Loch Lomond, for all its fame.[2] One song has, of course, gone all the world over. There is an old Celtic belief that when a man meets his death in a foreign land, his spirit returns home by "the low road". The song "Loch Lomond" is said to refer to the last moments together of two Scottish soldiers captured at Carlisle during the '45. One was to be set free, the other was to be executed on English soil. His spirit would thus go home by "the low road", while his more fortunate friend returned by the "high road" through the Cheviots. It is thus a Jacobite song, and not a love song; the passion which animates its melancholy cadences is not that of a man for a woman, but that of a broken man for his suffering native land.

Wordsworth, of course, made Eilean Vhow the scene of his poem "The Brownie's Cell". And it was at Inversnaid, with its foam-flecked, cascading waters, that he heard his Highland girl singing. "Will no one tell me what she sings?" he asked plaintively.

Something Gaelic, something modal, almost certainly. I have always thought it fortunate that no one could give him the answer he sought. He would never have heard of the song anyway, and

---

[1] George Eyre-Todd (1862-1937), a littérateur whose Abbotsford series of anthologies of Scottish poetry played a useful part in keeping the national literature before our people, lived for many years at Auchenlarich, a house a mile or two back from Gartocharn.

[2] After his walk to Scotland in 1618, where he stayed with Drummond of Hawthornden, Ben Jonson planned a poem on Loch Lomond. If he actually wrote it, it was probably destroyed, along with the memorials of his Scottish tour, when his library was burnt in 1623-4.

even a partial removal of the sense of mystery might have deprived us of the poem.

Scott made several poetical references to the loch and its history, and Alexander (" Behave yoursel' ") Rodger addressed some rather flat lines of apostrophe to Tarbet. But there is not much else. One reason for this dearth of written poetry is that the loch and the mountains that close in upon its northern reaches are themselves a kind of poetry: a poetry which alters subtly in form and texture with every wind that swirls around those mist-steamed Highland bens, and varies with every fresh sweep of the sun.

I well remember the reception the loch gave me when I first went to live beside it. I had not then made my home in Gartocharn, and our bield was to be a newly bought caravan. As we were about to set out from Glasgow (in a vintage Rolls-Royce— 1926), with the caravan jocketing behind, the heavens, which had been ominously grey all day, suddenly crumpled, and heavy drops of rain stotted and skittered over the city streets. By the time we were nearing Gartocharn, the swish of our wheels on the wet road, and the thin, steady drooling of rain that clearly intends to persist for a long time, had lulled us away from contemplation of the trials which inevitably await those who try to establish a caravan in a field for the first time.

We were reminded sharply of the problems before us the moment we jerked down the Ross Loan, and saw the track which led off into our field; for its two grass ruts were a green squelch beneath our gumboots, and the unmetalled surface between them had turned into a reddish paste. After much pushing, spattering and churning of slippery wheels, the caravan was eventually humphed into position on a firm mound beneath the dripping branches of an oak tree.

Later that evening, I walked down to the lochside. A drizzling mist had completely obliterated the mountains, and was rapidly rolling up the loch itself. Soon, all that remained visible was the tufted water's edge, where light-rippled fresh-water waves were breaking with a gentle, foamless splash on the sandy gravel. The air seemed to hang about me, soft and humid, the resinous smell of the damp trees giving off a fine, fragrant sweetness. Raindrops sat upon the spikes of the burgeoning blackthorn hedges, like tiny crystal blooms; the barks of the trees gleamed eagerly; the brown earth drank in the muddy gurgling moisture. Suddenly a blackbird burst out singing, as if Time itself depended on his song. No one who cannot enjoy the varied pleasures of wet weather can ever really hope to appreciate Scotland.

We had a strange experience that night. About two o'clock in the morning, we were awakened by a curious dunting sound. After each dunt, the caravan shuddered as if it had been playfully struck with the flat of some Fenian god's sword. We jumped up in alarm, and threw open the door. Immediately, our bulldog and our dachshund rushed out in a brave fury of barking. But it was no Fenian god with whom we had to deal. Around the caravan a herd of cows had gathered, marvellously fearless in the dark. They were huddled together in a way which suggested a primitive queue, as if each one was wanting its turn to have a knock. The dogs drove them off, and we went back to our bunks. But, soon afterwards, the dunting started again. There was nothing for it but to put on our clothes and build an improvized protecting fence round the caravan in the middle of a lashing rain-storm.

Morning broke in a gentle shower of gold. The rain had trailed far over the hills, leaving the innumerable growing things that crowd the verdant ditches of the lochside roads fresh and greened again. The waters of the loch were now warm blue; the hills were soaked in a rich flush of yellow light. As the sun climbed farther out of the east, heightening the angle of its rays, the hills took on a purpler hue, and beneath the wings of passing shadows the loch mirrored up its black, sloping depth. Bog-myrtle and honeysuckle laced the air as the day grew brighter, and the full flood of birdsong slackened in the heat.

I have never twice seen Loch Lomond under the same shifts of light and shade. But I have never seen it look more noble than once by midsummer moonlight. We had set out from Balloch, very late at night, in a motor-boat. A rowing-boat would have been a gentler craft, but the loch is no place for rowers or canoers, and we had no wish to add our names to the long list of those who have lost their lives on its waters.[1] In any case, the soft phuttering of the engine broke, not unpleasantly, the overwhelming stillness around us. The rugged hills, like legendary warriors, black and gold, sleeping on their tombs, lay silhouetted against the pale lemon sky. Here and there, a sharp light twinkled from the shore, as the beam of a distant car-headlamp stabbed its way round the curves of the winding road. The water lapped softly against our bow; the engine chug-chugged steadily. But around those sounds of our progress, there lay a huge and ancient silence. A Gaelic silence, I thought it; a silence whose benedictory overtones sounded a saining peace.

[1] In summer, hardly a week-end passes without some fatal tragedy occurring in the loch. Many parts are unsafe for swimmers; and because of the effects of sudden changes of wind, due to the channelling effect of the surrounding glens, it is dangerous for unskilled people in canoes or rowing-boats to venture far from the shore.

# CHAPTER IV

## STIRLINGSHIRE
## AND THE PERTHSHIRE LOWLANDS

*" Stirling, like a huge brooch, clasps Highlands and Lowlands together."*

ALEXANDER SMITH, 1853.

I

TOPOGRAPHICALLY, the greater part of Stirlingshire is essentially east coast in character. Yet it stretches from the Forth across Scotland to the shores of Loch Lomond, where it takes in the parish of Buchanan, once part of the Lennox estates. Three of the larger islands of Loch Lomond are in Stirlingshire. A winding road from Drymen twists down to Balmaha, sheltering in a woody bay opposite Inch Cailliach. Balmaha, which simply means " village on the water ", is a popular spot with those who run motor-boats on the loch, and during the summer months, the bay is flecked with white-and-silver craft nodding gaily at their moorings.

From Balmaha, a short but extremely steep hill, which has been the defeat of many an aged car, leads through the Pass of Balmaha up to Rowardennan. This autumn-sounding name means the Cape of Eunan's height, Eunan being a corruption of Adamnan, Abbot of Iona from 679 to 704, and the biographer of St. Columba. What Adamnan's connection with Loch Lomond may have been, no one has yet discovered.

As the loch narrows, it becomes deeper, in some places going down more than a hundred fathoms. Probably it was somewhere near Rowardennan that Robert the Bruce, after his Lorne defeat, crossed Loch Lomond with his followers on their way to the sanctuary of Rathlin. According to the poet John Barbour (1320?-1395?), they could find only one small boat. So Bruce and Douglas went over first and, as the others were being ferried across, the King read to his troops the popular romances of the day, including the tale of Fierrebras.

At Rowardennan, the public road ends. A few widely scattered cottages, the pier, a hotel, and a mansion that is now a Youth Hostel, make up all there is of the place. But it is the *point de depart* for most folk who ettle to climb Ben Lomond.

98

Other mountains in Scotland can claim greater height than Ben Lomond's 3,192 feet above sea level (3,170 feet above the surface of the loch); but because of its commanding position amongst the neighbouring hills and its proximity to the rolling Lowland fells, the Ben casts an aura of majesty over three shires. It is composed chiefly of gneiss, interspersed with considerable quantities of quartz. Near the top, immense masses of quartz weighing several tons are to be found, as well as micaceous schist, which on sunny days can be seen from the Luss shore, gleaming like summer snow.

The north and west sides of the mountain are very steep—the north side contains a sheer precipice of 1,800 feet—so it is from the southern approach that most would-be conquerors make their ascent. From the summit, it is possible on a clear day to see right across the narrow "waist" of Scotland.

Because of this animated map-like panorama, many visitors who would never dream of calling themselves mountaineers come to Rowardennan to tackle the climb. Towards the end of the eighteenth century, an anonymous English gentleman made the ascent, and thereafter inscribed some advice to his successors on a window at the inn:

"Stranger! if o'er this pane of glass perchance
  Thy roving eye should cast a casual glance,
  If taste for grandeur and the dread sublime
  Prompt thee Ben Lomond's fearful height to climb,
  Here gaze attentive, nor with scorn refuse
  The friendly rhymings of a tavern muse. . . .
  Trust not at first a quick advent'rous pace,
  Six miles its top points gradual from the base;
  Up the high rise with panting haste I passed,
  And gained the long laborious steep at last.
  More prudent you, when once you pass the deep,
  With measured pace ascend the lengthened steep;
  Oft stay thy steps, oft taste the cordial drop,
  And rest, oh rest! long, long upon the top.
  There hail the breezes; nor with toilsome haste
  Down the rough slope thy precious vigour waste:
  So shall thy wandering sight at once survey
  Vales, lakes, woods, mountains, islands, rocks and sea. . . .

  The scene tremendous shakes the startled sense
  With all the pomp of dread magnificence.
  All these, and more, shalt thou transported see,
  And own a faithful monitor in me."

Possibly that rather flat finish was caused by the poet's discovery that he had run out of window-space.

I have often wondered what implement was used by these fenestrial bardsters. They had, of course, the great example of Burns before them. He scratched verses on at least three Scottish inns, and legend has it that, after having versified his maledictions on the House of Hanover on a window of the Golden Lion at Stirling, he repented his indiscretion and smashed the window with the butt of his riding-crop. Even supposing eighteenth-century landlords to have been *a priori* in favour of versified windows, it is hard to believe that they could have looked with much favour on such a method of erasure!

A revival of this ancient art might offer intriguing possibilities. If poetically minded visitors to some of our Highland hotels could only be persuaded to cut on the dining-room windows their views on the standard of comfort and hospitality purveyed by the landlord, the results might be salutary indeed!

Although the public road up the eastern side of Loch Lomond ends at Rowardennan, Inversnaid is still within the Stirlingshire border. It looks across at the Loch Sloy Hydro-Electric power station whose concrete pipes vein the rugged hillside. There used to be an old fort at Inversnaid, built to keep in order the turbulent MacGregors. Its effectiveness may be gauged from the fact that it was three times burnt down by the Highlanders. General Wolfe, who later won fame for his exploits at Quebec, was stationed there as a junior officer. Half a century later, when Sir Walter Scott visited it, the garrison had been reduced to a single veteran. Now the ruins give shelter only to nesting sparrows.

The most distinguished son of Inversnaid was, of course, Rob Roy MacGregor, who designated himself as being of the place. Some of Rob Roy's exploits have already been mentioned; but since the Rob Roy country lies mainly in this part of Stirlingshire, and in the adjacent parish of Perthshire, a fuller account of Rob and his sons will not be out of place.

He was born at Glengyle, in the parish of Callander, in 1660, and baptized in the neighbouring parish of Buchanan. His father, Lieutenant-Colonel Donald MacGregor, was chief of a sept of the MacGregors. The persecution of the clan as a result of their rievings, terminating in the Glen Fruin affray described in the previous chapter, was still renowned in the time of William of Orange. Many MacGregors had adopted the names of those land-owners who suffered them to remain on their territory, and Rob Roy took his mother's name of Campbell.

Those who like to regard Rob Roy as a romantic hero, a helper of the poor and the weak, make out that the trouble began when the last and least wise of all the Stewart Kings, James the Seventh and Second, was driven from his London throne in consequence of his obduracy in attempting to enforce the Catholic religion upon his English subjects.  James, from his place of exile, sent forth an edict instructing his loyal subjects to make things as difficult as possible for the new government.  And the loyal Rob is supposed to have used the King's edict as justification for his later perpetrations.

This explanation is, however, quite unconvincing.  It was, after all, James the Sixth and First, the exiled King's grandfather, who first introduced the penal laws against the MacGregors.  Furthermore, loyal Rob, for all his Jacobite pretensions, did not feel moved to turn up at Sheriffmuir in defence of his "rightful" sovereign for the very good reason that he was pillaging the lands of those who had gone off to fight.

He had first demonstrated his prowess in 1691, when he led an excursion known as "the hership of Kippen".  A prominent Whig scion of the Livingstones of Callander had a herd of cattle fattened and ready to be sent to the market at Stirling.  This man, Alexander Livingstone of Bedlormie, had rendered considerable service to the Prince of Orange, so Rob decided that his cattle ought to be intercepted.  Rob and his men passed through Aberfoyle on their way to the Menteith district, where they forded the Forth and entered Buchlyvie.  The folk of this village became alarmed, and began to muster themselves, at the same time sending off to Balfron for assistance.  To avoid a conflict with the villagers, Rob and his men withdrew to Kippen Moor.  When Bedlormie's cattle appeared, the MacGregors swooped down on them.  The men of Kippen, thinking they were about to be attacked, joined in the fray.  And although the Highlanders used the flat of their broadswords (as they usually did when fighting with unarmed rustics) and easily won the day, they were so incensed at having been interfered with that, before they withdrew with their capture to the Highlands, they raided every byre and stable in Kippen.

For this offence, however, Rob managed to get himself forgiven; and, for a time, he worked the lands of Craigroyston, at the northeastern end of Loch Lomond, and later those of Inversnaid.  At this stage in his career, he took to cattle-dealing, an occupation which, traditionally, has always put a strain on honesty.  No doubt he was an astute bargainer.  Few would care to argue with this huge, red-bearded man who had such a reputation for strength and agility.

Either because of some fluctuation in the market, or for even less excusable motives, Rob absconded with a large sum of money entrusted to him for the purchase of cattle. A notice advertising his flight appeared in the *Edinburgh Evening Courant* in 1712.

Some say it was actually Rob's partner who absconded with the money, and that Rob fled to avoid being implicated. In any case, much of it belonged to the Duke of Montrose, and, accordingly, he claimed a portion of Rob's lands in payment of the debt.

For many centuries, Highland factors[1] had a shameful reputation for insensitive and unimaginative brutality. Graham of Killearn, Montrose's factor, arrived to carry out the eviction at a time when Rob was absent from home. According to Rob, his wife Mary (not the virago Helen, as portrayed in Scott's novel) and his bairns were rudely ejected and insulted.

To avenge this insult, Rob later captured Graham of Killearn while that worthy was collecting his master's rents near Gartmore. Graham was then treated to a period of confinement on an island on Loch Katrine, from where he was forced to write to the Duke explaining his situation, and requesting His Grace to forward ransom money. The Duke does not seem to have considered his servant worth paying for. At any rate, no money was sent. So Rob confiscated the rent-money, and returned Graham of Killearn and his rent-books to the Duke.

The Duke thereupon made several determined attempts to capture Rob, and finally succeeded in laying hands upon him near Balquhidder. But it was one thing to capture Rob, and quite a different matter to hold him. By "swimming and diving like an otter" whilst the party was fording a river, Rob escaped. In 1717, Rob gave himself up to General Carpenter, Commander-in-Chief in Scotland, but, repenting his weakness, escaped again two days later on one of his escort's horses. He was finally caught in 1727, but he obtained a pardon, and later turned Roman Catholic.

At last, old age began to filch the suppleness from his limbs, and gradually forced him to give over his activities. He was allowed to spend the last years of his life in peace at Kirkton, his farm at Balquhidder. The romanticists have given him an heroic, almost an operatic end. On Hogmanay (December 31st) 1734, a visitor, who had been on strained terms with Rob, called at Kirkton. Rob, now very weak, was lying in bed. But, before he received his guest, he made his family bring him his broadsword and his full

[1] Anyone interested in studying the depths of degradation to which human beings can descend should read Alexander Mackenzie's *Gloomy Memories*. This book, recently reissued under the title of *The Highland Clearances*, gives a vivid account of the behaviour of some Highland factors during the Clearances.

panoply of war. When the guest was ushered in, Rob received him sitting erect in his chair. Then, when the guest took his leave, Rob went back to bed. "Now call in my piper," he commanded, "and let him play *Cha tell mi tulli*" (MacCrimmon's Lament— "I'll return no more"). As the old year passed, and the strains of the ancient pibroch dirled against the frozen stillness of the night, the old warrior's soul took its flight. Or so they say. More likely he died alone in the early morning on a dirty ragged couch; but be that as it may.

Rob Roy was buried in the old kirkyard at Balquhidder. His grave was desecrated by a gang of vandals in the autumn of 1841. The idea was apparently to get hold of Rob's skull as a souvenir. All the intruders got was a few bones from the remains of a neighbouring old woman. When I visited the place some years ago, the mossy stone had become so overgrown with ivy that it was impossible to decipher the inscription. This, however, announces that his wife and at least two of their sons lie buried beside Rob.

There were five sons in all: Coll was a man of good character; Ronald and Duncan, outwardly respectable, came under suspicion for several offences which were never proved against them; James Mor (Big James) was an open Jacobite and, on the whole, a rather unsavoury character, though a good piper; while Robert Oig, the youngest, did his best to rival his father in a very much shorter space of years.

He was the central figure in two notorious episodes. One of these concerned the MacLarens, who had always been numerically strong in the country around Balquhidder; particularly MacLaren of Invernenty. After old Rob's death, this MacLaren made an offer for the farm of Kirkton, where the widow MacGregor and her sons were still living. Fearing they might be evicted in favour of a less notorious tenant, young Rob, then still in his teens, threatened to settle with MacLaren as soon as he got back from Doune a gun that was being repaired there. MacLaren heard of these threats, but paid no attention to them, thinking them merely the bragging of a headstrong boy. A few weeks later, however, in the spring of 1736, young Robin shot and mortally wounded MacLaren whilst he was ploughing outside his own farm. At the same time, forty head of MacLaren cattle were hamstrung and cruelly destroyed.

Young Robin then fled. But his brothers James, Ronald and a retainer were brought to trial. For lack of evidence, the main charge was found "not proven"—which, incidentally, is traditionally taken in Scotland to mean "we know you did it, but we can't pin it on you"!—but the two MacGregors were held to be reputed thieves, and made to find caution of two hundred pounds for their good behaviour during the next seven years.

Young Rob, who was outlawed, managed to clear the country. Later on, he fought with the Black Watch at Fontenoy, where he was wounded and taken prisoner. In due course, he was exchanged and released. Thinking that, in view of his services to the Government, it would now be safe to return home, he came back to the MacGregor country and married the daughter of a bonnet-laird, Graham of Drunkie.

Meanwhile, James Mor had fought with Prince Charles' army at Prestonpans and at Culloden. He behaved with great gallantry, and on both occasions he was wounded. Indeed, after the disaster of Drummossie Muir, he had to be carried back to his own mountains on a litter by his clansmen. He recovered sufficiently to bring the total of his own family up to the substantial figure of fourteen.

Young Rob's matrimonial affairs unfortunately did not develop in so satisfactory a manner, for Mrs. Rob MacGregor died within a year of her marriage. The widower thereupon decided to abduct a pretty young widow, nineteen-year-old Jean Kay, a Wright of Edinbellie, near Balfron. Her previous husband had died only a few weeks before the night of the outrage. A party of MacGregors surrounded the house of Edinbellie, where Jean was living with her mother and uncle, and, by means of armed threats, compelled her to " prepare for a journey " Her hands were tied, and she was thrown across young Rob's horse. They paused at the house of Leckie the maltman, at Milton of Buchanan, and thereafter proceeded through the Pass of Balmaha to Rowardennan. Here, the marriage took place—probably simply an old Scots marriage by declaration.[1] Thereafter the couple moved about rapidly from place to place.

To prevent MacGregor getting possession of his new wife's estate, her friends had the property sequestrated, and warrants were issued for the capture of the abductors.

Early in the New Year, Jean rode to Edinburgh, apparently accompanied by James, with a view to taking out a suspension of the sequestration. This suggested that she had, in fact, finally acquiesced in the abduction. But the authorities could hardly permit such lawlessness to go unpunished, so Jean was detained in Edinburgh. The brothers were brought to trial. James escaped from his prison in Edinburgh (causing the arrest and punishment of two " lieutenants and four private men "), and made his way to France, where he died in poverty in 1754. Before his death,

---

[1] Marriage by declaration remained valid in Scotland until 1939.

he attempted to deliver up to justice Alan Breck Stewart,[1] the supposed murderer in the Appin case, on condition that Robert Oig's life should be spared. Young Rob was captured in 1753 and executed in the Grassmarket of Edinburgh on 14th February 1754, some weeks before James' death. Jean Kay went to Glasgow to live with a ward, where she died of smallpox in October 1757.

Victorian commentators used to be fond of saying that Rob Roy and his son were anachronisms in an age which had got beyond the lawlessness of earlier days. Now, in the twentieth century, we might hail them as early examples of the modern " underground " fighter in enemy-occupied territory. It all depends on one's viewpoint as to whom is the proper enemy!

Balquhidder, " Bonnie Strathyre " and the Trossachs, all part of the Rob Roy country, lie within Perthshire. Sir Walter Scott not only made this lovely district famous by embellishing the story of the famous cateran in his novel *Rob Roy* but he also provided it with a set of more or less imaginary characters in his poem " The Lady of the Lake ".

Mountains are not very susceptible to poetic treatment, and, although many Scottish poets have tried to capture and tame their rugged grandeur within the rhythmic stresses of verse, to my mind, only two have succeeded—the eighteenth-century Gaelic poet Duncan Ban MacIntyre, in " In Praise of Ben Dorain "; and Scott in " The Lady of the Lake ". So rich is the variety of colouring in the Trossachs, so rapid the variations of light, and so subtle the woody fragrances which rise up from the ground at every step over bracken or heather, that no words yet fashioned are capable of describing these delicate, subtle things. Yet Scott's picture of Loch Katrine[2] as it first appeared to Fitz James will not easily be surpassed:

" . . . *One burnish'd sheet of living gold,*
*Loch Katrine lay beneath him roll'd;*
. *In all her length far winding lay,*
*With promontory, creek, and bay,*
*And islands that, empurpled bright,*
*Floated amid the livelier light,*
*And mountains, that like giants stand,*
*To sentinel the enchanted land.*

[1] The Stewarts of Appin were enemies of the MacGregors because of their connection with the MacLarens. Alan Breck's adventures form the basis of Stevenson's novel *Kidnapped*. James Mor is the father of Stevenson's *Catriona*.

[2] The name, rather surprisingly, derives from two Gaelic words meaning " the mists of Hell ", though Scott held it to have come from *cateran*, the name given to wild Highland robbers.

*High on the south, huge Benvenue*
*Down on the lake in masses threw*
*Crags, knolls, and mounds, confusedly hurl'd,*
*The fragments of an earlier world;*
*A wildering forest feather'd o'er*
*His ruin'd sides and summit hoar. . . ."*

If you intend to visit the scene of the exploits of James Fitz James (alias King James the Fifth) and Roderick Dhu, the probability is that you will sail up Loch Lomond to Inversnaid, and then go by bus—once it would have been by stage-coach—past Loch Arklet, to Stronachlachar, on Loch Katrine. Stronachlachar, the mason's promontory, is the northern pier for the loch's graceful yacht-like steamer *Sir Walter Scott*. Past wooded shores and beneath gently rounded hills the steamer sails out until it reaches the lower pier, sheltered beneath the Highland majesty of Ben Venue (said to mean in Gaelic, "little", as compared with the greater bulk of Ben Ledi, the hill of prayer), which towers its 2,873 feet above Loch Vennachar. Out in the bay lies Ellen's Isle (originally Eilean Molach, the shaggy isle) where the opening cantos of Scott's romance are set. But the "silver strand" from which Fitz James made his first crossing has been sunk beneath the waters, which were raised when the loch became Glasgow's reservoir.

The Trossachs hotel, a comfortable, turreted, mock-Gothic building beneath Ben A'an, stands almost at the junction of two equally enchanting roads. One road finds its way eastwards, down the shore of Loch Achray, past Kilmahog and Brig o' Turk, to Duncraggan and the shores of Loch Vennachar. At the eastern end of Loch Vennachar, Coilantogle Ford, where the fight between Fitz James and Roderick Dhu took place, is now a sluice-gate controlling the flow of water to the River Teith, which glides, glittering and serene, through Callander, to merge ultimately with the Forth. Lanrick Field, the mustering-place of the Clan Alpine, lies in a hollow about a mile from the western end of the loch.

The gorge of the Trossachs, which separates Loch Katrine from Loch Achray, was without a road until Sir Walter Scott's day. Earlier visitors had to follow:

*"Where twined the path in shadow hid,*
*Round many a rocky pyramid."*

Even now, the shores of Loch Katrine remain inaccessible.

Glasgow Corporation have restricted building in the area under their control, and, although they have gone in for sheep-farming and afforestation, their first concern has naturally been to preserve the purity of the water.

The old shooting-lodge of Brenachoil, Royal Cottage, built for Queen Victoria when she opened the undertaking in 1859, Stronachlachar House and Glengyle now serve the unromantic function of providing Glasgow's "cooncillors and bylies" with holiday residences. Glengyle, which decorates the north-western corner of the loch, has colourful associations. Once it was the seat of the Dougal Cior (mouse-coloured Dougal) sept of the house of MacGregor. The present building, erected in 1704, carries the initials of Gregor MacGregor above the lintel of the door. This man, known as Ghlun Dhu (black knees), had a remarkable career. At one time he laid claim to be chief of the clan, a claim he subsequently waived in favour of the more influential MacGregor of Balhaldie. Glengyle was "out" in both the '15 and the '45. During the second rising, assisted by James Mor, Rob Roy's son, he captured the Hanoverian garrison of Inverness.

In peace-time, Ghlun Dhu, like Rob himself, practised as a primitive insurance agent, levying blackmail on his Lowland neighbours, in return for which he guaranteed them against Highland rieving. Those who showed reluctance to pay usually changed their minds once their would-be protector had organized a demonstration-theft to open their eyes to the dangers of the uninsured state! Ghlun Dhu died in his bed in 1777, a very old man indeed. His old home retains much of its ancient fastness, for it can be reached only over a three-mile track from Stronachlachar or by water.

It was at the neighbouring mansion of Brenachoil that Dr. Archibald Cameron, brother of the "gentle Lochiel", sheltered after the '45. His "implication" consisted of having tended the wounded of both sides, for which crime he was arrested in 1752 and subsequently executed at Tyburn, to the lasting disgrace of George the Second and his ministers.

II

Doune and Dunblane both lie to the east of the Trossachs. Doune, between the Ardoch and the Teith, still possesses the ruins of a fourteenth-century castle, "the Doune of Menteith", as it used to be called. It was built by Robert, Duke of Albany, Earl of Menteith, Regent of Scotland, and father of that Regent Albany who died with the Lennoxes on Stirling's Heading Hill. Even in ruin, Doune Castle is a grimly awesome place, with its high battlements, its massive walls, its huge donjon towers, and its damp, deep dungeons. It was from Doune Castle that "the Bonnie Earl o' Moray" rode out on his last journey to Donibristle, where he was set upon and brutally assassinated by the Earl of Huntly, a royal warrant against Moray being used by Huntly as an excuse for personal revenge. The unfortunate Earl and his castle are both commemorated in one of the finest of the Scots ballads:

> " He was a braw gallant,
>   And he played at the glove;
> And the Bonnie Earl o' Moray,
>   O, he was the Queen's love.
>
> O lang will his lady
>   Look o'er the Castle Doune
> Ere she sees the Earl o' Moray
>   Come sounding through the toun."

Prince Charles used Doune Castle to house the prisoners his army took in 1746 at the Battle of Falkirk. One of these prisoners was John Home, the future playwright. He was confined in a high room, but, with seven other students, he escaped down a rope made of knotted sheets.

Dunblane centres round its ancient Cathedral, though more people are probably attracted by its prominent, ugly looking hydropathic on the hill. St. Blane founded his little kirk there during the eighth century, and David the First, that "sair sanct for the crown", so-called by girning nobles who thought religious patronage a sign of weakness, endowed the first cathedral during the twelfth century. Of King David's building, only the lower section of the tower has survived. Edward the Third of England caused the lead from the roof to be stripped to provide heavier ammunition for his stone-slingers, while besieging Stirling Castle. The Cathedral was also damaged at the Reformation, giving rise to Archbishop Laud's witticism that it was "a handsome church even before the Deformation". It lay roofless for over three hundred years. Sir Rowand Anderson (1839-1921), made a creditable job of its restoration, in spite of some protest from John Ruskin (who, incidentally, thought the scenery around Loch Katrine disappointing). The sage of Coniston worked himself into a rapture over the old building . . . "He was no common man who designed that Cathedral. I know nothing so perfect in its simplicity, and so beautiful so far as it reaches, in all the Gothic with which I am acquainted. And just in proportion to his power of mind, that man was content to work under Nature's teaching; and instead of putting a merely formal dog-tooth, as everybody else did at the time, he went down to the woody bank of the sweet river beneath the rocks on which he was building, and he took up a few of the fallen leaves that lay by it, and he set them in this arch, side by side for ever. . . ." The Cathedral still contains a fine set of sixteenth-century choir-stalls, a not inconsiderable part of the scant heritage of early Scottish woodwork to come down to us. They make the inferior nineteenth-century woodwork look decidedly gauche.

In the centre of the chancel, three slabs mark the burying-places of the Lady Margaret Drummond and her two sisters. Lady Margaret became the mistress of the young King James the Fourth at a time when his nobles were bending their diplomatic energies towards bringing about his marriage with the daughter of Henry the Seventh of England. Lady Margaret bore her monarch a daughter, and James kept putting off a decision on the English alliance. So one day, after partaking of a feast at Drummond Castle, their father's seat, the young unmarried mother and her two sisters were mysteriously seized with a violent illness which proved fatal before sundown. Within twelve hours, their bodies had been interred in Dunblane Cathedral. No investigation into the cause of their deaths was permitted: nor was it probably necessary!

Tradition has it—though on no real evidence—that James the Fourth celebrated his love for the Lady Margaret in the lovely Middle Scots poem, which begins:

> "When Tayis bank was blumit bricht
>     With blossoms blicht and braid,                [bright
> By that river ran I doun richt,
>     Under the ryss I red.                           [bushwood
> The merle melit with all her micht,
>     And mirth in morning made,
> Throw solace sound and seemly sicht,
>     Alswith a sang I said. . . ."                  [forthwith

The song was of his lady, the "mild, meek, mansuet (gentle) Margaret", whom he must have loved very dearly if he was, in fact, the author of the poem:

*" Her colour dear, her countenance,*
*Her comely crystal een,*
*Her portraiture of most plesance,*
*All picture did prevene;*       [surpass
*Of every virtue to avance,*
*When ladies praisit been,*
*Richest in my remembrance*
*That rose is rootit green. . . ."*

A group of pleasant seventeenth-century houses still preserves
the atmosphere around the Cathedral, while in the centre of the
town, another old house known as Bishop Leighton's Library
also keeps faith with the past.  Two miles to the south along the
Stirling road, Bridge of Allan shelters its population of retired
folk and livers-out from the cities.  A visitor to the place in 1827
called Bridge of Allan ". . . everything a village ought to be—
soft, sunny, warm; a confusion of straw-roofed cottages and rich
mossy trees, possessed of a bridge and a mill, together with kail-
yards, bee-skeps, collies, callants, old inns with entertainment for
man and beast; carts with their poles pointing up to the sky;
venerable dames in druggets, knitting their stockings in the sun;
and young ones, in gingham and dimity, tripping along with
milkpails on their heads".  There are still inns, a bridge and a
mill, though the wheel no longer turns; possibly, there are also
collies and callants.  But the straw-roofed cottages which so pleased
Dr. Chambers have long since given place to stolidly sizeable stone
villas; and the girls flaunt city nylons!  Allan Water, besides
giving the place its name, rippled alive a gentle and melodious
song in the mind of Burns.

Northwards, the road rises towards Blackford, Auchterarder
(the longest village in Scotland) and the Highland town of Perth.[1]
To the east of Dunblane, on the slopes of the Ochil Hills, lies the
Battlefield of Sheriffmuir, where the Jacobite forces of the Earl of
Mar were defeated in 1715.

III

When the heather has covered the hills with purple haze, the
heat of autumn begun to singe the sturdy bracken, and the first
sudden heralding gales of approaching winter are rudely shaking
the slender tresses of the birch-trees, till they sough in apprehen-

[1] In spite of its Lowland approaches, Perth is, I think, in spirit essentially
of the Highlands.  As such, it lies outside the scope of this book.

sion of their ruin—then is the time to make a journey over the Duke's road, which stretches from the Trossachs Hotel to Aberfoyle. Each twisting, tortuous bend of its fourteen miles, taxing the motorist as he groans up the summit of the steep ridge in low gear, reveals fresh vistas of loch and mountain, startling in their loveliness. Until the 1930's, this road was the property of the Duke of Montrose, and cars were not allowed over it, although stage-coaches made the daily journey. I remember the scene one morning on the village green at Aberfoyle when, as a boy, I wandered amongst an extraordinary collection of horse-drawn vehicles, while an auctioneer knocked down a hansom or a mail-coach or a common cab to collectors and scrap-dealers for a few paltry pounds.

Aberfoyle, although its Gaelic derivation means " above a bog or hole ", is a pretty little hill-shadowed village on the upper banks of the Forth. This river rises at the western extremity of Aberfoyle parish, and its main tributary, the Water of Duchray, rises on Ben Lomond and joins it near Aberfoyle. Two spectacular cascades tumble into Loch Ard. On a tiny island in the middle of the loch the ruins of another castle built as a retreat by the second Duke of Albany, cousin to James the First, and Regent during James' imprisonment in England. King James, however, saw to it that the Duke's retreat was of a more permanent nature than anything the island could offer!

At the head of Loch Ard, a crumbling laroch represents the remains of Jean MacAlpine's Inn. There, according to Scott, the worthy Bailie Nicol Jarvie did some handy work against the Highlanders with a poker seized red-hot from the fire. An old iron object which looks rather like a butcher's cleaver hangs upon an ancient tree opposite the Bailie Nicol Jarvie Hotel. This is supposed to be the famous poker, its moment of fictional glory being commemorated annually by the application of a coat of scarlet paint. " The Covenanters Inn ", on the Duchray Road, is so-named because it was here that the Scottish National Covenant was drawn up in 1949. This document, pledging the signatories to work by all constitutional means towards the achievement of Self-Government for Scotland within the United Kingdom framework, was subsequently signed by over two million people, a majority of the Scottish electorate.

Aberfoyle was the scene of the ministrations of the Reverend Robert Kirk (?1614-92), whose book, *The Secret Commonwealth*, or an Essay on the Nature and Actions of the Subterranean (and for the most part) Invisible People, " heretofoir going under the name of Elves, Faunes, and Fairis, or the lyke, among the Low-

Country Scots, as they are described by those who have the Second Sight ", was the first attempt at psychic research to be made in Scotland. It has earned him an eccentric's reputation, under the shade of which the fact that he produced the first complete translation of the metrical psalms into Gaelic is sometimes lost sight of. *Psalma Dhaibhidh A nMendrachd* was published in 1684.

The road from Aberfoyle down this side of Loch Ard leads past Loch Chon, to Stronachlachar on Loch Katrine, a bumpy branch road making its way to Inversnaid on Loch Lomond.

To the east of Aberfoyle lies the district of Menteith, a parish containing Scotland's only lake. On the larger of the lake's two islands stands the remains of the Priory of Inchmahome, founded in 1107, probably on the site of a Culdee place of worship. The village of the Port was erected into a burgh of barony in 1466 by James the Third. The island achieved still greater royal distinction when it became the residence of the Scottish court for about six months between August 1547 and the following February. After the lost battle of Pinkie, the Regent Arran had the child Mary, Queen of Scots, conveyed to Inchmahome so that she should not fall into the hands of the victorious English. From there, she was taken to Dumbarton Castle to await a ship for France.

The Lake of Menteith, were it not for those Highland hills which cluster around the northern and western horizon, would hardly seem a Scottish water at all. It is loveliest in spring, when a glory of daffodils dances about its banks, and the waters that surround the ivy-crumbled Priory and the neighbouring islet of Inch Talla, once a feudal stronghold of the Earls of Menteith,[1] catch the shifting sunshine in a silver net of ripples.

Much of the district of Menteith is taken up by a barren plain of heathery bog, a transformed remnant of the Caledonian Forest, known as Flanders Moss, which stretches from the Campsies to the Grampians. Through it, the Forth flows sullenly, in winter spreading its overflowing waters amongst the soggy rushes.

From a brae-side on the outskirts of the hilly village of Gartmore, Gartmore House, once the home of Robert Graham of Gartmore (1735-97), stares out beyond the park across the dreary waste where the mountain winds of winter scud through the skeletal heather. In this house, somewhere about the year 1780, Laird

---

[1] Menteith was the seat of an old Celtic earldom. Gilchrist, the first earl, lived in Malcolm IV's reign (1153-65). It changed hands several times by marriage. In 1427, it was granted to Malise Graham, but the title again became dormant in 1694. Inch Talla castle dates from 1427. Dog Island once contained the Menteith kennels.

Graham, a happily married man with a successful Jamaican civil-service career behind him, and owner also of the estate of Ardoch in Dunbartonshire, laid aside his port and his politics to write:

> *"If doughty deeds my ladye please,*
> *Right soon I'll mount my steed;*
> *And strong his arm, and fast his seat,*
> *That bears from me the mead.*
> *I'll wear thy colours in my cap,*
> *Thy picture in my heart;*
> *And he that bends not to thine eye*
> *Shall rue it to his smart.*
> *Then tell me how to woo thee, love;*
> *O, tell me how to woo thee!*
> *For thy dear sake, nae care I'll take,*
> *Tho' ne'er another trow me. . . ."*

Strange that such courtly music should have sounded from the wilds of the Highland fringe!

His descendant, Robert Bontine Cunninghame Graham (1852-1936), the last family laird of Gartmore,[1] had glittering literary accomplishments similar to those of that famous seventeenth-century writer, Sir Thomas Urquhart of Cromarty. A Spanish hidalgo, when he was known as Don Roberto, Cunninghame Graham spent much of his youth in the Argentine. He was passionately fond of horses. Like his ancestor, he represented a Scottish constituency—Lanark—in Parliament for a few years. He was ardently associated with Keir Hardie and his friends in the founding of the Labour Party, and, later on, with the founders of the Scottish National Party.

Cunninghame Graham's English prose has astonishing poise and lucidity, fretted though it is with a wealth of accurately observed imagery. His books are worth reading for their style alone, what-ever he may happen to be writing about. Like Urquhart, his range of interests was uncommonly wide. He lies buried on the island of Inchmahome.

When I visited Gartmore House, the wind that so often ripples the heathery sea of Flanders Moss, stirred through the overgrown shoots which now choke the once-orderly terraces. The place was taken over by the Army during the Second World War, when the

---

[1] He inherited Gartmore heavily burdened with debt, and in 1900 was forced to sell it. But he retained Ardoch, which is still in the family possession.

estate was much mutilated. Concrete hut-bottomings still littered the grounds, and rusted barbed-wire snaked through the tangled briars. The house itself, an enormous rambling place, with coarse nineteenth-century additions, has now become a Roman Catholic school.

Just how great a change has come over this "march" between Highlands and Lowlands can be gauged from a perusal of the First Statistical Account. Before 1771, the western parishes of Stirlingshire were all mainly Gaelic-spoken. In Drymen, there were still some folk who did not understand English. Improved methods of agricultural production were beginning to force the amalgamation of the many small farms into larger and more economic units. The old Lowland equivalent of the crofter-farmer found himself driven out; so he and his family moved south-westward to find employment in the new industries of the Vale of Leven, Blanefield or Glasgow.

Drymen itself stands above Strathendrick (the name comes from *druim,* an eminence). The lands of Drymen were said to have been given to a Hungarian nobleman called Maurice by Malcolm Canmore's wife Saint Margaret. Until they effected an exchange with an erstwhile Duke of Montrose for their present lands, the Drummonds, family of the Earl of Perth, had their seat in Drymen. The River Endrick sweeps relentlessly down from the Campsie Fells into Loch Lomond; so relentlessly indeed, that in winter it frequently floods the fertile strath. The geological basis of the strath is old red sandstone, giving the river-banks a curious reddish tinge. About ten miles before it passes beneath Drymen, the Endrick flows over the Falls of Gartness. Once, a castle stood above the rocky dell, and in it Napier of Merchiston (1550-1617) was born. For many centuries, the turbulent, rock-bound waters turned a mill-wheel. Napier is supposed to have asked the miller of his day to still the wheel when its monotonous "clack-clack" got on his nerves while he was working out his logarithms!

It is a fine sight to see the salmon pool at Gartness:

*All the released collusion of wide rains*
*twisted from ragged slopes in channelled rills*
*plunges its whiteness, lunges towards the plains.*
*Seawards the river spreads and over-fills,*
*swirling against the sandy fringe of fields*
*browed with loose meadow-grass and clutching sorrel*
*as soil gives up its mould, cracks, crumbles, yields,*
*and clouds itself beneath some sucking whorl.*

*In broad full-breasted surge the river rides,*
*tearing the earth-veined roots that bind its bed*
*till boulders bend and fold its narrow sides,*
*spume like an ocean's rears its spitting head,*
*plummets the precipice and pounds the pool*
*beneath, a boil of salmon pink with spawn,*
*a seethe of breathlessness, a steam of cool*
*precipitant force towards which these fish were drawn.*

*Instinct, wiser than words made by man,*
*ferries them back to find that hidden bank*
*hung under shade where first their lives began;*
*and so they lurk beneath this turgid, dank*
*peat-riven froth, and dare the slimmied rock*
*that gaps the torrent's hammer, gathering strength*
*to launch the twitch of their throw, to staunch the shock*
*of crashing water crushed along their length.*

*Out of this ceaseless rush they rise, like thoughts*
*tensed by some counter-force, to curve them high*
*above inertia's drift that drops or rots*
*away in endless falling. Oh! they fly,*
*flanks shimmering, one leap to take the lynn,*
*till all that measures is this fleshing will's*
*weak triumph wrapped in the dissolving din*
*of thunder melted from the silent hills.*

Like Drymen, the parish of Killearn, higher up Strathendrick, was also once part of The Lennox. The name means "the church of the west point", and obviously refers to Killearn's position at the western end of the Campsie range. Others maintain that the village stands on the site of the cell of St. Keiran. At any rate, the place itself is now a fashionable Glasgow dormitory-annex, although it retains a little of its village-like appearance.

In the farm of Moss, down the brae from the village, the great scholar, historian and Latin poet, George Buchanan, was born (1506-82). Buchanan studied at the Universities of Paris and St. Andrews; then he turned Protestant. His first poem "Somnium", which he published on his return to Scotland in 1537, was a bitter satire on Franciscan friars. It highly delighted James the Fifth, who thereupon made the poet tutor to one of the royal bastards. Buchanan next held academic appointments at Bordeaux, from where he was driven by the plague, though not before writing his two great Latin tragedies "Baptistes" and "Jephthes"[1] at Paris,

[1] English translations attributed to John Milton exist.

and at Coimbra, in Portugal, where the Inquisition threw him into prison. After further years of academic wandering, he came back to Scotland in 1560, to become classical tutor to Queen Mary, who appointed him to the revenue of the wealthy Crossraguel Abbey.

Seeing which way the ecclesiastical wind blew, Buchanan supported the Protestant lords in the ensuing tustle between the Marians and the Jamesites. In 1567, he became Moderator of the General Assembly. His "De Maria Regina" states the case of the lords against the Queen. In 1570, he became preceptor to the young King James the Sixth. Eight years later, he resigned most of his official positions to devote his remaining years to the writing of his *History of Scotland*.

Two contemporary word-pictures of Buchanan help us to visualize the old man, a strangely venerable mixture of strength and weakness. One comes from the memoirs of no less a person than Sir James Melville of Halhill, who was Queen Mary's ambassador at the court of her cousin Elizabeth. With diplomatic loftiness of judgment, he tells us that: "Master George was a stoic philosopher, and looked not far before the hand; a man of notable qualities for his learning and knowledge in Latin poesie, mekle made accompt of in other countries, plaisant in company, rehersing at all occasions moralities short and fecfull (pithy), whereof he had abundance, and invented where he wanted. He was also of gude religion for a poet, bot he was easily abused, and sa facile that he was led with any company that he haunted for the time, whilk made him factious in his auld days; for he spak and writ as they that were about him for the time informed him. For he was become sleperie and careless, and followed in many things the vulgar opinion; for he was naturally popular, and extreme vengable against any man that had offendit him, whilk was his greatest fault. . . ."

The second picture, more warm and friendly, occurs in the *Autobiography and Diary* of the Reverend James Melville[1] (1556-1614), a Reformation minister whose professional work was overshadowed by that of his more famous uncle, Knox's successor Andrew Melville, but whose shrewdness of observation made his book one of the most readable contributions to Scottish "private" literature:

"That September (1581) . . . my uncle Mr. Andro, Mr. Thomas Buchanan and I, hearing that Mr. George Buchanan

---

[1] Who was not related to Sir James. For more anent Melville, see Chapter VII.

was weak, and his Historie under the press, past owre to Edin-
bruche . . . to visit him and see the work. When we came to
his chalmer, we fand him sitting in his chair teaching his young
man that servit him in his chalmer to spell a, b, ab; e, b, eb; etc.
Eftir salutation, Mr. Andro says, 'I see, Sir, ye are nocht idle.'
'Better thus,' quoth he, 'nor stelling (watching) sheep, or sitting
idle, whilk is also ill!' Thaireftir, he schew us the Epistle
Dedicatorie to the King; the whilk, when Mr. Andro had read,
he tauld him that it was obscure in some places, and wanted
certain words to perfyt the sentence. Says he, 'I may do na mair,
for thinking on another matter.' 'What is that?' says Mr.
Andro. 'To die!' quoth he; 'but I leave that and many ma
(more) things for yow to help.'

"We went from him to the printer's work-house, whom we
fand at the end of the 17 Buik of his Chronicle, at a place whilk
we thought very hard for the time, whilk might be an occasion
of staying the hail wark, anent the burial of Davie (Rizzio).
Thairfor, staying the printer from proceeding, we cam to Mr.
George again, and fand him bedfast by (contrary to) his custom;
and asking him how he did? 'Even going the way of welfare,'
says he. Mr. Thomas, his cousin, schaws him of the hardness
of that part of his story, that the King would be offendit with it,
and it might stay all the wark. 'Tell me, man,' says he, 'gif
I have tauld the truth?' 'Yes,' says Mr. Thomas, 'Sir, I think
sa.' 'I will bide his feud, and all his kin's, then!' quod he:
'Pray, pray to God for me, and let him direct all!'"

Such, in outline, was the career of this remarkable son of Killearn. To few of those who gaze at the obelisk to his memory,
erected in 1788 (for some obscure reason the exact copy of a
monument erected in 1690 to William the Third at Boyne), does
his name convey anything. Yet his most famous tract, *De Jure
Regni*, stated the earliest Scottish case for constitutional
monarchy. And with the possible exception of Arthur Johnston
(1587-1641), Buchanan was the most considerable of the Scottish
Latinists, that little group of scholarly poets who went on address-
ing their verses to learned if limited audiences till the beginning
of the eighteenth century. Buchanan's most famous poem is
"Epithalamium for Mary Stuart and the Dauphin of France".
In it, he addresses the Dauphin, pays tribute to the beauty and
ability of his former pupil, and gives forth this noble passage in
praise of the stamina and character of his native land. . . .

"Not here will I tell you about the country's acres of fertile land, about its glens fruitful in cattle, its waters fruitful in fish, its copper-and-lead-laden fields, its hills wherein is found bright gold and hard iron, its rivers flowing through metaliferous veins—enriching commodities which other nations besides ours possess. These things let numbskull mob admire, and those who despise everything but wealth. . . . But the real boast of the quivered Scot is this: to encircle the glens in the hunting; to cross by swimming the rivers; to bear hunger; to despise the variations of cold and hot weather; not by moat and walls, but by fighting to defend their native land; to hold life cheap when their good name has to be maintained unimpaired; once a promise has been made, to keep faith; to revere the holy spirit of friendship; and to love not magnificence but character. It was due to these qualities that, when wars roared throughout all the world, and there was no land but changed its ancestral laws, made subjects to a foreign yoke, one solitary nation in its own home still bade on, and still enjoyed its traditional freedom. Here the fury of the Angles halted, here stuck fast the deadly onset of the Saxons; here the Danes stuck after defeating the Saxons, and when the fierce Danes were subjugated, the Normans too . . . here too, Roman victoriousness halted its heralding march. . . ."[1]

There is a curious gorge through the Stockiemuir, in the parish of Killearn, known as the "Whangie". Three hundred and forty-six feet in length, the gully has a depth of thirty feet, and in breadth it varies from ten feet down to two. Like the Campsie range, the Stockiemuir hills are made up of old red sandstone capped with trap. In the parish of Strathblane, there are two ruined castles—that of Duntreath, seat of the Edmoundstoune family, and once celebrated for its dungeons and appurtenances of torture; and Mugdock, which became a Montrose seat in 1646. The neighbouring mansion, Dougalston, has been bequeathed to Glasgow Corporation for use as a gallery to house the valuable art collection given to the city by Sir William Burrell. Those not interested in art may find the zoo and the children's pleasure-park more of an attraction. The fertile valley of the Blane, well wooded with firs, larch, willows, black poplars and oaks, is of itself a very lovely strath, though Blanefield, its principal village, wears rather a drab town-suburb look. The conical-shaped hill of Dumgoyne dominates the strath.

Campsie was an important parish in pre-Reformation days, since its minister was sacristan of Glasgow Cathedral. The pleasant

[1] Translated from Buchanan's hexameters by Hugh MacDiarmid.

Kirkton Glen is a favourite spot with Glasgow hikers. Lennox-town, in the words of the Reverend Gillespie, the Victorian reviser of Nimmo's *History of Stirlingshire*, is "a street set down in the centre of the strath for the purpose of accommodating the labourers employed in working the mineral and other manufactures". These "other manufactures" were calico-printing and bleaching. Campsie suffered severely at the time of the Calico collapse, and Lennoxtown's very obviously "set-down" street now constitutes the nearest imaginable approach to a country slum.

Kilsyth—church of the river of peace—has had its fame spread abroad because it was the scene of one of "the Great Marquis's" victories. In 1647, James Graham, fifth Earl and first Marquis of Montrose (1612-50), won his five rapid victories over the covenanting army at Tippermuir, Inverlochy, Auldearn, Alford and Kilsyth, before his Highland forces were heavily defeated in 1650 at Philiphaugh. His attempt to write Charles the First's epitaph "in blood and wounds" thereafter led to his capture and barbarous execution in the Grassmarket of Edinburgh. The Kilsyth battle probably frightened some of the unlucky "locals" into burying their valuables, for Montrose was rarely able to restrain his troops from indulging in pillage after victory. Numerous coins and domestic relics of the period have been dug up from time to time in Kilsyth and the neighbouring parishes.

Kippen, a village which straggles up a single hilly main street, was the birthplace of the Victorian architect Alexander Thomson (1817-75). Known as "Greek" Thomson because of his fixed dislike of the Gothic curve and his predilection for pillared proportion, Thomson built several Glasgow churches, of which St. Vincent Street U.P. Church and Queen's Park U.P. Church, destroyed in 1943, were the finest. Thomson, as the leading Scottish architect of his day, might reasonably have expected to have been asked to design the University. But he was passed over in favour of Sir Gilbert Scott, a slick London architectural shamster, whose taste was unexceptionally appalling.[1] Thomson's adverse criticisms of the Scott plans, delivered without any personal animus, have been endorsed as the verdict of posterity.

---

[1] Or almost so. St. Mary's Episcopal Cathedral in Edinburgh is a tolerable piece of sham Gothic. But does it count for much when set against St. Pancras Station and the Albert Memorial?

IV

From the braes of Kippen one looks out over a broad carse, across the flat parish of Gargunnock, to Stirling itself crouched up amongst its woody eminences. The road from Dumbarton to Stirling runs through this carse, and a long stretch of it is known as the "Kippen straights". The fertile farmland on the north side of the road was once a bog—Kincardine Moss—and the present road, laid upon a foundation of tree-trunks, follows roughly the course of a Roman road. Roman relics have been found in relative profusion throughout the southern parishes of Stirlingshire, for the line of the Antonine Wall (Graham's Dyke) traversed the country.

The rough course of the wall, which probably had nineteen forts, with watch-towers in between them, may be traced by linking them on the Ordnance Survey map. They were: Old Kilpatrick, Duntocher, Castlehill, New Kilpatrick, Balmuildy, Cadder, Kirkintilloch, Auchendavye, Barrhill, Croyhill, Westerwood, Castlecary, Seabegs, Rough Castle, Mumrills, Inveravon, Kinneil, Brideness, Carriden-on-Forth.

The forts (*praesidia* to the Romans, *caers* to the British) stretched in a chain across the isthmus of Scotland at intervals of about two miles. Sir George MacDonald[1] thinks that they were probably abandoned about half a century after they were built, the defenders having twice been driven from their positions in that time by the native tribes, and having twice returned. Interesting discoveries were made at Castlecary when digging was in process in connection with the construction of the Forth and Clyde Canal. In 1769, workmen came upon what proved to be the foundation-plan of an eight-apartment house, with a *sudorium* or bath attached. Two years later, fragments of coins and vases were uncovered, as well as brazen helmets and shields. Further discoveries were made when the railway viaduct was being constructed, the north-eastern end of it being planted in what is thought to have been the site of one of the forts. Now, the National Trust for Scotland owns Rough Castle, west of Falkirk, the least damaged of the forts. It was excavated in 1903 by the Society of Antiquaries for Scotland, and a still more comprehensive headquarters than that at Castlecary was uncovered. That

[1] *The Roman Wall in Scotland.* Since the above was written, a twentieth out-post fort has been discovered on the Renfrewshire side of the Clyde, apparently designed to prevent the line being turned by a river invasion from the south.

portion of the Wall which runs through Seabegs Wood is also owned by the Trust. Rampart, ditch and Military Way are all visible.

The most important Roman works in Stirlingshire, however, were those at Camelon, famous for its place in Arthurian legend. The Romans apparently had a fairly extensive camp at Camelon which may possibly have been the advanced base for the northern expeditions of Agricola, Severus and Caracalla. Relics have been found here, too, including bricks containing the impression of a dog's foot, which seems to have been a Roman "trademark", coins, an elaborate vase, the neck of a wine jar, and various iron implements.

George Buchanan tells us that, in his day, Camelon resembled the ruins of a moderate city, with ditches, walls and streets still standing. So little respect had our near-ancestors for these valuable remains of a vanished civilization, that Camelon was carted away stone by stone for the building up of dykes. Now an appendage to Falkirk, it boasts what is probably the largest bus-depot in Scotland!

Stone slabs in honour of Antoninus Pius, or commemorating the work of the builders of the wall (the Second or Augusta legion, whose badge was a sea-goat, whatever that may have been! the Sixth or Vanquisher Legion, with a badge of eagles' heads; and the Twentieth or Valiant and Victorious Legion, whose badge was a wild boar), have been found at various places along the course of the fortifications. Usually these slabs carried the date when the section being commemorated was completed, the legion's designation, the date, and perhaps a dedication to Antoninus. The legion had, of course, the assistance of "auxiliaries" and "pressed" Caledonians. But, as Buchanan boasts in his "Epithalamium", the efforts the Romans made against Scotland were entirely in vain. It is strange to look at these relics meant to commemorate the colonizing efforts of a great race for all time. Fragmented or worn thin by the crumbling action of the centuries, or the chipping of peaceful spade or plough, they lie now in dusty corners of museums, memorials to the impermanent nature of military conquest, and to the intransience of the glory of Man!

The last intact relic of Roman building in Scotland was probably the erection known as Arthur's O'on (oven) or Julius' Howf. This was "a perfect dome with a circular orifice at its apex, built in double courses of finely hewn stones, laid on each without mortar". Apparently, it looked rather like a large beehive. It may well have been a chapel where a legion kept its colours. Another, less probable, view is that it might have marked the tomb of King

Arthur, who was defeated and slain by Medrunt the Pict, uncle to St. Mungo, in 537. It stood a few yards to the north-east of the Forge Row, Carron, on the estate of Stenhouse, until, in 1743, a pig-headed laird, Sir Michael Bruce, removed it stone by stone, in spite of the protests of the leading antiquaries and historians of the day, to repair a mill-dam.[1] Such things still happen. I once knew an Orcadian farmer who discovered a sizeable Pictish dwelling on the cliff-fringe of his land. The sight of so ancient a memorial roused in him such affronted fury that its speedy destruction became an obsession. He had it completely pulled down, and used its stones to repair dykes and steadings.

The northern parishes of Stirlingshire have little to attract the visitor, however ancient may be their several stories. The Kilsyth Hills make waste a large tract of ground, and on the southern side of the strath which carries the Forth and Clyde Canal, the Glasgow-Edinburgh Railway, and the first road to link the two cities, mines and treacherous mosses abound.

Dunipace, at the eastern end of the Kilsyth Hills, once gave shelter to Edward the First of England during one of his Scottish forays. Now, joined to Denny, it forms one of the outer ramparts of Stirlingshire's concentrated industrial corner. From Kilsyth to Lauriston, in the south of the shire, and from Skinflats (a decrepit village which seems literally to be crumbling away) to Fallin on the east, pimple-bings of collieries sear the landscape. This disfigurement perhaps matters less hereabouts than in other parts of Scotland, for the agglomeration of heavy industries which has developed over a long period near the coal-fields has also worked its share of desolation on the land.

Some of the earliest coalmines in Scotland to be scientifically worked were those on the estate of Kinnaird, once owned by James ("Abyssinian") Bruce (1730-94), a man of Herculean physique who travelled on foot to the source of the Blue Nile (which he mistook for the Nile itself) and into the heart of then unknown Abyssinia. His contemporaries first refused to believe him until, in 1790, because of the insistence of Daines Barrington, the English jurist who produced a famous paper after examining the prodigious talent of the boy Mozart, Bruce wrote an account of his experiences. Scunnered at the literary world, which failed to give him the recognition he thought he deserved, he retired to his estate. There, having grown "exceedingly heavy and lusty", he would ride slowly over his estate to his collieries "mounted on a

---

[1] Thomas Pennant tells us gleefully that "within less than a year, the *Naides*, in resentment of the sacrilege, came down in a flood and entirely swept it away".

charger of great power and size ". Whiles, he would dress himself up in his Abyssinian costume, and sit musing on his past adventures. The manner of his death was gallant, if hardly heroic. Hurrying to hand a lady to her carriage, he missed his footing and pitched down the stairs of his own house, striking his head in the fall.

The River Carron rises in the Kilsyth Hills, and flows eastwards into the Forth at Grangemouth, an important port in the eighteenth and early nineteenth centuries. Now, it is the site of a large oil refinery, and the terminal end of an oil pipe-line which runs across Scotland from Loch Long, a more convenient harbour for American tankers.

The Carron features in the poems of Ossian; or, if you prefer, of James MacPherson! We are told that on its shores, about the year 211, the young Fingal defeated Caracalla, the son of Severus.

Where once the mountain-girt gods and heroes of ancient Alba played out their fierce and strenuous lives, mists of another sort now hover. For since 1760, when Dr. Roebuck of Sheffield founded the Carron Ironworks some three miles north of Falkirk, the area cornered by Bonnybridge, Falkirk, Stenhousemuir and Larbert has come to contain over thirty foundries employed mostly in the making of light castings. Grates, fuel-saving stoves and fires, pots and pans, as well as more warlike materials, have been produced in great quantity in this umquhile Ossianic quarter. During the Napoleonic wars, almost every country in Europe did brisk business with the Carron Ironworks in a piece of light artillery known as the Carronade. There are also several brick-making factories in the surrounding district. All night long, the sky above has a steady orange lining, as the flames of the furnaces leap up to lick the darkness. Burns, as he approached the Carron district, must have been struck with the similarity of the spectacle to the Presbyterian conception of Hell. At any rate, when he was refused admittance to the Carron Works, he wrote:

> " We cam na here to view your works,
>     In hopes to be mair wise,
> But only, lest we gang to Hell,
>     It may be nae surprise:
> But when we tirl'd at your door
>     Your porter dought na hear us,
> Sae may, shou'd we to Hell's yetts come,
>     Your billy Satan sair us! "

Falkirk itself, the largest town in Stirlingshire, is thought to derive from its Gaelic name of *Eaglaisbreac,* "spotted kirk", of which "*fach-kirk*" is supposed to be the Anglo-Saxon translation. The kirk in question is said to have been built during the reign of Malcolm Canmore from the blackened stones of Camelon, which was probably finally destroyed by fire. The old kirk was demolished in 1811 to make way for the present grim and graceless affair huddled between the town's two narrow, main, traffic-ridden streets.

A house in Falkirk once known as the Great Ludging gave shelter to Prince Charles and, as so often happened during that strange adventure, about a fortnight later, to his "cousin" the Duke of Cumberland.

As with so many other social and business gatherings of their kind, the great three-day fairs held annually during August, September and October, and known as the Falkirk Trysts, have been discontinued. For over a century and a half, farmers from every county in Scotland drove in great herds of beasts. The Victorian travel-writer Augustus Hare visited the Tryst on September 13th, 1865, and noted in his journal: "It was a curious sight, an immense plain covered with cattle of every description, especially picturesque little Highland beasts attended by drovers in kilts and plumes. . . ." Trade was brisk, and the ensuing merriment was hilarious. But the development of the railways put an end to the Trysts.

In the countryside around Falkirk and Stirling (or Snowdon, as it used to be called before it earned the name of "the toun of strife"[1]) four major battles have been fought.

Sir William Wallace, second son of a Renfrewshire laird, had begun to harass the English garrisons which Edward the First of England had planted at Gargunnock, Airth and north of the Forth. Edward, who was in France at the time, thereupon ordered two of his lieutenants to suppress the Scottish insurrection. The English army gathered itself together and marched north. It found the Scots army drawn up on the Abbey Craig. On the 17th of September 1297, after having had their offer of peace upon submission refused with the contempt it deserved, the English commanders hastily ordered an advance over the Forth, where an old wooden bridge stood. Either because of the strain put upon the flimsy structure, or, according to the poet Blind Harry (1450-92), because Wallace had caused the main beam to be sawn away—the bridge

---

[1] This popular derivation of Stirling or Strivelin is not borne out by J. B. Johnstone who, in his *Place Names of Scotland,* suggests *Struthlinn,* a river pool, after a Gaelic transliteration of the Brythonic *Ystrevelyn,* a dwelling.

suddenly collapsed, throwing many of the English soldiers into the Forth, and cutting their army in two.[1] During the confusion which followed, the Scots attacked, and won a clear victory. The section of the English army stranded on the south bank retreated towards the south, but they were harried by the forces of the Earl of Lennox, who had ambushed them from behind, and by the pursuing Wallace: so much so, it seems, that when the Earl of Surrey, the English commander, reached the safety of Berwick, his horse was so fatigued that it was not able to eat. Doubtless, its master was in little better shape.

Edward, on learning of this disaster, hastily patched up a truce with France, and marched north with an army of 80,000 foot-soldiers, as well as a large body of battle-experienced cavalry fresh from the French wars. He landed his army on the Forth, probably at Queensferry, and it spent the night there before the Battle of Falkirk at Linlithgow. There, according to one historian, the English King's horse trampled on him, breaking two ribs. It says much for the abominable tyrant's courage that he insisted on leading his army as usual next morning, the 22nd of July 1298.

Wallace's army of about 30,000 men was divided into three divisions—one led by Wallace himself, one by John Comyn of Badenoch, and one by Sir John Stewart of Bonkill, brother of the High Steward of Scotland. Precisely what happened in the councils of the Scottish leaders just before the battle has never been revealed. But a quarrel of some sort took place, as a result of which Comyn marched his men off the field in a huff.

When the English second line charged, the Scots at first stood firm, but, under a deadly shower of arrows, Sir John Stewart's division was surrounded and cut to pieces. Wallace and his infantry stood their ground, until their ranks were broken by the fire of the English archers. This forced Wallace to make a tactical retreat, which he did successfully, extricating most of his troops.

A less creditable version of the affair asserts that Wallace also held back his forces from the field after the Scottish quarrel, and that he only cut his way out when he saw that his own troops were in danger of suffering the same fate as those of Sir John Stewart. In any case, Wallace withdrew his shattered army to Torwood, and from there to Perth, where he disbanded it and resigned his office as Protector.

[1] Modern historians doubt this tale, and no longer believe that the old wooden bridge stood much up the river from the present old bridge.

A curious incident took place during the battle. Wallace had an interview with Robert the Bruce, who must have had doubts as to the honourableness of his English alliance, from the opposite bank of the Carron, as a result of which Bruce, for the first time, saw where his true interests and those of his country lay. Sir John Stewart and Sir John Graham, Wallace's second-in-command, both of whom fell, lie buried in the old kirkyard at Falkirk.

Wallace returned to private life for a few years, until he was trapped and handed over to Edward by Sir John Menteith of Ruskie. Thereafter, in 1305, he was given a "rigged" trial in London (at which no evidence was even led), and automatically sentenced to suffer death by a method devised by the Christian Edward himself, and much favoured in England for five centuries thereafter! The former Protector of Scotland was drawn, chained prostrate on a hurdle, to Smithfield, and there half-hanged, disembowelled, castrated, beheaded and quartered.

Christian Edward also supplied Hitler with another pleasant idea. On his deathbed, he instructed those about him to boil his body down and run off the liquid fat, so that his bones could be borne by his son's army against the Scots. His son, however, was apparently too squeamish to have this instruction carried out.

The state of leaderless Scotland during the years following the Falkirk debacle must have been pitiful indeed. They were dark days, in which the people had good cause to feel in actuality what the poet Barbour retrospectively put into their mouths over a century later:

> "Ah! Freedom is a noble thing!
> Freedom maiss man to have liking;
> Freedom all solace to man gives:
> He lives at ease that freely lives.
> A noble heart may have nane ease,
> Na ellis nocht that may him please,
> Gif Freedom fail. . . ."

—sentiments the savour of which too many Scotsmen have forgotten since those bitterly heroic days!

Edward the Second, though he baulked at rendering his father's corpse, was no less determined than his forbears to bring Scotland under English sway. In 1314, therefore, he resolved to march with a great army into Scotland, and settle the "insurrectionists" once and for all. Robert the Bruce was now the leader of the Scottish people, having been crowned in 1306 by the luckless Countess of

Buchan, who later fell into Edward's hands, and was kept in a cage until she died. Bruce had had his troubles since his encounter with Wallace, and more than once it must have seemed that the forces of Scottish resistance might collapse altogether. But Bruce was apparently a man of hardy physique and indomitable courage. He does not perhaps impress us as being initially motivated by the same impersonal patriotism as Wallace—who, after all, had nothing to gain by taking up arms, and everything to lose, as events subsequently proved. Bruce, on the other hand, was more or less forced to come down on the patriotic side once and for all, the moment his angry dagger pierced the blood of the Red Comyn at Dumfries in 1306. Yet Bruce's leadership, once the fighting days were over, was of a firm and wise kind that hardly seems to justify the accusations of his detractors that he was "just a Norman adventurer".

In any case, there can be no doubting his courage on that spring day in 1314, when he learned that Edward the Second was marching against him with 100,000 men, the biggest army ever to cross the Border. Bruce collected in all about 30,000 men, many of them Highlanders with whom he was popular. The story of the reckless preliminary gallantry of Edward Bruce,[1] the King's brother, and of the care with which the King selected his site, from the burn of the Bannock to the village of St. Ninian, so that even the rays of the sun might be on the side of the Scots, is familiar enough.

The English King thought that the mere sight of his host would frighten the Scots into submission. When he saw them all suddenly kneel in prayer, he turned to one of his commanders, Sir Ingram Umfraville, and, in Barbour's words, said:

> " ' Yon folk kneeleth to ask mercy.'
> Sir Ingram said, ' Ye say sooth now,
> They ask mercy, but none at yow;
> For their trespass to God they cry.
> I tell thee a thing sickerly,
> That yon men will all win or dee,
> For doubt of deid they will not flee. . . ."

Win or die! And so it was. The English began the battle with a vigorous cavalry charge. But, as they galloped up the brae, they came upon prepared spiked pits lightly covered over with camouflage turf. Down came riders, the bellies of their horses ripped

---

[1] Later, for a few years, King of Ireland.

and torn, they themselves shaken and shattered. Early in the battle, one ambitious knight, Sir Henry de Bohun, galloped up to the King of Scots himself, hoping to slay him in single combat and so end the battle at a blow. But Sir Henry's blow missed, and the King struck him dead instantly with a stroke the force of which snapped the shaft of the royal battle-axe. The success of the anti-cavalry trap, together with the King's demonstration of courage, immensely heartened the Scottish troops, and, although the battle raged throughout the day (June 13th), and there were moments when the tide of victory might have settled in either way, the Scots won the field. A party of excited Scots baggage-men suddenly appeared on the horizon, and the English, thinking them reinforcements, broke off battle and fled. The English King refused to leave the scene of his defeat until one of his commanders laid hold of his horse's bridle and led him away.

Much of the curious, often unformulated anti-Scottish behaviour of English politicians down the centuries, to say nothing of the post-1746 barbarities, seems to me to derive from the psychological effects of Bannockburn. That the English, who failed to take Scotland by force, succeeded in the end by guile and bribery, merely indicates a steady decline in the temper of the Scottish character. But official persistence, even down to our own day, in ignoring Scottish feeling whenever it is more convenient for English complacency to do so, seems to me incapable of any other explanation; especially since, in many other respects, the English display a breadth of judgment and a generosity towards the people under their sway unparalleled amongst the nations of Europe.[1]

The third battle to be fought in these parts was that of Sauchieburn. It was, on the whole, a shameful affair, the principal victor wearing a chain about his waist to which he added a link every year, as a mark of penance for having taken up arms against his father.

James the Third was the father; but, whatever may have been his virtues as a parent, he was the weakest character of all the Stewarts. Weakness is not foolishness—James the Seventh and Second out-measured him in this latter quality!—but for all practical purposes, it was equally dangerous in the Scotland of the 1480's. James the Third's weakness was that he had an inordinate love for the refinements of a gentleman—music, dancing, fencing, good clothes. He even preferred the society and council of those who purveyed these pleasures to that of his senior nobles. This

[1] "We have catched the Scots at last and we mean to hold them fast," declared an English politician in 1707.

preferment was so indiscreet and tactless that, in the end, his nobles took the law into their own hands. Archibald, Earl of Angus, seized the luckless favourites and hanged Cochrane, the leader, over Lauder Brig, for which he afterwards earned the nickname of Archibald Bell-the-Cat.

There was nearly a battle between the royal forces and those of the nobles over this affront; but a truce was patched up, in which the King promised to abjure such unconventional councils. He also had to promise not to give any more pardons for crimes of violence or cases of treason such as that of the Duke of Albany, who was suspected of plotting with Edward the Fourth of England. Apparently, however, James did not keep his word, and more and more hitherto loyal nobles joined the ranks of the dis-affected.

The thing which "fired the train" was the King's proposal to allocate the revenue of the Priory of Coldingham to the endow-ment of the choir of the Chapel Royal. The local lords, Hume and Hepburn, considered that Coldingham's revenues were not the King's to redispense. James flew to the North, where he reckoned he could count on royal support.

If James had attacked the rebel lords with his Northern army, he would almost certainly have beaten them. Instead, he wasted time in parley, and finally pardoned the rebels and disbanded most of his own army. He then found that the rebel lords had not, in fact, disbanded their forces, and that the gates of Stirling had been shut in his face.

On the 11th of June 1488, the two forces met at Sauchieburn, a little to the south of Stirling. James' boy son, already pro-claimed King by the rebels, was with the opposing army, so that the Lion Standard moved against the Lion Standard. The real King's horse bolted from the field and made towards Bannockburn. Possibly James had the idea that if he reached Admiral Sir Andrew Wood's ship, anchored in the Firth, he would be safe. At any rate, his horse threw him to the ground outside Beaton's Mill. He was carried inside and tended by the miller's wife (the sight of whose pitcher is said by the imaginative to have caused the horse to stall in the first place!). When he recovered a little, he asked for a priest, that he might confess. The miller's wife asked him who he was. "This day at morn I was your King," came the reply. At once, the woman went out crying after a priest for the King. A passing stranger claimed to be one. After listening to the King's confession, he leant forward and stabbed him to the heart with a whinger.

The last battle to be fought in Stirlingshire—the second battle of Falkirk—was part of Prince Charlie's rearguard action as he marched north from Derby. In the New Year of 1746, the town of Stirling was invested (unsuccessfully) by the Prince's troops. That coarse and brutal English commander, Lieutenant-General Hawley, hastily mustered his army at Edinburgh, and moved to the relief of Stirling. He encamped at Falkirk, near the site of the earlier battle. Hawley had been appointed to command the Hanoverian army in succession to Sir John Cope, who had been defeated the previous year at Prestonpans, and whose rout is celebrated in Adam Skirving's rousing song, "Hey! Johnnie Cope are ye waukin yet?" Hawley went to dine at Callander House, Falkirk, with the Countess of Kilmarnock. There was double irony in this, because not only did this social indulgence help to cause Hawley's subsequent defeat, but the husband of his hostess, herself a Jacobite, actually held a command in Prince Charles' army.[1]

Meanwhile, Prince Charles decided to attack. A Hanoverian Colonel rode to Callander House to tell Hawley of the impending danger, and Hawley was seen to rush from the grounds on horseback, his grey hair streaming in the wind. By modern standards, what followed was a scrummage rather than a battle. Hawley's army had to retreat: but a portion of Prince Charlie's army dispersed under the mistaken impression that they had lost the day! The Jacobites thereupon blew up their powder magazine—the old parish kirk of St. Ninians—leaving only the steeple standing. After spending a night at Bannockburn House, where he may have seen Clementina Walkinshaw, Charles followed his army northwards. Hawley, of course, was replaced by the gross and cruel Duke of Cumberland, who, at Drummossie Muir a few months later, exacted considerably more than a just revenge on the poor Highlanders for what he called "the small stain of Falkirk".

## V

Stirling is more closely associated with the Stewart kings than any other place in Scotland. Stirling Castle, for over five hundred years, from the days of Alexander the First to those of James the Sixth, was a favourite Royal Palace, and it is impossible not to go through it to-day without being deeply conscious of the part both castle and burgh have played in the making of Scottish history.

[1] On which account he later lost his head.

"Stirling," an observant traveller, John Macky, noted in 1723, "is situated much like Edinburgh, with its castle on an eminence to the west, and the town running down the descent of the hill to the east. The market-place is spacious, with a handsome town-house in it; and from the Earl of Mar's house to the bottom of the town may be about half an English mile, all upon a descent, with good houses." In point of fact, the similarity of Old Stirling to Old Edinburgh is closer than Macky perhaps imagined, because both are about a mile long by a quarter of a mile broad.

Long before this pleasant and compact burgh had developed, Stirling had become a place of importance because of the strategic value of its rock and its position at a river-crossing. There may have been a Pictish stronghold on the rock before Agricola forti-fied it. It is said to have been the Round Table on which King Arthur trained his forces, and the poet Barbour refers to it by that name when he remarks that Edward the Second and his retainer, fleeing from Bannockburn, went "Richt by the Rownde Tabill their way".

The Northumbrian King Egfrid is said to have established an Anglican Bishopric at Abercorn, on the Forth, in 675, and to have taken possession of Stirling Castle. Ten years later, on May 20th, 685, this attempt by the Angles to gain Pictish territory was de-feated by Bruidhe, King of Picts, at the decisive battle of Nectans-mere.[1] The bishopric was no doubt withdrawn at this time and the Castle, which would be made of wood, destroyed.

One of the last struggles between the Picts and the Scots before they finally came together in the ninth century is supposed to have taken place beneath the rock. The wolf is said to have got itself into the Stirling coat-of-arms about the close of this century, when the town was threatened by a Danish investment. A sentinel at the South Port fell asleep, but was awakened by the growl-ing of a wolf in time to sound the alarm. Such stories are picturesque, the more so since they can neither be verified nor disproved!

It was certainly King Alexander the First (1107-24), son of Mal-colm Ceann Mor, sometimes called the Fierce, and owner of the finest collection of pearls in Europe, who founded the original Chapel Royal on the rock. He also made the town into a royal burgh and died there.[2] His brother, Malcolm's ninth son, King David the First, caused Cambuskenneth Abbey to be founded in

[1] Probably Dunnichen, near Forfar.
[2] At any rate he refers to Stirling as his "royal burgh" in a charter of 1108. David the First confirmed the town's statutes as a royal burgh in 1150.

1147, one tower of which has survived the Reformation and the actions of later domestic quarrels. The grave of the luckless James the Third was discovered here during the reign of Queen Victoria, who caused a granite covering to be raised over the last resting-place of her "illustrious ancestor".

That King William, so ineptly named "the Lion" (1165-1214), pledged the stronghold of Stirling to Henry the Second of England as part of his ransom bargain under the term of the Treaty of Falaise after he had been captured on an imprudent forward reconnaissance whilst besieging Alnwick Castle in July 1174.[1] Forty years later, King William returned from an expedition into Moray, to die in the castle. It was from Stirling that King Alexander the Second (1214-49) proclaimed the law which first established trial by jury in Scotland. King Alexander the Third (1249-86) laid out the Royal Park.

When the poet-king, James the First (1406-37), returned from his English captivity, he frequently held court at Stirling. There, he sat in judgment over Regent Murdoch, Duke of Albany, his sons and his father-in-law, the aged Lennox, condemning them to be beheaded on the Heading Hill. This stern, though probably just, measure, however, antagonized many other nobles, and was ultimately responsible for James' assassination in Perth by Sir Robert Graham, who was in due course also executed on the same spot, preliminary tearings by red-hot pincers and crownings with red-hot crowns being part of the punishment contrived for him by the widowed Queen Joan.

James the Second (1437-60) made the Castle a dower house for his Queen, and frequently stayed in it himself. He, too, was alarmed at the power of the Douglases, and he also chose an unwise method of attempting to limit it. In February 1452, he invited William, eighth Earl of Douglas, to dine with him at Stirling Castle, luring the Douglas with a letter of safe-conduct. After the meal, the King invited his guest into an inner chamber to confer. The King wished the Douglas to break off his alliance with the Tiger Earl of Crawford, an alliance the King rightly regarded as constantly menacing himself. In spite of all persuasion, Douglas refused, whereupon the King, in a temper, drew his dagger, and plunged it into the Earl's throat. Hearing the noise, Sir Patrick Gray, who was on duty at the door, rushed in, followed by the guard. In a few moments, the lifeless body of the last Earl but one of the Black Douglases had been pushed through the window into the courtyard below, from where it was hastily buried in a sunken garden by the ramparts. It requires

[1] Richard the First (Cœur de Lion) restored Stirling to the Scots.

only a cursory examination of the room which is supposed to have witnessed this bloody deed, to see that it is of more recent construction than the date of the murder.

James the Third (1460-88) was born in Stirling Castle in 1451. He it was who built the Great Hall, and founded the second Chapel Royal, possibly to the design of his prime favourite, Cochrane, who met so rude an end over the parapet of Lauder Bridge.

James the Fourth (1488-1513) made further improvements, and laid out the "King's Knot", an intricate knotted garden still preserved in outline beneath the Castle in a field by the Stirling-Dumbarton road. James the Fourth went in for splendid tournaments, which must have brought a rich blaze of colour to the grey environs of the Castle buildings. He also dabbled in alchemy, which in his day passed for scientific experiment. Thus it came about that when a plausible foreigner, John Damien, Abbot of Tungland, claimed he had invented a pair of wings which would enable him to fly, King James caused the court to assemble to watch the bird-man flutter from the ramparts of the Castle. Of course, the experiment was a failure, and the Abbot was picked up with a broken thigh. His explanation of the failure was that a mistake had been made in the construction of his wings. Instead of having been made up entirely of eagles' feathers, hen feathers had also been introduced: and as hens cannot fly to any great extent, how could his wings possibly operate?

A better man had a better explanation. William Dunbar (?1460-?1520), the greatest poet Scotland has produced, Burns apart, also witnessed the proceedings. His passionate, frustrated, saturnine muse only required some suitable topical occasion to bring it into brilliant action. The Abbot of Tungland's downfall was too good an occasion to be missed. So Dunbar sat down in his castle room, where no doubt many of his astonishingly intricate metrical *tours de forces* had been evolved in the past, and wrote "The Fenyeit Friar of Tungland", a magnificent piece of scurrilous abuse.[1] After he has stripped the Abbot of his religious pretensions, and scorned his so-called "cures"—a laxative "to gar a wicht horse want his life": a purgative "to mak a thief to dee without a widdy" (gallows), which anticipates Burns' "Death and Dr. Hornbook"—Dunbar goes on to describe the reaction of the birds of the air as the Abbot made his undignified descent. Finally, the birds attacked him as he lay helpless on the ground.

[1] Nevertheless, as Dr. T. Crouther Gordon pointed out in a recent article on John Damien in *The Scotsman*, Damien was not such a fool as Dunbar made out. Nor did his flying disaster cause James to lose confidence in Damien's abilities.

> "*They set upon him with a yowl*
>     *And gaif him dint for dint.*
> *The golk, the gormaw and the gled,*        [cuckoo, cormorant,
> *Beft him with buffets while he bled;*                    kite
> *The sparhalk to the spring him sped,*
>     *As fierce as fire on flint.*
> *The tasall gaif him tug for tug,*        [male peregrine falcon
> *A stenchell hung in ilka lug*              [kestrel, ear
> *The pyat forth his pens did rug,*        [pulled out his feathers
>     *The stork strak ay but stint. . . ."*        [without reserve

In the end, while attempting to escape, the Abbot slipped out of his feathers, and fell up to his eyes in a myre.

> "*The air was dirkit so with fowls,*              [darkened
>     *That came with yammers and with yowls*
> *With screiching, screaming, and with scowls,*
>     *To tak him in the tide. . . ."*

And because the noise of the birds was so great as to disturb the poet and disagreeably haunt his memory, Dunbar cursed "that canker't rowte".

Like his father before him, James the Fifth (1513-42) spent much of his boyhood at Stirling. When he was sixteen years old, the Earl of Angus gained possession of him, and took him to Falkland Palace. The young King escaped on horseback and, much to the joy of the Captain of Stirling, made safely over the bridge, ordering the gate to be closed behind him and every Douglas who should approach within twelve miles of his person to be denounced as a traitor. The historian Lyndsay of Pitscottie (1532-78), describes this adventure with relish, and tells us that after the King was safely in the Castle, the Captain shut the gates, let down the portcullis and "pat the king in his bed to sleip because he had ridden all nicht".

James the Fifth is supposed to have been fond of disguising himself as a commoner, slipping out by the eastern postern known as the Ballengeich Road, and mingling incognito with his subjects. When thus abroad, he called himself the "guid man of Ballangeich". He is credited, on not very conclusive evidence, with having recorded his "Ballengeich" adventures in two vigorous poems, "The Gaberlunzie Man" and "The Jolly Beggar". Under the guise of Fitz James, Scott makes him the hero of "The Lady of the Lake". In courtly mood, James was fond enough of assembling the rank and beauty of Scotland on the Ladies Hill, to watch tournaments in the gardens below; fond also of hunting and hawking; of watching his pet lion in the Lion's Den; and of sailing the royal barges on the pleasure canal which once glistened through the green fields around the rock.

James the Fifth did more than any of the earlier monarchs to beautify the Castle. In 1549, he had the Chapel Royal rebuilt. The Palace was built in 1539 to the design of the rascally Protestant-persecuting architect, Sir James Hamilton of Fynnart, who also built the Palace of Linlithgow. Hamilton, described by Lindsay as "that bluddie bouchour ever thirstand for blude", finally fell into the King's disfavour, and was beheaded. Judged purely by their architectural abilities, how would not we in Scotland have benefited if many later architects had suffered a similar fate early in their careers!

Mary, Queen of Scots (1542-67), was crowned at Stirling in 1543, and her son, James the Sixth (1567-1625), was also crowned there, in 1566. There was a good deal of bloody scuffling for the place between the Jamesian and the Marian nobles during the Regency, but in the end, James' supporters gained ultimate possession. His heir, Prince Henry, was baptized with a sumptuous splendour hitherto unknown in Scotland, in 1549. Even the representative of Elizabeth of England, the Earl of Sussex, appears to have been impressed.

After 1603, when he had become James the Sixth and First, and betaken himself to London, Stirling Castle declined in importance. James came back to it twice, and both Charles the First and Charles the Second paid a brief visit. The Cromwellian General Monk besieged the hereditary keeper (the Earl of Mar) in the Castle during August 1651, knocking the domes off two of the four towers of the "foir-face", and pitting the outer walls with holes that may still be inspected. The Jacobite rôle of the Castle during the 1715 rising, and its Hanoverian rôle during the '45, have already been recounted.

Architecturally, Stirling Castle contains three of our finest treasures. The Great Hall, where the Parliaments of Scotland so often met, once had an "open oak roof of hammer-beam construction". Externally, the outstanding features of the building were the windows—projecting oriels of finely wrought masonry, and deeply recessed windows set in pairs, with boldly designed rybats.

Anent the Palace, George Scott-Moncrieff says, "in the young sixteenth century the familiar Scottish castellated forms . . . suddenly burst out before an early breath of the Renaissance, into a superimposing grace of singular seriousness heightened by the fantastic statuary, grotesques that lean out with sensual breasts and lips. . . ." The King's rooms were in the northern half, the Queen's in the southern. We learn from the Royal Household Accounts of the story-telling tapestries that once adorned the walls. The King's Presence Chamber was roofed with large, carved-oak roundels. In 1777, one of the roundels fell down, killing or at least injuring a soldier. The whole roof was there-upon stripped, and but for the presence of mind of the Governor of Stirling prison, one Ebenezer Brown, who saved some of the roundels from the rubbish heap, all of them might have perished. As it is, twenty-eight are preserved in the Smith Institute at Stirling, and three in the National Museum of Antiquities at Edinburgh.

At about the same time, the Government of the day spent a large sum of money turning these noble buildings into a military barracks. The Great Hall was split up, and the Palace partly stripped and denuded. The Chapel Royal and the Royal Mint became stores.

" How disgraceful it is to the nation," wrote Lord Cockburn in 1845, " and particularly to the Government, that the scenes of its history should be converted to such base uses. The place where the Parliament met, a barrack room! And every other sacred spot equally debased! I have often and positively been assured that about the beginning of the last war, 1804, the Government of the day wished virtually to obliterate the Castle altogether. . . ."

When I visited it (1952), the same sorry state of things still per-sisted. A magnificent fireplace in the Queen's apartments was bricked up with red lavatory tiles. Cheap plaster smothered the stone-work everywhere; exciting arches and internal pattern-work were ruthlessly bisected by military walls. The place is now under the care of the Ministry of Works, and there is some talk of belated restoration. But shortage of money is always the difficulty, especi-ally where the restoration of buildings with special significance to the spirit of Scotland is concerned! In any case, what is one to make of the citizens of a nation which passively tolerates such an affront to present honour and former glory?

Although much of Old Stirling has been preserved, partly by chance and partly by the far-sightedness of her administrators aided by the Thistle Trust, in more recent times, much that could have been saved has been pulled down. A few years ago, I set out to inspect an eighteenth-century building called the Coffee House. I was horrified to find the demolition men scrambling over it, and only the lower walls standing! If Stirling is to retain its character, it is essential that most of the ancient buildings, at any rate in Broad Street and St. John Street, should be restored.

Stirling has still a richer heritage of seventeenth-century houses than any other burgh. She should be zealous in preserving it.

The finest of the domestic dwellings, if one could so call the Renaissance palace known as Mar's Wark, was built by the 6th Earl of Mar, Regent of Scotland, between 1570 and 1572, largely out of stones removed from the body of Cambuskenneth Abbey. Since about the middle of the eighteenth century, only the ruined façade has dignified the upper end of Broad Street.

The Argyll Ludging has been more fortunate. It was put up by Sir William Alexander of Menstrie, first Earl of Stirling (?1577-1646), about 1630, to the plans of his second son, Sir Anthony. Alexander was a zealous courtier-poet who helped James the Sixth with his version of the Psalms, wrote his "Monarchick" tragedies of "Darius", "Croesus", "Julius Caesar" and the "Alexandrian Tragedy" in the Senecan manner, as well as an enormous epic poem "Doomsday", and a series of love-complaining sonnets, "Aurora", which were inspired by the daughter of Sir John Shaw of Sauchie. From James the Sixth he received the grant of Nova Scotia, and he later became Secretary of State for Scotland, a position which brought him obloquy because of his master's growing unpopularity amongst the Scots. He was, however, a most interesting character, and, contrary to the opinions expressed by many literary historians, passages of considerable force and vitality are to be found even in his longer works.

Obviously, such a man had to have an impressive town "ludging". The Argyll Ludging, so called because it was later sold to the Argyll family, is, in fact, both in scale and design, by far the most impressive town-dwelling to survive in Scotland. Two kings—Charles the Second and James the Seventh (when Duke of Albany) lodged there, as did also the Duke of Cumberland. It has been a military hospital since the later eighteenth century. Such a use has, at any rate, caused it to be preserved outwardly in perfect condition.

Smaller "ludgings" may be seen at 36-38 Broad Street, 30-32 Broad Street, 72-74 St. Mary's Wynd, 26-28 Bow Street, 19-27 St. John Street and 2 St. John Street, to list only a few.

The Cowane Mansion, a ruined building (which in the opinion of the architect, Mr. Ian G. Lindsay, could yet be restored—and certainly should be), was once the home of John Cowane, one of Stirling's greatest benefactors, and an umquhile Dean of Guild. He it was who bequeathed money for the building of Cowane's Hospital. This building went up between 1636-49, and is a delightful crow-stepped structure with a central bell-tower, and a niche over the entrance containing a statue of the founder. It looks north towards the Kirk of the Holy Rude, and has a balus-traded terrace and an early eighteenth-century bowling-green. Its original purpose was to shelter "twelve decayed Gildbreithers". In 1852, the interior was altered to form the present Guild-Hall.

Spittal's Hospital, put up by another of Stirling's benefactors, Robert Spittal, tailor to King James the Fourth, may or may not have been located at 82 Spittal Street. This old house, despoiled to some extent in the late nineteenth century, was at any rate the tailor's home from 1521 until he died, very old, in 1550.

Two other public buildings are worth attention—the Parish Church of the Holy Rude, which consists of a "western tower, an aisled nave of five bays, crossings and trancepts, an aisled choir of three bays, and a deep eastern apse". Just short in length of 200 feet, Holy Rude is one of the largest pre-Reformation burgh kirks to survive in Scotland.

The present Tolbooth of Stirling was built in 1702-4 to the design of Sir William Bruce. It has a fine tower with a pavilioned roof. The old Mercat Cross which used to stand in front of it was removed in 1792, and the present approximate copy was put up in 1891.

It was somewhere hereabouts that a shocking spectacle took place in 1820. Andrew Hardie and John Baird, two humble West country weavers, were publicly hanged, then beheaded, the executioner holding up poor Hardie's mangled head by the hair and crying, "This is the head of a traitor." His treason con-sisted in having led a bunch of radical weavers to Bonnymuir in a futile demonstration in favour of Parliamentary reform. The two men have since become known as the Radical Martyrs. And was their martyrdom, if far less justifiable, a whit less noble than that of George Wishart and Patrick Hamilton?

VI

Alexander Smith was of the opinion that the finest approach to Stirling is from the field of Bannockburn. (Incidentally, the "field" is now owned by the nation. A large price was paid for it, in spite of the fact that the weight of historical evidence points to its being the wrong field!) That may have been so in the 1850's, when he passed through Stirling *en route* for *A Summer in Skye*. Now, this approach is so disfigured by housing schemes and coal bings, that the vista is smudged. The approach from the north, over the Old Brig, with its eighteenth-century replacement arch necessitated by the destruction of one span during the '45,

is disfigured by an enormous acreage of pre-fabricated houses, giving the distant impression of a field upon which some new and deadly fungus has sprung up. The finest approach nowadays, in my view, is along the Kippen Strait. Against the background of the Ochils, the Wallace Monument—that strange, mock-baronial tower put up in 1861 on the spot where the Scottish army was drawn up before the encounter at Bannockburn—may be seen perched on the wooded Abbey Craig. To the right of it, the Castle watches and waits on its separate eminence, as it has done for so many centuries. And wherever one looks to the north, hills rise out of the plains.

Modern Stirling is no longer a royal seat. Now, bustling amongst its antiquities, the life of a county town whose industries are mainly associated with agriculture and floriculture, goes busily on. The nearby coalmines, however, keep it in touch with the atmosphere and the problems of industrialism. In some ways, Stirling not only clasps Highlands and Lowlands together; it unites past traditions with present innovations, and brings together Scots men and women from many different walks of life.

" 'Tis a royal borough," wrote Thomas Morer, an English traveller, in 1689; " was formerly the king's palace, and the seat of Parliaments, is well built, and continues still in much reputation and honour." One might add that whether or not future ages will echo this last clause must very largely depend on the care with which Stirling guards and restores the irreplaceable stone-and-mortar treasures that have been left to her by so many vanished ages.

*Perthshire: The Lake Menteith in winter*

# CHAPTER V

## CLACKMANNAN AND KINROSS

*" O gin I were a doo*
*I wad fly awa the noo,*
*Wi my neb to the Lomond and my wings wavin' steady,*
*And I wadna rest a fit*
*Till at gloamin' I wad sit*
*Wi' ither neebour doos on the lums o' Balgedie."*
                    " HUGH HALIBURTON ", 1872.

I

HAD "Hugh Haliburton" indeed been a doo, instead of Mr. J.
Logie Robertson, for many years head English master in the Edinburgh Ladies College, such a method of transport from Queen
Street to the shores of Loch Leven would no doubt have been
possible.  Things being as they were, however, he could either
have crossed the Forth by the railway viaduct, or by Queensferry (now, of course, the Forth Road Bridge); or else he would
have had to make the journey by road via Stirling Brig.

For most travellers in Scotland, it would not be a bad thing if
ferry and viaduct could be considered temporarily out of action.
The road trip would then be forced upon them, and they would
make the entry into Fife through Clackmannan and Kinross, two
pleasant little counties which are otherwise apt to remain un-
visited.

Clackmannanshire, the smallest county in Scotland, gets its
rather sombre character from the domination of the Ochil Hills,
which lie in a north-easterly direction, stretching almost from the
Forth to the mouth of the Tay, and forming a large part of its
natural northern boundary with Perthshire.  Structurally, the
Ochils are a continuation of the Campsie and the Lennox Hills.
Geologically, they are made up of red and grey granite whinstone,
and different kinds of schist.  Strings of silver have from time to
time been discovered in them, mostly too thin to be profitably
worked, although between 1761 and 1764, Sir John Erskine of
Alva is reputed to have produced silver ore to the value of about
£50,000.  Thereafter, the vein became exhausted, and Sir John
lost most of his fortune sinking a useless mine in the hope of

coming upon another string. Towards the end of the eighteenth century, cobalt was also discovered and mined in limited quantities. The porcelain works at Prestonpans used it to colour their blue products. Lead and copper seams were found in the hilly parts of the county, but, like the silver, they never proved profitable to work. The one mineral that has been mined with profit is coal. There are several coal-fields, some of them surface-mines, within the county.

Alloa,[1] the largest town in Clackmannanshire, and a burgh of barony which now includes the ancient parish of Tullibody, is largely given over to industry. Bottle-making has been carried on in Alloa since the eighteenth century, and, for almost as long, its brewers have ensured that most of the bottles do not go out from the town empty. Passing winds carry the malty tang of the breweries over the surrounding countryside, so that Alloa announces its main occupation from afar. Burns' "Dear Kilbaigie", regarded for long as the finest whisky in Scotland, came from the nearby village of Kilbaigie, which is now more famous for its paper-mill.

Like most of the east-coast ports, Alloa must once have been engaged in a substantial general trade with the Continent before the west coast of Scotland was opened up to shipping. Because of the three islands which lie in the Forth off Alloa, only small vessels nowadays venture as far up the river. During the summer, little pleasure-steamers used to ply between Stirling and Leith. They were taken off during the First World War, and never replaced. Indeed, there has been a steady decline in the available sailings on Scottish waters since that time, mainly due to the development of the motor-bus. Yet to be cramped inside a jolting bus is surely a poor substitute for the gentler charms of sailing on loch or river!

For several miles along the Clackmannan and Fife coastlines, there occurs in good weather during the neap-tides, what sailors call a "leaky tide". After the water has flowed in for about three hours, it then runs back for an hour and a half, returning during the next hour and a half to its former height. This "leak" occurs during both flood and ebb tides, so that at these seasons there are actually double the number of tides in the Forth than anywhere else. As recently as 1933, a vessel ran aground in the river because its skipper was ignorant of this phenomenon.

Alloa was once a royal residence. King Alexander the Second (1214-49) built a "mote-and-bailey" tower, an affair of mud and

---

[1] Celtic *ath-luath* (pronounced *ah-loa*), "a swift ford", according to **Dr.** McLean Watt.

wattle, on Mar's Hill in 1225. Long before that, the Romans probably used this eminence as a summer outstation for Camelon, on the other side of the Forth. Incidentally, it should be remembered that the land has risen considerably during the last two thousand years, and that both Camelon and Clackmannan were once sea-ports.

In 1362, King Robert the Second gave Sir Robert de Erskine the barony of Alloa and the Forest of Clackmannan for services rendered to the Stewart cause. So began the long association of the Erskines with the district, an association that has persisted, in spite of the vicissitudes of history, for 600 years. The Erskines, Earls of Mar, who took their family name from their estates at Erskine on the Clyde, have been hereditary Governors of Stirling Castle since 1366. For a time, they also had the Governorship of Edinburgh and Dumbarton Castles, but these were later taken from them, partly for geographical and partly for political reasons.

Alloa still has a donjon tower, dating from about 1497, which replaced King Alexander's fortification. It became the Erskine home. Over the centuries, it was enlarged by the addition of a fine house which stood out from the tower, but the house was destroyed by fire in 1800. The conflagration consumed some valuable family relics, including a late portrait on copper of Mary, Queen of Scots, given away by the Queen before her execution at Fotheringay. James the Fourth stayed at the tower in 1588, its owner being his Lord High Treasurer. After his father had been killed at Flodden, the young James the Fifth was kept at Alloa Tower for a time until he was moved to Stirling, where he was brought up under Lord Erskine's care until Archibald, Earl of Douglas, managed to abduct him to Falkland. In 1565, only four days after the birth of her son, the future James the Sixth, Queen Mary came to Alloa, making Lord Erskine Earl of Mar. The Mars remained Jacobites, and it was the eleventh Earl who lost the battle of Sheriffmuir in 1715. Thereafter, the estates were attainted, but they were bought back into the family by Mar's brother, Lord Grange. Grange it was whose wife became so troublesome that he had her kidnapped and removed first to the Hebridean Island of Heisker, then to St. Kilda, where he kept her for seven years, and finally to Skye. Alloa witnessed the spectacle of a grand mock-funeral to the lady some months after her disappearance. But the ruse was not sufficiently convincing to allay suspicions, and Grange's conduct caused quite a stir in the Capital. According to Simon, Lord Lovat—perhaps hardly a good judge in such matters, since he himself was a cruel husband—Grange was "quite justified, there being no mad-houses at the time"!

The present Alloa House was put up by the fourteenth Earl, whose saying, "Puddings in the belly are better than bullets", indicates that he was perhaps wiser than his posthumous reputation as an eccentric suggests.

There is another donjon tower, roofless and much decayed, at Sauchie, a mile or two to the north of the town; and a third at the village of Clackmannan itself. The Clackmannan tower had an interesting history, for it was a residence of King Robert the Bruce (1306-29), before it became the home of the Bruces of Clackmannan—once related to the royal line—and the seat of the last chief of the clan, Henry Bruce, who died in 1772 without male issue. His widow, Mrs. Katherine Bruce, a venerable dame who survived until 1791 and whose features are preserved in a sketch by David Allan, received Burns during his Highland tour of 1787.

Burns, who had been visiting Harviestoun House, near Dollar, staying with the mother and sister of his close friend Gavin Hamilton, the attorney of Mauchline, had as his travelling companion one Dr. Adair of Harrogate, and the worthy medico left this account of their reception:

"A visit to Mrs. Bruce of Clackmannan, a lady above ninety, the lineal descendant of that race which gave the Scottish throne its highest ornament, interested his (Burns') feelings. . . . This venerable dame, with characteristic dignity, informed me, on my observing that I believed she was descended from the family of Robert Bruce, that Robert Burns was sprung from her family.[1] Though deprived of speech by a paralytic affection, she preserved her hospitality and urbanity. She was in possession of the hero's helmet and two-handed sword with which she conferred on Burns and myself the honour of knighthood, remarking that she had a better right to confer that title than some people. You will, of course, conclude that the old lady's political tenets were as Jacobite as the poet's. . . ."

Dr. John Jamieson, the lexicographer responsible for *Jamieson's Dictionary of the Scottish Language*, paid a visit to Mrs. Bruce a few years later, and was rewarded with a similar honour.

The old mansion of the Bruce's, which stood alongside the tower, has been demolished. The tower itself, weakened by

[1] Actually, the Bruces of Clackmannan claimed descent from a younger brother of Robert the Bruce's father.

underground workings, recently cracked down the middle of the outer walls. The Ministry of Works, who now have it under their care, are making strenuous efforts to preserve it by under-pinning.

The old village of Clackmannan struggles up a steep hill crowned, as it were, by the hoary remains of the old tower, which is visible for many distant miles. The village has a solid air of seemly dignity, its pantiled houses and crow-stepped gabled cottages rising stepwards up the slope. Unfortunately, many of them have been allowed to fall into a state of abandoned decrepitude. They could, and should be restored. It is all too easy for local authorities to order the demolition of such properties. Along comes a bull-dozer, and, in a very short time, the stout old walls are conveniently turned into road-bottoming. But in places like Clackmannan, where the destruction of much of the old property would also destroy the charm and character of the village, every effort at preservation should be made. Alas, the imaginative powers of the average Scot can rarely visualize the possibilities of reconstruction, so that it is only the more enlightened, though numerically less powerful section of the community who are willing to raise their voices against the wanton destruction of old, restorable property. In the minds of some folk, age itself is an overwhelming argument in favour of destruction. Not long ago, when my wife and I had newly moved into our recently restored cottage at Gartocharn, a local tradesman was calling upon us. He looked round about him in critical scrutiny, then said to my wife, " Ay, this must have pit ye to some expense. Hooever, if ye jist bide in the village lang enough, ye'll mebbe qualify for one o' thae coonsil hooses over by." The new " coonsil hooses over by ", needless to say, are hideosities erected without any regard for their aesthetic suitability to their surroundings.

Clackmannan affords a good example of another kind of preservation which, though better than no preservation at all, rather resembles the keeping of one's tonsils in a pickle-bottle. The steeple of the old Tolbooth, and one of the walls, stand in the centre of the village, obvious, though interesting relics of a past age. The blend of force and grace in the pavilioned tower, which dates from the sixteenth century, moved me so deeply that I had not the heart to search out whatever building does present duty in housing the local civic dignitaries.

The curious stone which now stands on a pinnacle beside the steeple and the Mercat Cross has a bearing on the name of the place. " Clack " is from the Celtic, meaning " stone ", while " mannan " has reference to the Celtic sea-god Mannan. This god's spirit was supposed to reside in the stone, which would once be nearer the sea than it is now.

Legend offers another explanation of more than ordinary ingenuity. When King Robert the Bruce was living at his Castle, he went out hunting in the Forest of Clackmannan. During the day's sport, he lost his glove. On the way home, he sent Sir James Douglas back to look for the glove, directing him to the brae on the south side of the town where, at the stone or *clach*, he was to "look aboot" for the glove or *mannan*. The brae is called Lookabootye Brae to this day, which would seem to give weight to the legend's authenticity, were it not that the name is demonstrably older than the fourteenth century. Another point relating to the first explanation is that the district which lies at the head of the Forth was called Mannan by the eighth-century historian Nennius and others. Slamannan—the moor of Mannan—is still the name of a village a few miles from Falkirk.

When "Hugh Haliburton" was sojourning in the Ochils tuning his pastoral note, he must often have travelled along the northern road across the county. Winding its way round the wooded Abbey Craig, on which stands the monstrous Wallace Memorial (containing, besides icy-looking marble busts of the poets, the hero's eighteenth-century sword!), the road enters Clackmannanshire through the parish of Logie. Blairlogie was once famous as a health resort for invalids who sought the popular goats'-milk cure —less absurd than it seems to us now, when we remember that goats' milk is richer in nourishment than cows', and is also tubercle free. Logie has earned more permanent fame from the fact that, in the parish kirk, one of the incumbents wrote a poem that marked a new departure in Scottish literature. The poem was "Of the Day Estivall", the author, Alexander Hume (?1500-1609), a younger son of the House of Polwarth, trained for the Bar, which he forsook to become a courtier at Holyrood. Eventually, he tired of the courtier's life too, and he ended up as a rather gloomy Calvinistic Presbyterian minister.

"Of the Day Estivall" describes the progress of a summer's day with an accurate use of sensuous nature-imagery not rivalled by any Scottish poet for a hundred and fifty years. At high noon, for instance, he tells us:

> "The time sa tranquil is and still
> That na where sall ye find—
> Saif on ane high and barren hill—
> Ane air of peeping wind.

*All trees and simples great and small*
  *That balmy leaf do bear*
*Nor they were painted on a wall*
  *Na mair they move or steir.*[1]

*Calm is the deep and purpour sea,*
  *Yea, smoother nor the sand;*
*The waves that welt'ring want to be,*
  *Are stable like the land. . . .*

*The rivers fresh, the caller streams*
  *Ower rocks can saftly rin,*
*The water clear like crystal seems,*
  *And makes a pleasant din.*

*The flourishes and fragrant flowers,*
  *Throw Phoebus' fost'ring heat*
*Refresh'd with dew and silver showers,*
  *Casts up ane odour sweet. . . .*

*The breathless flocks draw to the shade,*
  *The frechure of their fald,*
*The startling nolt as they were mad*
  *Runs to the rivers cald.*

*The herds beneath some leafy tree,*
  *Amids' the flowers they lie;*
*The stable ships upon the sea*
  *Tends up their sails to dry. . . .*

*Back from the blue paymented whun,*
  *And from ilk plaister wall,*
*The hot reflexing of the sun*
  *Inflames the air and all. . . ."*

Hume must have been a tortured soul indeed, haunted, like so many post-Reformation Scottish poets, by the belief that beauty is sinful—an artistic guilt-complex which has singularly impoverished the native personality. Only one other of his poems

---

[1] George Eyre-Todd has drawn attention to the similarity of rhythmic pattern between this poem as a whole, and Coleridge's *Ancient Mariner*, particularly to the similarity between Hume's penultimate line in the second of the verses quoted above, and the English poet's image of a " painted ship upon a painted ocean ".

has even half the merit of " Of the Day Estivall "; and this secondary effort contains a revealing stanza:

> " O poets, pagans impudent,
>     Why worship ye the planets seven?
>   The glore of God by you is spent
>     On idols and the host of heaven,
>   Ye pride your pens men's ears to please
>     With fables and fictitious lees. . . ."

The second line perhaps seems less bewildering—unless, of
course, it was meant as a " take-off " of Hume's Catholic contemporary, Alexander Montgomerie (1545?-1611?), who specialized in
" celestial " effects[1]—when one remembers that " seven " is one of
the few rhymes for " heaven "!

A few miles to the east, in Menstrie Castle, another " pagan im-
pudent " once sunned his courtly and ambitious muse.  He was
Sir William Alexander (1574-1640) who, during the course of his
extraordinary career,[2] became the first Earl of Stirling, and a
colonizer whose influence has been compared with that of
England's Sir Walter Raleigh.  He was also a close friend of
Hume, as is shown by the fact that the older poet appointed
" the guidman of Menstrie ", as he calls him, " counsellor to his
wife and bairns " by the terms of his will.

Menstrie Castle has been happily restored as housing flats. The
old village of Menstrie, with its red-pantiled houses nestling close
beneath the Ochils, makes a poetic picture in strong contrast to
the concrete ugliness of the new village sprawled about the main
road.  Menstrie stands beneath a dumpling of a hill which bears
the onomatopoeically appropriate name of Dumyat.

Alva, a douce-looking little weaving town, had the distinction
for many years of being the only place to return a Scottish
Nationalist as its Provost.  Tillicoultry, which has a distillery,
has no special feature of architectural interest, although the
parish contains a Druid circle and a legend about St. Serf or
Servanus.  The prior of Inch Serf, on Loch Leven, Andrew of
Wyntoun (fl. c. 1395-1424), the chronicle poet, records the incident.

[1] See, in particular, Montgomerie's sonnet:
    " The royal palace of the highest heaven,
      The stately furneis of the starry round,
      The lofty might of wandering planets seven ". . . . etc.

the nature and course of which may all be contended with; but
    " Only of this master love we doubt,
      Whose crafty cure no cunning can find out."

[2] See Chapter IV.

A ram which used to accompany the saint was one day stolen. . . .
When the suspect was brought before St. Serf he denied all knowledge of the beast. But he soon blushed red with shame, for
the ram bleated aloud in the thief's stomach, and so gave him
away.

Dollar was the scene of the defeat of the "Scots" in A.D. 877
by the Danes, who then chased them to Inverdovet, and killed
their king, Constantin, son of Kenneth MacAlpin. This is the
one battle known to have been fought on what was then Fife
soil.

Dollar owes its most recent fame to the presence of its academy.
The main building was put up in 1819 by Sir William Playfair
(1781-1857), the most distinguished disciple of the Adam brothers.
It is in the classical Georgian style of the period, and the additions
erected in 1868, 1892 and 1909 have not destroyed the general
balance. But Dollar has older associations than those of learning.
The name—*dolour*—means sadness, and from the glen behind the
town, the Burn of Care and the Burn of Sorrow tumble down
rock-bound acclivities. On a pinnacle at the height of the glen
stand the ruins of Castle Gloum, or Castle Campbell, as it later
came to be called. The nomenclature, allegedly bestowed by
some unhappy lady while a prisoner within the Castle walls, is
romantic, and so is the situation of this extraordinary fortress.

The oldest part of the Castle dates from the fifteenth century.
In 1465, it came into the hands of Colin Campbell of Lochow,
first Earl of Argyll, by his marriage. He had the name altered to
Castle Campbell by Act of Parliament. At the time of the Reformation, it was the residence of Archibald, fourth Earl of Argyll,
who was the first nobleman in Scotland to go over to the Protestant
religion. Here, in 1566, John Knox preached and dispensed the
sacraments. Here, too, Queen Mary came for the marriage of
Argyll's sister. The Castle was partially destroyed in 1645 by
detachments of Montrose's army, as the Great Marquis marched
south towards Kilsyth. Argyll had been responsible for the burning of the "Bonnie Hoose o' Airlie" in 1640—an act of pure booty-
snatching, ill-disguised as political necessity, in which Argyll
behaved with callous brutality towards the young Lady Ogilvie—
so Castle Campbell was sacked in revenge. The path through the
glen was not then in existence, so it must have been a well-nigh
impregnable stronghold. Tradition has it that when the McLeans
fired burning arrows on to it from the shoulder of the adjacent
hill, most of the defenders are reputed to have been out foraging.
Tradition, however, is by no means infallibly accurate, for, according to another source, the McLeans did approach the Castle, but

retired again without damaging it, contenting themselves with destroying all but two houses in the parish, these two being spared only by accident. General Monk, writing to Cromwell on 29th July 1654 anent his pursuit of the Earl of Glencairn's Royalist troops, put the matter beyond doubt when he reported that " Some small parties of the enemy are abroad, and on Monday and Tuesday night last burn't Castle Campbell, an house belonging to the Marquis of Argyle ".

The Jacobite poetess, Caroline Oliphant, Lady Nairne (1766-1845), lamented in song the fate of the interesting old place:

> " Oh! Castell Gloom! thy strength is gane,
>     The green grass o'er thee growin',
> On hill of Care thou art alone,
>     The sorrow round thee flowin'!
> Oh! Castell Gloom! on thy fair wa's,
>     Nae banners now are streamin';
> The howlit flits amang the ha's,
>     And wild birds there are screamin'.
>
> Here ladies bright were aften seen,
>     Here valiant warriors trod;
> And here great Knox has aften been,
>     Wha feared nocht but his God.
> But a'a are gane! the gude, the great,
>     And naething now remains,
> But ruin sitting on thy wa's,
>     And crumblin' doun the stanes! . . .
>
> Oh! mourn the woe, oh mourn the crime,
>     Frae civil war that flows;
> Oh! mourn Argyle, they fallen line,
>     And mourn the great Montrose."

The donjon tower still stands intact, and part of the mansion has been restored as a home for the keeper. The place is now in the hands of the Ministry of Works, and when I visited it they were excavating the floor of the old hall. There, before my eyes, lay the old slates newly uncovered and still clinging to the charred embers of those rafters that must have crashed down with a fearsome flurry of sparks so many years ago. I saw also the fist-size aperture in the carved drawing-room ceiling through which rush-lights once were lowered. It was temporarily visible only because the floor above had been stripped for renewal.

The Argylls must have been well in advance of their time, for the Castle contained two long-drop W.C.s more hygienic than many of the primitive shunkies still in use in town and country to-day.

A perpendicular gully, in which the remains of steps cut out of the stone may still be seen, leads from the front of the Castle lawn down to the cleft in the rock where the Burns of Care and Sorrow meet. No doubt it was used as a means of supplying the Castle with water during a siege, or, in extremity, as a means of escape. The name of Willie Kemp, one of those sturdy, lovably improbable rascals in which Scottish folk-lore abounds, is now associated with it, because of an alleged escapade in which he stole the King's dinner from Dunfermline Palace. After further un- specified escapades of this sort, he is supposed to have been be- headed and thrown into the River Devon at a place still known as " Willie's Pool ".

The Devon was celebrated by Burns, in his best Augustan manner, during his first visit to Harviestoun House:

" *How pleasant the banks of the clear winding Devon,*
*With green spreading bushes and flow'rs blooming fair!*
*But the bonniest flow'r on the banks of the Devon*
*Was once a sweet bud on the banks of the Ayr. . . ."*

The pretty compliment was addressed to Charlotte, Gavin Hamilton's sister, with whose cousin Peggy Chalmers the poet fell in love to the extent of proposing marriage to her. Dr. Adair was with Burns when he paid his second visit to Harviestoun, and although Peggy Chalmers would have none of the poet, Charlotte in due course became Mrs. Adair. Burns was not often defeated when he set out to win the hearts, if not the hands, of the fair. As in this case, most of his rare defeats were with women of higher social class than himself. This experience no doubt conditioned his outlook on the local scenery, which he seems to have found disappointing.

The Devon rises in the parish of Blackford, in Perthshire. It runs eastward through the Ochils for about eleven miles, and then takes an acute turn to the west. This turn is known as the Crook of Devon. Although its source is only six miles away from Cam- bus, where it enters the Forth, the Devon covers a course of about thirty miles in getting from one point to the other. Salmon come up from the Forth in season, and trout and par are to be had in those deep pools where pearls were found in the eighteenth century. In 1766, when the development of waterways occupied much public attention, none other than James Watt was engaged to report on the possibilities of making the lower reaches of the Devon navigable for the benefit of Clackmannanshire's coal trade. However, the project, which was to cost two thousand pounds, came to nothing.

During its winding course, the Devon (or "little Dovan", as it was anciently called) is frequently constricted into rock-pent cascades and lynns. In the Devil's Mill, so called because of the curious clacking sound made by the water as it presses its way through the gorge, there is a cave which was the scene of a curious Jacobite adventure. Hector McEachen, a nephew of a Lord Provost of Glasgow, was arrested on his way to join Prince Charles' army, and imprisoned in Castle Campbell. Whilst there, he aroused the interest and compassion of Hannah Haig, the daughter of a neighbouring laird. She contrived his escape, by means that are not vouchsafed to us, and hid him in the Devil's Mill cave until the hue and cry had died down. He did succeed in fighting for his Prince, but he was captured again, and this time he was sent to stand his trial at Carlisle. But for some fault in the evidence, he would almost certainly have shared the death sentence meted out to his companions. When the judge announced his acquittal, a young woman in the court burst into tears. But they were tears of relief, for she was none other than Hannah Haig, who had come down to Carlisle to get a last glimpse of the man she loved. Their subsequent marriage puts the story dangerously near that category which might prove acceptable to an American film-magnate in search of a heather-scented, tartan-girt, real-life romance!

There are further cascades at Rumbling Bridge, and at the Caldron Linn, before the Devon really begins to assume that placid character so formally noted by Burns.

## II

Kinross, the next smallest county to Clackmannan, was once part of Fife, when both were known as the Ross, after the Gaelic word *ros*, a promontory; but Kinross has had a separate identity for more than five hundred years. Loch Leven, lying back between the Lomond Hills, the Cleish Hills and the Ochils, occupies about a sixth of the county's area. It is around the shores of the loch that much of the county's history has been played.

No doubt the Romans, on one of their excursions over the Forth, passed through Kinross. But there is no evidence that they ever really conquered "the district between Kinross and Muck-ross", as our Celtic forbears called, in their apt way of naming places, the head and the snout of the well-defined promontory that we know as Fife and Kinross. To march through territory is not necessarily to conquer it.

St. Serf made a more lasting impression on the county. The exact period of St. Serf's ministrations is not really known, although there is no doubt about his having existed. According to one authority,[1] St. Serf was probably a pupil of St. Ninian at Candida Casa, Wigtownshire. He settled at Culross, had a retreat at Dysart (which means a desert or hermitage) and kept a tame robin. But in Kinross-shire he visited Portmoak, on Loch Leven, where an early church bore his name, and he inspired the build-ing of a later foundation on the island in the loch named in his honour.

But the Picts and the Scots had long since united, Christianity the common bond between them then, by the time the monas-tery of St. Serf had its most famous prior, Andrew of Wyntoun (c. 1350-c. 1420). Andrew whiled away the hours not spent in devotion by writing his *Orygynale Chronikyll of Scotland,* a poem in nine books. Although he was not much of a poet, and an indifferent historian, his account is of value because of the material relating to his own times. Incidentally, the story of Macbeth and the three weird sisters makes one of its earliest appearances in Wyntoun's *Chronikyll.*

The castle of Loch Leven stands on another island near the middle of the Loch. The local poet, Michael Bruce, described its appearance in the eighteenth century:

> " *No more its arches echo to the noise*
> *Of joy and festive mirth; no more the glance*
> *Of blazing taper through its windows beams*
> *And quivers on the undulating wave;*
> *But naked stand the melancholy walls,*
> *Lash'd by the wintry tempests, cold and bleak,*
> *And whistle mournfully through the empty hall,*
> *And piecemeal tumble down the towers to dust. . . ."*

Now, the Ministry of Works at least see to it that no more of the Castle shall " piecemeal tumble down to dust ". Legend has it that Loch Leven Castle was founded about a thousand years ago by Congal, a Pictish king, as a royal residence. Wallace is said

---

[1] Diana Leatham: *Celtic Sunrise.* Further conjectures about this Saint are to be found in Chapter VI.

to have captured it from an English garrison by first swimming across the loch and bringing back the boat needed to ferry his men over to the island for the attack. In that adventure, thirty Englishmen were slain in their beds. Unfortunately, it is more than possible that the manner of the attack, if not the deed itself, is another fiction of Blind Harry. The castle certainly withstood the later siege of Balliol, when Sir Alan Vipont swept the English away by piercing a dam originally designed to trap the invested garrison.

Loch Leven Castle has its place in Scottish history not so much because it was used as a prison for the first Stewart King, Robert the Second (1371-90), and his lawless son, the Wolf of Badenoch; or even because it once housed Patrick Graham, a presumptuously outspoken Primate of Scotland in the reign of James the Third; but because another prisoner, the twenty-five-year-old Mary, Queen of Scots, made a daring escape from its grim walls.

She came to it first of her own accord in 1565. On the 15th of April, she met Knox there in what is reported to have been the least stormy of their interviews. She was all smiles, it seems, and she even went so far as to present the dour reformer with a watch. But at this interview, Knox formed his unalterable verdict that her heart was for ever closed against God and His Truth— His Truth, that is to say, as it was so confidently perceived by John Knox. Thereafter, as Marion Angus put it:

> " Master John Knox was no friend to her
> She spoke him soft and kind.
> Her honeyed words were Satan's lure
> The unwary soul to bind. . . ."

In the end, of course, it was Knox who did the binding, for Mary returned to Loch Leven on the 17th of June 1567, the prisoner of the Protestant nobles. She remained in captivity until her escape on the 2nd of May 1568.

Her jailer was Lady Douglas, mother not only of its young owner, Sir William Douglas, but of Murray, afterwards Regent, the natural son of James the Fifth, and thus Queen Mary's illegitimate half-brother. The circumstances leading up to her escape have been worked into Scott's novel, *The Abbot*, and are known to us in considerable detail because of the account which she dictated, years later, at Fotheringay, to Nau, her faithful secretary.

Her room was situated high in a corner tower. She had been forced to sign a Deed of Abdication in favour of her son by Lord

Lindsay of the Byres: and she had just had a miscarriage. Yet she spent her time not only in embroidery, but in laying plans. First, she won the heart of George Douglas, Sir William's son. Because of this, he was expelled from the island. Next, she set about his brother, the 18-year-old Willie, by all accounts rather a simple lad. Her first attempt was foiled by the vigilance of James Drysdale, the Captain of the guard. Her next attempt succeeded.

She indulged in boisterous play with Willie Douglas, rehearsing openly with him how she would escape. In a performance of the old folk mummery-play the *Abbot of Unreason*, Willie played the part of the lay Abbot, and she romped after him round the grounds till everyone laughed "as if he were drunk or simple"!

But Willie was not so simple. On the chosen night, the 2nd of May, he fastened with pegs the chains of all the boats except one. And he removed the key of Mary's prison from under Sir William's nose in a white napkin.

Meanwhile, Mary, who had been praying in her chamber, provided herself with a cape for disguise, and a red handkerchief for signalling. At a sign from Willie, she ran down the stairs, past the room where Sir William was still savouring the bouquet of his guid reid wine, through the unlocked gate which was then relocked, to the shore where the boat lay rocking. The alarm was given while the boat was still in passage. On the mainland, George Douglas was there to greet her, with Lord Seton and others of her party. An expert horse-woman, she rode off through the town of Kinross, and on without a halt to Queensferry, where she crossed the Forth to her first resting-place at Niddrie, Lord Seton's home.

But, alas, her gallantry availed her little. From Niddrie, she rode forth to watch the final defeat of her army at Langside, and thereafter, against the pleading of Archbishop Hamilton of St. Andrews, to gallop into England, from which her ultimate escape eighteen years later was through the block to her grave.

Those who walk down the lochside from the town of Kinross to-day pass the long wall of Kinross House. It was built by a native of the town, the architect in Scotland to Charles the Second, Sir William Bruce (d. 1710), at the end of the seventeenth century, for the Duke of York should the Exclusion Bill require him to live furth of London.

George Scott-Moncrieff calls Kinross House "a gracious piece, with shallow wings and pilasters, mezzanine floors, a vaulted base,

and a fine range of chimney-stacks ". At the shoreward corner of its spacious park, there is an old churchyard with a tower built at the time of the "Resurrectionists" to house the nightly guardians of the newly dead.

Kinross is a solidly prosperous nineteenth-century-looking little town, its hostelries, "The Green Hotel" and "Kirklands", well known to anglers who come from afar in search of Loch Leven trout.

The only other sizeable place in the county is Milnathort, its name probably derived from a Gaelic phrase meaning "mound of burial". It was the birthplace of J. Logie Robertson ("Hugh Haliburton"—or "Roguie Lobertson", as his students affectionately called him), the poet of the Ochils (1846-1922).

The ruins of Burleigh Castle, the ancient home of the Balfours of Burleigh, stand on the outskirts of Milnathort. At the beginning of the eighteenth century, Robert Balfour, the Master of Burleigh, fell in love with the governess of one of his younger sisters. His father refused to sanction a match with Janet Thomson, who was actually the niece of the parish minister of Orwell, so he sent his son abroad to cool his ardour. Before he set out, Robert told the girl that if she married anyone else during his absence, he would kill her consort. She paid little attention to this wild threat, however, and on the 6th of December 1705, she married Henry Stenhouse, schoolmaster at Inverkeithing. More than a year passed before the Master of Burleigh came home and heard that Miss Thomson had become Mrs. Stenhouse. On the 9th of April 1707, he rode out of Burleigh Castle with a few retainers, arriving at Inverkeithing while the market was in progress. There, he searched out and found Stenhouse, whom he had never seen before, and shot him dead before Janet's eyes.

Two years later, the murderer was condemned to death. But in those days, there was still one law for the rich and another for the poor. His family manœuvred his escape from the Tolbooth of Edinburgh, dressed in his sister's clothes, and he fled to the safety of the Continent. His father died in 1713, and on the 29th of May 1714, the new Lord Balfour appeared at the cross of Lochmaben, in Dumfriesshire, to proclaim the Old Chevalier James the Eighth. His title was thereupon attainted; and, though he again escaped to dree out an exile's life on the Continent, it was a hundred and fifty years before there was another Balfour of Burleigh. The castle now stands roofless, preserved as an ancient monument. In a nearby field are the Standing Stones of Orwell, mute memorials to the forgotten rites of pre-Christian days.

*Stirlingshire: The Guildhall, Stirling*

Balgedie lies on the eastern shore of Loch Leven. It is a tiny village with no recorded history, although the visitor who passed through it on a sunny day may sympathize with "Hugh Haliburton's" desire to be there rather than in his Edinburgh classroom. Kinnesswood, in the parish of Portmoak, numbers amongst its sons: Andrew Wyntoun, who is supposed to have been born thereabouts; more certainly, John Douglas, the first "tulchan" bishop of St. Andrews; and Dr. Alexander Buchan (1829-1907), the meteorologist, who plotted his famous five annual Cold Spells and his much less famous three Warm Spells. Most celebrated of Kinnesswood's sons, however, was Michael Bruce (1746-67), "the gentle poet of Loch Leven". The son of a hand-loom weaver, young Bruce set out to become a minister of the Secession Church. He died of privation and consumption at the age of twenty-one. His birthplace has been preserved as a museum, and every year the Michael Bruce Trust organizes a memorial service in Portmoak Parish Church. When I was invited to give the address at the service a few years ago, I took as my theme the value of minor poetry in a nation's literature. Bruce did not live long enough to "find" himself as a poet. The language he spoke was undoubtedly Scots, so that the English he wrote had often a strained and artificial air. In spite of the exaggerated praise which has been bestowed on Bruce's best-known poem, the "Ode to the Cuckoo"—really a very slight piece—it seems to me that he achieved his highest flights in some of the paraphrases which he wrote originally to provide non-sacred practice-words for psalm tunes, but which are now used as praise by the Church of Scotland:

> "No strife shall rage, nor hostile feuds
>     disturb those peaceful years;
> To ploughshares men shall beat their swords,
>     to pruning-hooks their spears.
>
> No longer hosts encount'ring hosts
>     shall crowds of slain deplore;
> They hang the trumpet in the hall,
>     and study war no more."

These words have a sturdy grandeur and a rugged vision which has lifted up generations of Scottish hearts. Thousands of Scottish worshippers sing this and Bruce's other paraphrases every year without even being aware of the author's name. Bruce's real fame is thus happed in anonymity; ironically so, since a rascally fellow-student, John Logan (1748-88), did his best to claim Bruce's poems as his own shortly after Bruce's death. The Bruce-Logan controversy still provides matter for those who thrive on such tea-cup literary troubles; but the Rev. T. G. Snoddy, Bruce's latest biographer,[1] has put the matter beyond all reasonable doubt, firmly in Bruce's favour.

Kinesswood is almost a deserted village. It can have altered very little from Bruce's day. The old houses climb the lower slopes of Bishop's Hill. The cobbled streets are untended, and many of the houses are crumbling to ruin. Strange it is to reflect in such surroundings upon the fire and fervour of that little weaving community whose praises for his early rhymings urged on the young Michael Bruce to become a poet, and whose fiery faith made the pulpit of the Secession Church seem the noblest of all earthly goals!

### III

No one who tries to understand the temper of Lowland Scotland can avoid coming up against the religious disturbances which led to the various secessions from the Scottish Reformed Church. Since this " hiving-off " activity was nowhere stronger than in the western districts of Fife and Kinross, this seems an appropriate moment to trace their development in outline.

By about 1560, the Reformation had triumphed in Scotland. Not only was it anti-papistical in orientation—the vices with which Sir David Lyndsay charged the " Auld Kirk " in *The Thrie Estatis* and in *Ane Dialogue betwixt Experience and ane Courtier* have mostly been substantiated with chapter and verse by W. Murison in his stimulating study, *Sir David Lyndsay: Poet and Satirist of the Old Church in Scotland*—but it was also part of a wider surge of individualism which flowed over the western world, an aftermath of the Renaissance.

Individualism has always been a Scottish characteristic. It leads to an inclination for dispute. After the transfer of political Authority to London, many disputatious political matters had been removed from the arena of contention, focusing attention on religious matters; the more so as both James the Sixth and First and Charles the First were rashly bent on bringing about Episcopalian religious conformity between the two kingdoms.

The Presbyterians insisted upon the absolute right of the Church to control its own affairs. In Scotland, most of them

[1] *Michael Bruce* (1946).

combined this attitude with loyal support of the Monarchy, although the monarch himself was doing his best to vitiate what his Scottish subjects regarded as a vital principle. This principle found expression in the two seventeenth-century Covenants, the second of which was regarded as binding the Scottish nation and King Charles the Second, who signed it, not only to maintain Presbyterianism at home, but also to establish it in England and Ireland. The oldest of the existing dissenting bodies in Scotland, the tiny "remnant" of Reformed Presbyterians, descends from those extremist Covenanters who refused to forego this part of the Solemn League and Covenant, even when the Presbyterian Church of Scotland was re-established by the Revolution of 1688-1689. From this time, too, dates the Episcopal Church in Scotland as a dissenting organization, at first almost wholly Jacobite.

The Revolution Settlement gave Church of Scotland congregations the right to choose their own ministers within certain limits. Like the other privileges of the Kirk, this right was thought to have been carefully safeguarded by the Treaty which united the Scots and English Parliaments in 1707. Unluckily, a High Tory Government, devoted to the interests of the Anglican Church, soon came to power in London. In the hope of mortifying Presbyterianism in Scotland and protecting parish ministers who were really Episcopalian at heart, this Government passed an Act abolishing the congregational right of election, and giving the appointment of ministers to lay patrons, in most cases the leading landowners of the parishes.

Most of the troubles and divisions of the Scottish Church sprang from this breach of the Treaty of Union, though no doubt that stubborn spirit of individualism, very characteristic of Lowland Scotland, had a good deal to do with fomenting them. The leaders of the first important movement of protest were the brothers Ebenezer and Ralph Erskine. Ebenezer, who had been minister of Portmoak, was one of a group of ministers who, on November 2nd, 1733, signed an Act of Secession at Gairneybridge, in the parish of Cleish, Kinrosshire, in protest against lay patronage.

The new body, the Associate Synod, was itself struck by secession after secession, dividing into Burghers and Anti-Burghers (on a purely theoretical scruple about its members' relations with the State); again into New Lights and Old Lights (Auld Lichts) on a theological point; and even into Lifters and Anti-Lifters on a dispute about the handling of communion elements.

Further disputes over patronage produced new secessions from the Established Kirk itself, the most important being the Relief

Church, a relatively tolerant body, founded in 1752. Early in the nineteenth century the process of fission began to reverse itself. By 1847, most of the dissenting sects had come together in the United Presbyterian Church, though there was, and still is, a tiny residue of Original Seceders. Four years before, however, the biggest and most famous split in the Church of Scotland itself had taken place. Once again, the Government in London had refused, during a prolonged crisis, to modify the law on the question of patronage. The previous quarter-century had seen a great revival of the Kirk's evangelical and social activity, with the building of many new churches in the growing industrial areas. The leaders of this movement took a particularly high view of the Church's rights to regulate its affairs, with the protection of the State, but without State control. It was four hundred and seventy of these men who, headed by Dr. Thomas Chalmers, a Fifer, marched out of the General Assembly in 1843 to form the Free Church of Scotland. Within little more than a year, they had succeeded in duplicating the Church's organization in almost every Scottish parish: an astonishing feat, financial as well as spiritual, which illustrates the intensity of the interest taken by early Victorian Scots in Church affairs.

The Disruption is still a famous date in Scottish memories. But within less than half a century, the movement was again towards reunion. The Established Church itself demanded and achieved the abolition of patronage; and by 1900, the two great dissenting bodies, the Frees and the United Presbyterians, had come together in the United Free Church. In 1929, the process was completed by the Union of the United Free Church with the Church of Scotland, which then became the only Protestant religious body of national importance, much stronger, proportionately speaking, than the Church of England is in its own country. The reunited church, though "established by law", has absolute control of its own affairs, and it may be said that, legally, the long, costly and disruptive struggle of the Scottish Church against the British State has been won.

Each movement towards reunion, however, has left out a small body of irreconcilables. Two of these, the "Wee Frees" (remnant of the old Free Kirk) and the Free Presbyterians, are often treated by the London press as if they were equivalent to the great body of English Free Churches—the Nonconformists. In fact, the Scottish "Frees" have very little influence over the majority of their fellow-countrymen. They are almost entirely confined to the remoter Highlands, where Calvinism, shielded to some extent by geography from the influences of later reason, still holds antique sway. For its victims, the Devil is still a real person, and all who do not share their own intolerance and bigotry are his hired agents. Eternity hinges on the turning of a wireless knob on Sunday; immortality on the avoidance of Sunday golf. Often, their fantastic and pompous pronouncements bring disgrace and ridicule upon Scotland, since the country as a whole is credited with holding the views of its religious " lunatic fringe ".

The art of religious secession has indeed taken us some distance in time and space from Kinross-shire. But it was in those airts that the strong winds of dissent first fanned up the flames which did much to destroy the respect and authority that a unified Presbyterian religion might well have commanded.

IV

Round the south end of Loch Leven, past Benarty Hill, and almost within sight of the mining district of Fife, lies Blairadam. It was built early in the eighteenth century by the architect William Adam. Of his four sons, Robert (1728-92) achieved more personal fame than his older brother James (d. 1794). Together, they built the Adelphi; Edinburgh's Register House; the Glasgow Royal Infirmary,[1] and many noble houses throughout the United Kingdom. Their classical style set the keynote for much of the best building of the age, and was copied by their immediate successors. Robert was for a time Member of Parliament for Kinross.

It was Robert's son, William, who founded the Blairadam Club in 1816. To Kinross on a Friday evening would come, from time to time, the nine members, one of whom was Sir Walter Scott. Saturday was spent in riding to some historical scene or monument within easy distance of the house. On Sunday, the members attended Cleish Church (the Kirk of Cleishbotham in " The Abbot ") and thereafter indulged in discussion, touching, no doubt, amongst other topics, upon the identity of the mysterious author of *Waverley*. There would be another outing on the Monday morning and then most of the party would return to Edinburgh, where their host was Lord Chief Commissioner of the Jury Court.

It was at the old House of Cleish that Squire Meldrum was born in 1493, the ruins of whose later home are still to be seen near Paranwell. After a career given over to fighting in the interest of chivalry, and culminating in his lusty affair with

[1] Not the present building.

Marion Lawson, which led to that ambush in which his rival, Stirling of Keir, left him for dead, having hacked off his arms and legs, the doughty squire rallied sufficiently to become Sheriff of Kinross, dispensing law and medicine with equal ability.

The landscape of Kinross, in its eastern parishes, is similar to that of Fife in quality and tone. It is almost entirely shut off by the Cleish Hills from the mining area which reaches right up to its southern borders. The peaceful loch and the gently rounded hills about it make it easy to appreciate why guide-book writers are so fond of referring to it as "the sleepy hollow of Scotland". To the north, the Ochil Hills ridge it off from the Perthshire Lowlands, though a picturesque road runs north-west through Glen Devon to join the main Stirling-Perth road between Blackford and Auchterarder, and another road branches off to Dunning. Eastwards, the Lomonds break the bitter North Sea winds that often blow so strenuously across the Kingdom of Fife.

# CHAPTER VI

## THE KINGDOM OF FIFE

*" Fyffe . . . is rich in all manneir of grain crops as any pairt of Scotland; quhare na corns are, it is richt profitable in store of bestial. . . . In Fyffe are won black stanes, quhilk hes so intolerable heat quhan they are kendellit, that they resolve and meltis irne, and are therefore richt profitable for operation of smiths. . . ."*

HECTOR BOECE, *trans.* John
Bellenden, 1536

THE earliest inhabitants of Fife of whom we know even the name were a branch of the Picts, called in their own tongue, Cruithne. According to legend, Fibh was one of the seven sons of Cruithne, the father of the race who gave it its name. This much we learn from Nennius, the historian. But Cruithne and Fibh are probably imaginary characters credited to explain existing national or tribal names.

We know so little about the Picts that, at this late hour, it is virtually impossible to disentangle fact from legend. Legend, however, may reasonably be assumed to have had some remote basis in fact; fact, misapplied by patriotic authors for the greater glorification of their race. Even the circumstances under which the early saints came to Fife are happed in controversial mystery.

Very little is known of St. Serf, to whom was mainly due the conversion of Fife to Christianity in the sixth century. Various legends credit the saint with exotic antecedents. For instance, according to one of the more improbable legends, he was the son of a Caananite king and an Arab princess. Nor is it any more likely that he was Pope for seven years, as another legend claims.

The two most probable legends are these.[1] That St. Serf was the adoptive father of Kentigern (or Mungo), whose mother Thenew, daughter of King Loth, had been set adrift in a currach off Aberlady Bay, because she preferred a swineherd to the suitor chosen by her father. A fierce storm drove her ashore at Culross, where Serf found her and her newly born infant on the shore.

---

[1] See also Chapter V, p. 152, where Serf's connections with Kinross are discussed.

162

The second legend makes Serf a contemporary of Adamnan, the pupil and biographer of St. Columba. Serf is said to have met Adamnan at Inchkeith, an island on the Firth belonging to Fife, when the senior saint told him to let his followers "inhabit the land of Fife from the hill of the Britons"—probably Largo Law —"to the hill called Okel" (the Ochils). Thereafter, Serf founded a church and cemetery at Culross, where his own bones are laid; he visited Portmoak, on Loch Leven, where an early church bore his name; he visited Dysart; he preached at Tullibody, Tillicoultry and Alva in Kinross-shire, and at Airthrie in Clackmannanshire. The church on Inch Serf, in Loch Leven, was probably established after his lifetime, though in his honour.

The Pictish king whom Serf converted is said to have been Brude, a common name amongst Pictish kings. It was a later Brude—Brude, son of Dergoil, the last of the Pictish kings—who give Inch Serf to the saint's Culdee followers.

The churches connected with St. Serf, however, were overshadowed by two other foundations—that at Abernethy on the Tay, in Perthshire, probably founded by a sixth-century mission from the church in Ireland; and that at Kilrymont. Abernethy became the chief ecclesiastical seat of the whole Pictish kingdom, whose capital was latterly at Scone, near Perth. After the union of the Picts and Scots under Kenneth MacAlpin, St. Andrews gained in importance until it became the principal ecclesiastical seat in Scotland, a position it maintained until the Reformation.

One Cainnech, or Kenneth, of Kilkenny is thought to have been preaching Christianity at Kilrymont towards the end of the sixth century. But his fame was soon to be eclipsed by St. Regulus, or St. Rule, a monk of Patras,[1] who was warned in a vision to emigrate westwards with certain relics of St. Andrew, and in company with "a priest, two deacons, eight hermits, and three devout virgins". After a stormy voyage, St. Regulus's ship was wrecked on the rocks at St. Andrews Bay, and this oddly assorted party scrambled ashore, bringing with them, "the armbone, three fingers of the right hand, a tooth, and one of the lids of the knee", all allegedly having belonged to the person of the Apostle. Here, St. Regulus encountered a certain Pictish King Angus, who lived between A.D. 700 and 800—at least a century after St. Regulus himself!—and had come down to the shore to pillage the wreck. But the saint converted the King, who

---

[1] St. Andrew, martyred in Patras, was first buried there, then removed three centuries later to Constantinople on the orders of Constantine. Finally, his body was brought to the Cathedral of Amalfi, near Naples, where his remains are said still to be entombed.

saw a vision of a white cross against the blue sky, and who there-upon adopted St. Andrew as his patron saint.

It makes a pretty story. Unfortunately, it is very largely the fabrication of diligent twelfth-century monkish scribes who were seeking to prove to the Pope, and incidentally the English King, that their church was older than that of England; and that, as the chosen people of Andrew, brother of Peter, they were entitled to the special support of Rome. Be that as it may, their fabrication came to be accepted as fact, and helped many simple folk to sustain their religious faith; Kilrymont became St. Andrews; and St. Andrew became the patron saint of Scotland, his badge—derived from a monogram made out of the Greek capitals XP, the letters CHR of our Lord's name—the flag of Scotland. In spite of this, St. Andrew remains a pale, enigmatic figure, much less potent as a patriotic or religious stimulant than, for instance, Ireland's St. Patrick, or even Iona's St. Columba, who is not a "national" saint.

Other saints also left their traces in Fife. Adrian or Magridin, by legend a Hungarian, settled on the island of May, off Crail, where marauding Danes martyred him in the ninth century. His companion, St. Monan, is responsible for the name of St. Monance, while St. Fillan, an Irish saint of the eighth century, though he had his church on Lochearnside, left a cave named after himself in Pittenweem.

That, then, is the background to the story of Fife—a background of shadowy Pictish kings and their peoples, once, no doubt, revering Druid nobles and priests, then coming under the converting spell of the early Celtic saints. These saints were, of course, monastic. After the expulsion of the Iona monks by King Nechtun of the Picts in 717, the saints themselves gave place to the Culdees from Ireland, priests who were not under monastic vows. Of settled Roman influence in Fife there is scarcely a trace, though numerous relics of itinerant columns have been found. Agricola is supposed to have landed at Burntisland in the summer of A.D. 83, and to have traversed the kingdom, while his ships made their way round the coast to the Tay. But that excursion was probably something in the nature of a summer manœuvre.

Fife is, in many ways, that part of Scotland where the slow traditions of evolving days have been best respected. It still contains a higher proportion of good old buildings than most other counties; and, except perhaps in its industrial belt, it still seems somehow to wear an air of being graciously at harmony with itself.

II

Medieval Scotland—Scotland from that point in its history when the Celtic influence was challenged and gradually began to wane before alien forces and ideas—has its roots in the town of Dunfermline.

In the middle of the eleventh century, Malcolm Ceann Mor (Canmore or Great Head—1057-93), son of King Duncan the First (1034-40), recovered the throne of Scotland from Maelbeatha, or Macbeth (1040-57), Duncan's cousin, who had usurped it after slaying Duncan in battle.[1] Malcolm had reigned for eight years when, in 1066, William the Conqueror got possession of the English throne as a result of the Battle of Hastings. For a time Malcolm supported the rightful Saxon heir, Edgar; but, as he proved a weakling, and the Normans had clearly come to stay, Malcolm eventually made a treaty with William.

Amongst those members of the deposed Saxon royal family who fled north to Scotland—their boat is said to have put in at the little bay in the Firth of Forth known to this day as St. Margaret's Hope—was Edgar's sister, Margaret. Her mother was a Hungarian, and Margaret herself had been brought up in Hungary. She was fair and beautiful; scholarly and possessed of statesmanlike qualities; but, above all, she was pious. She intended to take up the veil. Instead, Malcolm persuaded her to become his Queen.

She it was who, for better or for worse, brought Scotland into touch with the latest trends of European thought—ecclesiastical trends leading towards the centralization and standardization of the Church under Rome; secular trends leading towards the establishment of feudalism, at any rate in the Lowlands.[2] In particular, aided by her confessor, Bishop Turgot, she forced the Celtic Church to conform with Rome in some ways not exactly known to us now. She is credited with having introduced table-linen to Scotland for the first time, and with having refined and improved the Scottish court's standards of living. Like all reformers who cause irrevocable changes which reverberated down

[1] The real Duncan did not die in his bed at the hands of Lady Macbeth, as does Shakespeare's Duncan. And Macbeth, unlike his stage reincarnation, was in fact a good, strong king during the seventeen years of his reign.

[2] Feudalism of a kind—the Clan system—was already established in the north-west. It survived until the nineteenth century. The terrible Clearances of the early nineteenth century might perhaps have seemed a little less shameful had it not been that clan trust in their chieftains, by now anglicized and uninterested in their people, still burned strongly in the hearts of the ordinary Highlanders.

the centuries, Saint Margaret—until recently the only female Scottish saint to have a place in the Roman Calendar—has had her critics. She has been accused of anglicizing Scotland, just as her husband has been accused of having given the English their first "modern" claim upon Scotland's sovereignty by his treaty with William the Conqueror. Margaret's ideas were bound to have reached Scotland sooner or later, argue those who "support" her. A Celtic Scotland without Margaret's Saxo-Norman influence, say her critics, might well have developed along lines similar to those of Ireland, a country which retained its Celtic character, in spite of later invasions and colonizations, until the eighteenth century, and still retains an uncommonly sturdy passion for liberty.[1]

Certainly, it is utterly absurd to suggest that our Celtic ancestors were crude and uncultured, until Margaret "civilized" them. The trappings of their religion, their finely wrought crosses, and those of their jewels which have come down to us, show them to have been artists of fresh invention and craftsmen of astonishing skill.[2]

Margaret and Malcolm lived at first in a tower stronghold in Pittencrieff Glen, until their new palace at Dunfermline was ready. The ruins of its foundations are still to be seen beside those of the Abbey buildings. They were married in the nearby Culdee Chapel. In honour of their union, Margaret caused to be founded on the site of it a new Church of the Holy Trinity.

In 1093, in order to forestall an English invasion by one of the Conqueror's sons who sought to claim the submission of Scotland under the terms of his father's treaty with Malcolm, the Scottish King marched south of the Border. He was stabbed with a lance outside his own tent by an English ambassador carrying a white lily. In striving to avenge his father, the Crown Prince Edward was also killed. The news of this disaster was brought to Margaret by another son, Edgar, as she lay dying at Edinburgh Castle. She passed away with a sad prayer on her lips.

They brought her body back to Dunfermline to be buried in the great church she had caused to be built. The operation was only accomplished with difficulty, for already Edinburgh Castle was invested by Donald Ban, the children's uncle, who sought

[1] Ireland, however, has the decided advantage of being an island!
[2] The absence of Iona Crosses in eastern Scotland, where the Picts held sway, suggests that the finest artists were, in fact, the Scots-Irish of the west. Pictish art was hunter's art to a large extent.

the throne on behalf of Duncan, Malcolm's eldest son by his first wife. This Duncan, bred in England, where he had remained a loyal Norman all his days, got the throne and tried to hold it (1094-95), but he was murdered after only six months. Uncle Donald and Edmund, St. Margaret's second son, then shared the throne between them for two years, to be defeated and deposed in turn by that Edgar who had borne the sad tidings to his mother at Edinburgh.

While Donald Ban's soldiers were poised at the entrance to the Castle, another son, Ethelred, and Bishop Turgot carried Margaret's body through a postern door on the west side of the rock. Thereupon, a sheltering haar descended, enabling the party to reach Queensferry in safety, from where they rowed over to Fife. Haars come over the east coast of Scotland with astonishing suddenness, but the providential nature of this particular haar caused it to be regarded as a miracle.

The English King gave his permission for Malcolm's bones to be disinterred at Tynemouth, and taken to Dunfermline. Then, as Andrew of Wyntoun puts it . . .

> " Before the rude altar with honoure
> Scho was layd in haly sepulture:
> And with thame her sonnes twa,
> Edmund the first and Ethelred. . . ."

Even in her death, Margaret severed another Celtic link, for, hitherto, Iona had been the burying-place of Scotland's kings: but, after her time, for almost four centuries, Dunfermline became their last resting-place. Edgar and Alexander the First, with his queen; David the First with his two queens; Malcolm the Fourth; Alexander the Third, with his first wife, Margaret, and their sons, David and Alexander; Robert the Bruce and Elizabeth, his queen; the bones of all these princes make royal the dust around Dunfermline Abbey.

The place has been three times sacked. On the 10th of February 1304, King Edward the First instructed his soldiers to burn down the monastery, so that it should not in future breed patriotic plotters. But the Romanesque nave survived the flames. King Richard the Second of England burnt it again in 1385. The Reformers took further toll of the monastic buildings (which had been rebuilt after Bannockburn), sparing only the church because they intended to use it for their own worship. In 1753, the steeple collapsed, and, in 1807, the south-western tower fell, struck by lightning. Still the nave survived. The restored Abbey, built around the ancient nave, went up in 1818. In an excess of patriotism, the architect caused the name of King Robert the Bruce to be written in stone fretwork round the top of the tower.

Whilst workmen were excavating amongst the stones and rubble in preparation for the foundations of the new building, they came upon a vault containing a stone coffin, in which lay a skeleton wrapped in thin lead. Shreds of gold cloth still clung to the bones, and some of the teeth were still in the head. By accident, the remains of the greatest of all Scottish kings had been discovered, his breastbone sawn away so that Sir James Douglas could take out his heart.

A guard was mounted, and a new tomb built. Before the King was reinterred, he lay in state. Scott, who made a pilgrimage to the bier, tells us that . . . " as the church could not hold half the numbers, the people were allowed to pass through it, one after another, that each one, the poorest as well as the richest, might see all that remained of the great King Robert the Bruce, who restored the Scottish monarchy. Many people shed tears; for there was the wasted skull, which once was the head that thought so wisely and boldly for his country's deliverance;[1] and there was the dry bone, which had once been the sturdy arm that killed Sir Henry de Bohun, between the two armies, at a single blow, on the evening before that Battle of Bannockburn. . . ."

The palace remained a royal residence until the sixteenth century, although it seems to have found less favour with the later Stewart kings than did Falkland and Stirling. Bruce's son, King David the Second (1329-71), and the poet-king, James the First, were born within its walls; walls that were extended by both James the Fourth and James the Fifth.

Dunfermline has one other piece of religious history. Ralph Erskine, who, with his brother Ebenezer, was responsible for the break-away of the Secession Church, had the gaunt kirk in Queen Anne Street built for him by his followers when, in 1740, he was deposed by the Church of Scotland. His Abbey pulpit came into the collecting hands of Sir Walter Scott at the time of re-building, and it now occupies a place at Abbotsford in the form of two hall side-tables!

There are still one or two old houses standing in Dunfermline

---

[1] There are those who tell us that the Bruce was never able to think to any broader pattern than that of a feudal baron. Even if this were true, the conditions under which he came to power called more for the rule of a kind of super-baron, than for that of a king with softer and more civilized ideas.

—the Abbot's house in Maygate, for instance, with its advice over the doorway:

> "*Sin vord is thrall and thocht is fre,*
> *Keip veill thy tonge I counsel the*"

—advice very necessary in the Scotland of the Reformation.

Dunfermline has its literary associations. Robert Henryson (?1425-?1500), gentlest and most lovable of the Old Scots Makars, is stated by his fellow-makar, Dunbar,[1] to have died in Dunfermline, where, according to an early title-page, he was "sometime cheif schoolemaster".

In one of the introductory stanzas to his greatest poem, "The Testament of Cresseid", Henryson tells us how he came to bring Chaucer's masterpiece to its pitifully logical conclusion:

> "*I mend the fyre and beikit me about,*
> *Than tuik ane drink my spreitis to comfort,*
> *And armit me weill fra the cauld thairout:*
> *To cut the winter nicht and mak it schort,*
> *I tuik ane Quair, and left all other sport. . . .*"   [book

In his *Moral Fables*, delightful studies of humans in animal guise, based on the Fables of Æsop—Henryson shows acute powers of observation, as well as warm tenderness for the weaknesses of humanity, making him seem to-day somehow the most "modern" of the old Scots makars. The cold Fife winds that blew about his schoolhouse in winter; the spiritual completeness of his freshly coloured medieval world; the warmth and geniality of the poet's nature, and the breadth of his culture and knowledge; these things come over to us through his pages, so that, although not one authenticated biographical scrap has survived, we feel we are in contact with a "whole" man whom it surely would have been good to know in the flesh; good to share fire and drink with, and to listen to, as he read his smooth Scots iambics in his Fife-tinged Middle Scots!

Dunfermline was also the physical starting-point in the ballad of "Sir Patrick Spens". The king who:

> "*. . . sat in Dunfermline toun,*
> *Drinking the bluid-red wine . . .*"

—was not Alexander the Third, as is still commonly believed, but James the Sixth, who, in 1589, had despatched Sir Patrick

[1] Dunbar's *Lament for the Makars.*

Vans (not Spens) to negotiate a marriage between the King and Anne of Denmark. There was, in fact, no shipwreck: but rumours were current that Vans and his men had been overtaken by such a disaster.

The town of Dunfermline, made a royal burgh by James the Sixth, was almost wholly destroyed by fire in 1624. Its later prosperity grew out of its development as a centre of linen-weaving. The British Linen Company, originally more concerned with manufacturing than with banking, set up one of its earliest branches in Dunfermline in 1749. Until the beginning of the nineteenth century, great quantities of flax were grown in Fife—had been grown, indeed, since Henryson's day, as a reference in one of his poems shows—and linen-weaving became a thriving industry not only in the larger centres like Dunfermline and Kirkcaldy, but also, on a smaller scale, at Falkland, Cupar, Leven and Strathmiglo. When the English novelist, Daniel Defoe, came to Scotland in 1727, he found Dunfermline to be outwardly "the full perfection of decay its decayed monastery, palace and town, the natural consequence of the decay of the palace". But of the inhabitants he reported that "the people would be poorer if they had not the manufacture of linen—the damask and better sort being carried on here and in the neighbouring towns with more hands than ordinary". Many of these "hands" were, of course, those of humble weavers working in their own cottages. Nowadays, food crops have taken the place of flax. The raw material has to be imported. Some of the looms of Dunfermline have taken to weaving cotton goods, but the town is still famous the world over for the high quality of its linen and its rayon.

Outwardly, modern Dunfermline is not a prepossessing town. It abounds in mock-baronial public buildings of the most absurd kind, and, although the munificence of its famous patron, Andrew Carnegie, has preserved Pittencrieff Glen as a flowery park, much as it may have seemed to Henryson, his attempts to benefit the place in other ways have not always been without unlooked-for repercussions. A Free Library and Reading Room; a School of Music; Baths and a College of Hygiene in the town itself; a number of Trusts with, between them, a fabulous capital, the revenues of which have benefitted educational establishments and poor scholars not only in Dunfermline, but all over Scotland, England, Canada and the United States—these are the monuments to Carnegie's munificence.

All this is very admirable. Unfortunately, however, it has tended to turn Dunfermline into the Scottish centre of the "local-boy-makes-good" cult wherein the ability to make money becomes the highest of mortal virtues. It is not the gentle Henryson who is popularly regarded as being the first Dunfermline citizen of Elysium; nor is it even the blessed Saint Margaret. It is the "American" railroad and steel magnate, who was born in a little cottage in Dunfermline in 1835, the son of a humble damask-weaver. Behind the house, there now stands a museum which houses the caskets and illuminated addresses presented to Carnegie during his lifetime. Carnegie, in the material sense, "got on in the world", as no other Scot has "got on" before or since. And "getting on" is, in Scottish eyes, still the sign of the truest greatness.

Dunfermline stands at the edge of the West-Fife coal seams, and has, indeed, mines of its own. From Saline eastwards to Kirkcaldy, and from Kirkcaldy northwards to Leven, Markinch (the home of "John Haig" whisky, and one of Fife's paper-making centres) and Leslie, industry has staked its grim and dis-figuring claim on the countryside. The Scottish Coalfields Com-mittee, set up to ascertain the reserves of coal in various parts of the country, estimated in 1944 that more than half the total reserves of the whole of Scotland lie in the Fife-Clackmannan belt. This means that West Fife is bound to become more and more industrialized during the second half of the twentieth century.

As long ago as 1291, the owner of Pittencrieff was giving to the monks of Dunfermline the right to work coal. The monks were thus the first "miners", if they could be so-called, since the coal they worked was, of course, surface coal. An early Scottish traveller, Aeneas Silvius, afterwards Pope Pius the Second, visited Scotland during the reign of James the First. One of the things he commented on was how "the poor at the Church doors received for alms pieces of stone with which they went away quite contented and burnt in place of wood". The first Scottish mine to be sunk with a shaft was on the estate of Sir George Bruce of Carnock. The workings ran under the sea and came out on Pres-ton Island, in the Forth. When James the Sixth visited it in 1617, he made a famous and characteristic exhibition of himself. Coming up at the island end of the workings, he took one look at the water around him, and at once began to shout "treason". Sir Gerloge was able to calm his brave sovereign by pointing to the pinnace which was awaiting to take them all back to the mainland. The King, however, insisted on returning via the mine! John Taylor, the Water-Poet, visited the mine the follow-ing year, and left an interesting description of it in his pamphlet The Pennyless Pilgrimage, an account of his Scottish tour. The mine was "drowned" in the great storm which swept Scotland in March 1625.

The early mine-workers in Fife, as in the west, were, until 1775, in fact if not in name, heritable serfs bound to their owners by collars with their names on a tag. To-day, Fife coalfields are amongst the best equipped in Europe. The pit at Comrie, opened by the Fife Coal Company in 1940, was until recently the most up-to-date in machinery and amenities in the country. Now, with the shift-over of coal production from Lanarkshire to Fife, two new towns are being built to house the extra workers—at Kennoway and at Glenrothes—and new pits are being opened at Rothes, Dysart and Seafield.

Lanarkshire has been seared and pocked by the bing method of disposal of the rubbish from the big nineteenth-century pits. Greedy capitalists are usually blamed for this despoliation of the country's fair face. There can be no excuse for any further disfiguration of Fife by the National Coal Board.

### III

King James the Fifth is credited with having described the Kingdom of Fife as a "reuch Scots blanket wi' a fringe o' gowd". In his day, the hinterland of West Fife was mostly undeveloped woodland, while along the coast nestled snug little Flemish-looking ports busily trading with the Continent. To-day, the position is reversed. The "gold" lies beneath the woodland soil, and the villages and towns of the coast have lost much of their former importance, though happily not all of their loveliness.

Almost at the extreme western coast of Fife, Kincardine road bridge, built in 1936, links Fife with Stirlingshire. There are other links between the two sides of the Firth, the most obvious of which is the Forth Bridge carrying the railway from South Queensferry to North Queensferry. The idea of a Forth Bridge was first conceived by an English civil engineer, Sir Thomas Bouch (1822-80), the builder of the first Tay Bridge, which links Fife with Angus. When his Tay Bridge collapsed in a storm in December 1879, a committee was appointed to re-examine Bouch's plans for the Forth Bridge. It was found that, as in the Tay Bridge plans, he had under-estimated the degree of wind-pressure likely to be exerted upon the Forth structure.[1] New plans were prepared by John Fowler and Benjamin Baker, and their bridge was completed in 1890. When it was opened, it was regarded as

[1] See Chapter VII, p. 217.

one of the world's engineering wonders. It is still an awe-inspiring spectacle, dominating every vista of the Forth for miles around. Fifty-seven men lost their lives in its construction and five hundred were injured. Fifty tons of paint are needed to give the bridge one complete coat. The work of painting the girders never ceases, and twenty painters are employed all the year round. The bridge is patrolled every night, and watchmen are constantly stationed at each end.

The Queensferry crossing-place is supposed to be so-called because of its use by Queen Margaret, though no doubt it is even older than that. Pettycur was the northern terminus of an early ferry. Recently, a car-ferry complete with cocktail bar plied between Granton and Burntisland.

It was not, however, the sea-links with the Lothians that gave the "golden fringe" its medieval prosperity, but trade with the Continent of Europe, principally with France and the Low Countries, and there is still a Flemish flavour about many of the old towns and villages along the coast. George Jameson of Aberdeen (d. 1644), our first Scottish portrait painter of identifiable distinction, was trained in Holland, as were several of the composers of the Scottish polyphonic school. The Reformers did much to cut the link between East Scotland and France; the Unions of 1603 and 1707 attached Scotland firmly (too firmly in the view of many to-day!) to England, thus further discouraging the direct Continental market: and the opening up of the west ports in the early eighteenth century finally removed the ancient livelihood of Fife's smaller ports.

At the western end of the "fringe", Kincardine-on-Forth, long before the road bridge graced its shores, was a natural crossing-place and a juncture of the old drove roads, since the narrowness of the river at that point made it possible for cattle to swim across.

Culross ("Cooross" to the natives), like Kincardine, was actually a part of Perthshire until a readjustment of boundaries in 1891. Although it once produced tar, naphtha and salt, and was famous in the eighteenth century for its scone-girdles, all these sources of profit have long since vanished. Having been for so long a by-water, it has fortunately escaped that destruction of ancient loveliness which industrial change so often entails. Culross embodies the essence of Scots burgh architecture of the sixteenth and seventeenth centuries. No fewer than twenty of the buildings are now under the keeping of the National Trust for Scotland. Of these, the most imposing is the "Palace", the oldest portion of which was built by Sir George Bruce, the coal-owner, in 1597. Its delightful dormers, its painted barrel ceilings and seventeenth-century mural decorations (supposed to have been specially done in honour of the visit of James the Sixth), and its terraced garden give it a happy and unostentatious charm. When James the Sixth made Culross a royal burgh in 1588, Sir George received from the Town Council, to whom he had loaned £1,000 to enable them to press their claim, a grant of all the profits from the saltpans.

Bishop Andrew Leighton's study, a little tower in which he no doubt reflected upon the vanities of the mortal state, is also a building of quiet and unusual charm. The old tolbooth has an ogee cap and forestairs. Up the brae, Culross Abbey retains its associations with St. Serf, although its oldest stones did not come together until 1217 when the Earl of Fife founded it for the Cistercian order. The tower and the choir remain. Culross Abbey was secularized in 1567. One of the incumbents before this transformation took place was Abbot Inglis, Chaplain to James the Fifth and secretary to his queen. Inglis is supposed to have written " ballads, farces and plays ", none of which have come down to us. A great quantity of medieval Scots literature must have gone up in flames at the time of the Reformation. Dunbar, in his *Lament for the Makars*, names poets of whose works we have not a trace: and Dunbar, who was not notable for his charity, seems hardly likely to have been upset by the deaths of mediocrities. The case of a poet, much of whose work has come down to us, serves as a further illustration of the mutability of the pre-Reformation literature. Sir David Lyndsay, if his own word is to be believed, wrote a great deal more than we possess to-day. His dramatic masterpiece, *Ane Satire of the Three Estatis in Commendatioun of Vertue and Vituperation of Vice*, does not suggest that he was exercising a 'prentice hand at theatre-craft. So Abbot Inglis's missing literary output may quite well have been considerable.

The real charm of Culross lies not so much in the public buildings, as in the ordinary pantiled houses scrambling up its hilly streets. The biggest of these houses, the old mansion-house, has been allowed to crumble away to ruin. A hideous railway-line, no longer in use, spoils the sea-front. Although no preserver of ancient beauty can restore the higher level of the sea and so wipe out the over-extended foreshore, at least those rusty, disfiguring lines could be removed. It would be a good thing, too, if the absurdly hideous modern housing scheme on the hill-top could also be removed; but that, perhaps, is expecting too much! Still, perhaps it is not profitless to be forced to compare old Culross with new, and to meditate upon the lamentable decline of domestic architectural standards.

Torryburn, the next village on the "fringe", has a vigorous record of witch-burning, the last victim, Lilias Adie, dying in Dunfermline prison in 1704. It was here, too, that Alison Cunningham, nurse to Robert Louis Stevenson, was born in 1822. The village clings precariously to the rough coast, its red-roofed, pantiled cottages contrasting with the blackness of the splashed rocks at high tide. Coal and salt were worked on Preston Island, in the bay, early in the nineteenth century.

Until it became a naval base in 1903, Rosyth was a tiny village in a woody bay of the Forth, dominated by the crumbling ruins of its old castle, in which a quite unverifiable tradition asserts that Cromwell's mother was born—a legend which Queen Victoria echoed in her diary for 6th September 1842, after crossing the Forth in a steamer. The oldest parts of it probably date from the fifteenth century.

Inverkeithing, which also has naval connections, and is now famous for its ship-breaking yards, was the birthplace of Sir Samuel Greig (1735-88), the founder of the Russian Navy, of which he was supreme Admiral. His house in the High Street still stands. William the Lion gave the town its charter as a burgh in the twelfth century, although Inverkeithing claims to have been a burgh before then. In any case, its Mercat Cross with the four heraldic shields—one for Robert the Third and his son the Duke of Rothesay, who was killed by Albany at Falkland; one for Annabelle Drummond, Robert's queen; and one for the Earl of Douglas—is more than five hundred years old, though it was only moved to its present vantage point from the north end of High Street in 1799. The Town House, built upon an older building in 1755, has a curious lantern-shaped and slated cupola. It is still used for its original purpose. The tower of St. Peter's, all that remains of the fifteenth-century church destroyed by fire in 1825, and the Friary Hospitium in Queen Street, also of the fifteenth century and now used as a Public Library, help this busy modern town to remember its gracious past amidst the clanging hammers of the present.

When King James the Sixth despatched his messenger, whose orders sent Sir Patrick Vans (Spens) to "Norroway over the faem", that worthy mariner "was walking in the strand", according to the ballad. The strand, beneath the Hawk Craig at Aberdour, is a long silver stretch of sand, since then ribbed by the ripple of immemorial tides, and shifted by the drying winds of every airt, yet still no doubt much the same as it seemed to Sir

Patrick on that fatal morning. A stone and mortar memorial of the times older either than Sir Patrick or his great ballad—in its portrayal of two contrasting social levels of that early age, the rugged sailors and the elegant lords, and in the stately inevitability of the telling, surely one of the greatest of all the Scots ballads?— is the Church of St. Fillan, where the mariner probably worshipped. It was built early in the twelfth century, and it remained in continuous use until 1796. The folk of the late eighteenth century, flushed by the vision of "progress" which the Industrial Revolution seemed to hold out before them, were singularly insensitive to the stone-and-mortar values of the past. The Church of St. Fillan was allowed to fall into ruin. The roof crashed down, and the unrelenting grass, that final conqueror of every civilization, prised apart the stones. In 1926, the Reverend Robert Johnson, with a reverent feeling for the church's lineage, brought abor . its restoration. There used to be a leper's window in the kirk, through which the lepers, forbidden to come inside, could hear divine service. The window is now closed with the Pilgrim's Stone, which was once thought to contain a spell beneficial to those suffering from blindness.

Outside the town, the great spangled gates of Donibristle remind us of the Bonnie Earl of Moray, who, perhaps because he was too friendly with James the Sixth's queen, or because he had the misfortune to be the late Regent's son-in-law, but certainly because the Earl of Huntly hated him personally, was murdered on the sea-coast. On the 7th of February, the King's warrant in his pocket, the Earl of Huntly left Holyrood, having let it be known that he was going to a horse-race at Leith. In fact, he was on his way to Queensferry, where no boats but his own were allowed to cross. With forty men behind him, Huntly arrived at Donibristle. Moray barred the door, and Huntly's men set fire to the castle. Moray could not decide whether to come out and be slain, or bide and be burnt. In the end, his friend, Sheriff Dunbar of Moray, who was in the castle at the time, went out first in the hope that he might be mistaken for the Earl. This was precisely what happened: the gallant Sheriff was set upon and slain, and in the confusion the Earl escaped to the shore. Unfortunately, a silk string of his hood took fire unknown to him, and by its smouldering attracted the attention of the murderers. Gordon of Buckie struck the first blow, but insisted that Huntly should drive home the final stroke. Moray, who was vain of his youthful beauty, used his last breath to taunt Huntly with having spoiled a fairer face than his own. That it was a fair face is borne out by the chroniclers. The murder created a popular indignation that did not readily die down. Hence, indeed, the existence of the lovely ballad, which put into James' mouth the words:

> *" Now wae to thee, Huntly,*
>     *And whairfor did ye sae?*
> *I bad ye bring him wi ye*
>     *But forbade ye him to slae."*

There, however, the poet erred. For when, two days later, Lady Doune, the Earl's mother, brought over the two bodies to present them to the King, James took care to be out hunting to avoid witnessing the spectacle. He also failed to punish Huntly for the double murder. The present Donibristle is the third building to stand on that site, the one visited by Defoe having also been burned down.

Burntisland is said to have been chosen as a naval base by Agricola in the year 83. Subsequently, there may have been a tower on the site of the later castle of Rossend. Here, the unfortunate French poet, Pierre de Boscoul de Chastelard, earned his subsequent execution by secreting himself under the Mary of Scots' bed. He had done much the same thing a few weeks before at Holyrood, and had been generously pardoned. But Mary's nineteen-year-old beauty fired him with an insatiable passion. She may even have encouraged him—Knox infers as much when he tells us that the Queen chose him to be her partner in a dance called " The Purpose ", and leaned on his shoulder. At any rate, when she found him in her bedroom at Rossend, she called for help. Moray—father-in-law of the Bonnie Earl—entered, and the Queen ordered him to despatch the poet instantly. Moray, however, denounced and arrested Chastelard instead. He was later tried and beheaded at St. Andrews.[1]

In a bad French sonnet—he was not even a good minor poet—Chastelard had asked the Queen of what use it was to possess kingdoms, cities, towns, prisons, and to command nations: to be respected, feared and admired by everyone: yet to live a lonely widow, cold as ice? He went to the block declaiming the Hymn to Death by his friend Ronsard[2]:

---

[1] See G. Whyte Melville's novel, *The Four Maries*, for a fictionalized account of the affair.

[2] Chastelard does not seem to have been an " accredited " member of Les Pleiades. Probably he was but a desultory songster, like so many youthful French poets of the time. Some of them, however, had surprising minor talent, as Professor Alan Boase's recent rediscovery of the poems of Spode shows. Chastelard forms the subject of the first of Swinburne's three tragedies in the Elizabethan manner.

*" Such cruel martyrdom is love*
*No lover may contented live:*
*And death true happiness may give,*
*Since love no more his heart may move. . . ."*

As well as a number of pleasant houses, Burntisland has a remarkable old kirk, one of the first to be built after the Reformation. It is built on the top of a hill in the middle of the town, on a four-square plan to signify the equality of all believers, and shows Dutch influence. An outside stair leads to the Sailor's Loft, and round the galleries there are paintings of sailors and ships and guild insignia. It wears an air of solid homely strength, like a good Scots psalm-tune, of which it is a sort of stone equivalent.

Part of the sea-wall is still known as Cromwell's Dyke. He came there with his troops in 1651, and the first shot from his cannon shattered the provost's china-shop. This chance blow apparently somewhat weakened the provost's desire to resist further.

Burntisland, later the northern terminal of the Granton ferry, once received the first train-ferry in the world, the paddle-steamer *Leviathan*, in 1849. The rails on her deck linked up with rails at both the shore termini.

To-day, Burntisland is a strange mixture of shipbuilding town and holiday resort. The ring of hammers and the chattering of riveters' gear sound over the green links by the sea where folk from Dunfermline and the surrounding mining villages take their holiday ease. The raw red wounds of the aluminium workings show up for many a seaward mile. The only Scottish craftsman at present (1952) building harpsichords is, oddly enough, a Burntisland shipyard worker, who makes the instruments in his spare time.

Kinghorn was the scene of one of the greatest tragedies ever to befall Scotland. It took place on a stormy night in 1265. King Alexander the Third, delayed late in council at Edinburgh, insisted on crossing the Forth to be with his fair young second wife, Queen Yolette, to whom he had only been married four months. He crossed the Forth safely at Queensferry, in spite of a raging storm, but, riding blindly over the cliffs at Kinghorn, his horse wandered, stumbled, and threw him to the shore. His neck was broken by the fall. For a long time, the place of tragedy was marked by a simple cross. Now, overlooking the railway, there stands a marble obelisk, unveiled in 1847 by the Earl of Elgin.

At the King's wedding in Jedburgh, the Spectre of Death is said to have showed itself, stalking the players of a masque and casting a gloom over the gay festivities. If such a spectre did, in fact, appear—our authority is the *Scotichronicon*—it must have been stage-managed by someone; unless, of course, the masque was a too-vividly portrayed Dance of Death, which would, however, be an odd choice for a wedding piece.

Some writers have hinted at foul play. There is evidence of none. The barons apparently did their utmost to prevent the King leaving Edinburgh. The ferrymaster tried to dissuade him from crossing the Forth. The saltmaster at Inverkeithing was horrified to find his King travelling in such a night, and reluctantly provided guides. But, in the angry darkness, guide and guided became lost and the horses went their own ways.

Thomas the Rhymer of Earlston, who claimed to be a seer, prophesied in early March that within twelve days there would be heard the sorest wind and tempest that ever was heard in Scotland. On the last day of the period, Patrick, Earl of Dunbar, sneered at the prophet for his falsity. Within a few hours, the news of the King's death was brought to Dunbar Castle, and Thomas was vindicated. Alexander's death at the age of forty-two was, indeed, a sore tempest. It ended a period of relative peace and prosperity which had lasted for two centuries, since the days of Malcolm and Margaret. It encouraged English Edward to begin his greedy attempts to make Scotland his own. And it gave rise to the oldest extant piece of Scots poetry: an anxiously beautiful lament[1]:

> "*When Alexander our king was deid,*
> *That Scotland lede in lauche and le*   [led
> *Away was sons of ale and breid*   [plenty
> *Of wine and wax, of gamyn and glee.*
> *Our gold was changit into lede.*   [lead
> *Christ, born into virginity,*
> *Succour Scotland and remeid*   [help her
> *That stade is in perplexite.*"   [sunk deeply

Of Kirkcaldy, Thomas Carlyle testified, in his somewhat tortuous fashion, that it was ". . . a solidly diligent, and yet by no means a panting puffing or in any way gambling 'langtoun'. Its flax-mill machinery, I remember, was turned mainly by wind, and curious blue-painted wheels with oblique vanes rose from many roofs for that end". Carlyle was then a schoolmaster in the place, living in Kirk Wynd, and friendly with Irving the religionist. The year was 1816.

---

[1] It survives only because Andrew of Wyntoun apparently shared this opinion, and preserved it in his *Chronikyll*.

Kirkcaldy's early interest can be read in the names of some of her older streets—Sailor's Walk, which contains pleasing old pantiled houses, one of which, probably once the home of a wealthy sixteenth-century trader, has an interesting painted ceiling, and has been restored by the National Trust; Coal Wynd; Pottery Street; and Prime Gilt Box Street. She owes her modern prosperity very largely to the development of that manufacture which literally scents her environs. The linen trade, which began in Kirkcaldy, after the civil wars of the seventeenth century had ruined her shipping trade, became second only to that of Dunfermline. Then Mr. Michael Nairn, later knighted, a member of a well-known local family, had the idea of making more durable cloth which would be suitable for covering floors. Out of the fibre of cork and oil-paint, he succeeded in making linoleum. The cork came from Spain, and the whale-oil from the ships Kirkcaldy sent to the Greenland hunting-grounds. (Now, the wholesale entry of Russia and Germany into the whaling industry threatens even the continuance of the species, so heavy is the yearly toll taken on whales, and linseed oil is used instead of whale oil.)

The grimy claws of industry have pushed into the background Kirkcaldy's historical past. But, round about the town, there are still many old castles and mansions. Raith, possibly built by MacDuff, an Earl of Fife, now houses a collection of Roman relics. Balwearie was the home of a family whose most famous representative was Michael Scott (*c.* 1175-1234), the so-called wizard. He became tutor and astrologer to the exotic Emperor Frederick the Second of Sicily. In later life, Scott's experiments in astrology and alchemy earned him a shivery reputation:

> " *What gars ye gaunt, my merry men aa*     [look pale
> *What gars ye look sae eerie,*
> *What gars ye hing your heids sae sair*
> *In the Castle o' Balwearie?* "

—perhaps commemorates the view of him taken by the Scottish peasantry. The poet Dante stood in no such awe of the wizard. For in the eighth Circle of his Inferno is a " round valley " where

> " *Each appeared strangely to be wrenched away*
> *Between the upper arms and lower face.*
> *For towards the reins the chin was screwed, whereby*
> *With gait reversed they were constrained to go . . .*"

—one of the unfortunates

> " *Was Michael Scott; and verily he knew*
> *The circle of magic and its frauds to limm. . . .*"

Ravenscraig, the ruins of which are still fairly extensive, was built by James the Second for his Queen, Mary of Guilders. James was killed when one of his new cannons burst at the siege of Roxburgh Castle, and he did not see Ravenscraig completed. We learn from old records that the timber used in its construction was cut on the Allan Water, and floated from Stirling down the Forth. The property came into the hands of William St. Clair, Earl of Orkney and Caithness, who exchanged his Orkney lands for these. Thereafter, by descent and marriage, Ravenscraig went to the Erskines of Alva, who also inherited the Roslyn title of another branch of the St. Clairs. In 1896, the then Earl of Roslyn sold Ravenscraig and Dysart House to Sir Michael Nairn, head of the linoleum family.

The Grange, south of Kirkcaldy, was once the home of the family of Kirkcaldy of Grange. William Kirkcaldy of Grange, the bravest soldier of his time, held Edinburgh Castle for Queen Mary long after all the rest of Scotland had gone over to the Protestant lords. For this loyalty, he suffered death on the scaffold.

The Boswells also have a connection with Kirkcaldy, for at the farm of Balbarton, now a hollow beside the railway, Bozzy's pompous song-writing son, Sir Alexander Boswell of Auchinleck, fought and lost a famous duel in 1822. Sir Alexander was carried dying to Balmuto House, which belonged to the Boswells of Balmuto from the fourteenth century to the middle of the twentieth. Sir Alexander had chosen to write some articles in a Glasgow paper reflecting upon the character of Mr. James Stewart of Dunearn. When an apology was demanded Boswell refused to recant, so in due course he received a challenge. The court action which followed Boswell's death cleared Stewart of all blame. This was probably the second last duel to be fought in Scotland, the last being fought in 1826, also at Kirkcaldy, by two honour-overconscious local gentlemen, Londale and Morgan.

Kirkcaldy produced one of the greatest citizens of the eighteenth century, the economist Adam Smith (1723-90). After studying at Glasgow University and at Oxford, Smith was appointed to the chair of Moral Philosophy in his Scottish *alma mater*. Whilst there, he issued his *Theory of Moral Sentiments*. But he retired to Kirkcaldy to write most of his masterpiece, *The Wealth of Nations*, which appeared in 1776, and which Edmund Burke judged, with characteristic over-emphasis, to be " in its ultimate results, probably the most important book that had ever been written ". Certainly it was the first attempt to set down the principles of political economy scientifically, and basically these principles have been little altered.[1]  Kirkcaldy was also the scene of the brief little life of Marjory Fleming (1803-11), whose precocious literary talent won her the friendship of Scott, who called her " Pet Marjorie ".

Modern Kirkcaldy has never made a strong impression on me. The pleasant square by the railway station suggests a spaciousness which is not borne out by the cramped reality to be found down the side streets, excepting, of course, its four-mile-long Main Street, which earned Kirkcaldy its ancient sobriquet of "the lang toun".  Many of the nineteenth-century parts of the town have decayed, and the press of expanding industry has necessarily swept up most of the older houses.  Down many a side street, the sea tilts excitingly away from the front of a hilly wynd.  But the sea-front itself has been made depressingly formal.  As at Dunfermline, solidly prosperous-looking suburbs extend into the surrounding country.

Wemyss—which gets its name from the Celtic word *weem*, a cave, with the English plural added on, because there are several caves and an East and West Wemyss—has a history which reaches back an untraceable distance.  So, indeed, have most places: but, in the case of Wemyss, there is the ancient evidence of the caves themselves to remind us that the blue sea, the salty spray, and the golden suns of Fife were enjoyed by the men of pre-history—the men of the Bronze Age, 4000 B.C.  All that has survived to tell us of their existence are drawings and scratches on the walls, some of which probably had a religious significance. Nine caves have so far been discovered, the Michael cave as recently as 1929.  Some have since collapsed because of the adjacent mine-workings or the sea's encroachment.  The Michael cave, in the heart of a coal-mine, had to be filled in with concrete soon after it was discovered, in the interests of safer coal-getting: fortunately, not before the antiquary George B. Deas had taken photographs and made casts of some of the wall markings.  These are now to be seen in Kirkcaldy Museum.  Castings of a ship figure, the earliest representation of a ship in these islands, found in Jonathan's cave, may also be seen in Kirkcaldy, as well as in the National Museum of Antiquities in Edinburgh, and the Naval Museum, Greenwich.

Traces of layers of successive civilizations are to be found in these caves—carvings of Scandinavian origin; markings of Iron

[1] Burke also declared Michael Bruce's " Ode to the Cuckoo " to be the finest lyric in the English language!  Even allowing for the poem's pre-Romantic Movement date of composition, this was a strange judgment.

Age Picts, and of the Early Christians. On the cliffs to the west of the caves, there stands the relic of another and, by comparison, a modern civilization, the Castle of Wemyss, whose foundations date from the thirteenth century. It was in this castle that Mary, Queen of Scots, in February 1565, heard Darnley, "the best proportioned lang lad" that she had seen, propose to her. Although she did not immediately accept his ring, she had probably already made up her mind to marry, the experience with Chastelard having perhaps demonstrated the difficult position of a pretty husbandless nineteen-year-old queen. The Castle still belongs to the Wemyss family, who claim descent from the Earls of Fife, the remains of whose earlier tower lie a little to east.

David, Second Earl of Wemyss (1610-79), devoted the greater part of his life to the management and development of his coal-mines. He left a diary in which his ideas and improvements were duly noted. He built the harbour at Methil to export his coal, and he tells us that: "on 15th September 1664, Andrew Thomsone in Leven did load his boat in the New Herbure of Methil with coals from the coal of Methil, being 60 loads of coal; and he did take them to Leith on 17th September 1664, which was the first boat that did load with coals at the Herbure. The coals was well loved at Leith and since thorrow all sea parts of Scotland. . . ."

On either side, the Castle is hemmed in by the press of industrialization. To the south lies Dysart, now attached administratively to Kirkcaldy, which once did a great Continental trade in salt. By the end of the eighteenth century, nail-making had become its main occupation. But the richness of its coal, first mined as long ago as the fourteenth century, has proved the town's outward undoing, and only the fragments of St. Serf's tower, built in 1503, remind us that St. Serf came here to argue with the Devil. The Devil seems since to have made great gains. A fragment of the place's ancient character was preserved by Burns in 1787, when he heard a snatch of a local fisherman's song, and round it made the only song of his which has an unmistakable east coast ring:

> "*Up wi' the carles o' Dysart,*
> *And the lads o' Buckhaven,*
> *And the kimmers o' Largo,*
> *And the lassies o' Leven.*
> *Hey, ca' through, ca' through*
> *For we hae muckle ado;*
> *Hey, ca' through, ca' through,*
> *For we hae muckle ado. . . ."*

To the north of the Castle, the factory lums of Leven blacken the blowy sky. Leven was once one of the most substantial of the east coast ports. The sordid sprawl of its nineteenth-century expansion has turned it into one of the ugliest towns in Scotland. True, you may still see traces of its dignified past down some of its older side streets, and its ancient Mercat Cross is preserved outside the ornate façade of the Greig Institute. But these fragments survive, one feels, on sufferance. The broad promenade on the sea-front carries a large number of holiday-makers in summer: mostly, I am told, Glaswegians, who presumably can only feel at home against a background of industrial squalor.

The "lads o' Buckhaven" are said to be descended originally from the stranded crew of a Dutch vessel. Their once-alien character made them appear to their Scots neighbours rude and stupid, hence the traditional description of an uncouth Fifer as being "of the college of Buckhaven". In Defoe's day, the fishing-village seemed "a miserable row of cottages". Coal-mining has transformed it into a town to which that descriptive adjective "miserable" might still be applied with justification, at any rate to the visual aspect of the place. It contains a pre-Reformation Church shifted holus-bolus from St. Andrews at the end of the last century. The stones of this kirk were brought by Buckhaven fishermen in their own boats from the harbour of St. Andrews to the now abandoned harbour of Buckhaven.

IV

Thus far has industry spread through Fife. The coastal towns that have fallen within its grasp all contain surviving traces of their old burgh character. But the East Neuk of Fife, as the easternmost stretch of the coast is called, has remained largely unspoiled.

Lower Largo, the slope of the field, crouches snugly round its harbour beneath Largo Law. It has the modern disadvantage of looking across at Leven. But the main charm of Lower Largo lies in its unspoiled character. It has been the home of many sailors, several of whom have become immortalized in literature. Who has not heard of the *Flower* and the *Yellow Carvel*, and of their Admiral, Sir Andrew Wood, the friend and counsellor of both James the Third and James the Fourth? In 1498, Sir Andrew fought his famous engagement against the English when, behind the Isle of May, he captured three English ships and the English

Admiral Stephen Bull. Bull was sent back to his royal master in London with the slightly contemptuous warning that future English sailors caught marauding in the Forth would not get off so lightly!

James the Fourth presented the lands of Largo to Sir Andrew for his services. In the grounds of Largo House, the remains of his castle may still be seen, as well as the dried bed of the canal which he caused to be dug, so that when he was too old to walk to the kirk, he could still sail there in his barge manned by eight oarsmen.

The son of the Captain of the *Yellow Carvel*, young Andrew Barton, in due course carried on the brave work. Barton cleared the Forth of pirates, and took measures against the Flemish, the Portuguese and the English to stop their depredations on Scottish merchants. On one occasion, Barton sent his sovereign the present of a large barrel filled, not with herring, but with the heads of Flemish pirates! Barton's last engagement took place off the coast of Northumberland, when the Earl of Surrey captured Barton's ship, the *Lion*, and shot her master through the heart.

According to a ballad version of the encounter, the Scottish sailor died exhorting his men:

> " ' Fight on, my men,' Sir Andrew says,
>    ' A little I'm hurt, but yet not slain;
> I'll but lie down and bleed awhile
>    And then I'll rise and fight again.
> Fight on, my men,' Sir Andrew says,
>    ' And never flinch before the foe;
> And stand fast by St. Andrew's cross
>    Until you hear my whistle blow.' "

The English took his head to London, where it was triumphantly displayed.

> " . . . in came the queen and ladies fair...
>    To see Sir Andrew Barton, knight:
> They weened that he were brought on shore,
>    And thought to have seen a gallant sight.
>
> But when they see his deadly face,
>    And eyes so hollow in his head,
> ' I would give,' quoth the king, ' a thousand marks.
>    This man were alive as he is dead. . . .' "

Actually, Henry the Eighth quoth no such humanitarian sentiment, but contemptuously remarked that kings should not concern themselves with the fate of pirates.

Vengeance for Barton's death was one of the causes which led
James the Fourth to embark upon the disastrous Flodden project.
He had built the great *St. Michael*, a warship two hundred and
forty feet long, fifty-six broad, and armed with thirty-five cannon
and many smaller guns. She carried a complement of over three
hundred sailors, one thousand soldiers or " marines ", and a hundred and twenty gunners. Her building laid waste most of the
woods in Fife, and cost thirty thousand pounds, a sum roughly
equivalent in contemporary values to the price of the *Queen Mary*
and the *Queen Elizabeth* together. Yet the *St. Michael* never
fired a warlike shot, for she proved totally unwieldy, and, after
Flodden, was disposed of to the French.

Alexander Selkirk (1676-1721) also came from Largo. He was
a hot-tempered young man who was hauled before the kirk session
for beating his young brother who, it seems, had the temerity to
laugh when Alexander mistakenly drank a can of sea-water! It
was his hot temper that in 1704 led to trouble on board the
*Cinque Ports*, the ship on which he was sailing-master. He
quarrelled with his skipper, Thomas Stradling, who landed him
on the uninhabited island of Juan Fernandez by way of punishment. There, Selkirk remained for four years and four months,
until he was rescued by Captain Woodes Rogers, R.N. Two years
later, Selkirk fell in with Daniel Defoe at Wapping. Defoe became so fascinated by Selkirk's story that he made it the basis of
his novel, *Robinson Crusoe*. The poet Cowper, in his " Verses
Supposed to be written by Alexander Selkirk ", put these famous
words into the sailor's mouth:

> "*I am monarch of all I survey,*
> *My right there is none to dispute;*
> *From the centre all round to the sea,*
> *I am lord of the fowl and the brute.*
> *Oh, solitude! where are the charms,*
> *That sages have seen in thy face?*
> *Better dwell in the midst of alarms,*
> *Than reign in this horrible place. . . ."*

The citizens of Largo have put up a statue to Selkirk in front
of the house by the harbour where he was born—no bad harvest
of fame from the seeds of personal indiscipline!

Once, Largo was a fishing village. My friend the poet Sydney

Goodsir Smith—himself of East Neuk stock, Goodsir being a patronym of this airt—describes its decline in a vivid lyric:

> " *Ae boat anerlie noo*                    [only
> *Fishes frae this shore,*
> *Ae black drifter lane*
> *Riggs the cramassie daw—*          [crimson dawn
> *Aince was a fleet, and nou*
> *Ae boat alane gaes out.*
>
> *War or peace, the trawlers win,*
> *An the youth turns awa*
> *Bricht wi baubles nou*
> *An thirled tae factory or store;*
> *Their faithers fished their ain,*
> *Unmaistered; ane remains.*
>
> *And never the clock rins back,*
> *The free days are owre;*
> *The warld shrinks, we luik*
> *Mair t'oor maisters ilka hour—*
> *Whan yon lane boat I see,*
> *Daith and rebellion blinn ma ee."*

Unfortunately, even "rebellion" does little enough to strengthen the weakening position of the individual in the modern world, since the "rebellion" can at best be merely a personal, intellectual one. The world shrinks, and the Scots, who were essentially individualists and craftsmen, look more to their "masters": and their "masters" have perforce to look across the Atlantic.

At a crossroad north of Upper Largo, on the road to Ceres, a tumulus known as Norrie's Law provides an interesting treasure-legend. It once held real treasure, as an enterprising tinker of 1819 discovered. One night he opened the mound, and came upon a hoard of Celtic silver ornaments. Thereupon he sold them to local jewellers, who with that respect for the lovely things of the past which is so often the hall-mark of the commercial man, promptly melted them down.[1] Fortunately, the tinker bungled his burglary in the darkness, and further silver pieces were later found after an expert excavation had been carried

---

[1] Fifers, it may here be said, are essentially practical men, lacking in imagination, which is demonstrated by their relatively poor output of folk-art, and by the fact that they have produced few artists from their numbers.

out. These pieces are now safely entombed in the National Museum of Antiquities at Edinburgh.

Largo slopes steeply down to the sea from the face of its Law— not much of a hill by Highland standards, but a landmark on the flat coastland of Fife. Earlsferry and Elie join together around Elie Ness, the lower "jaw" of the Fife snout. Earlsferry, royal burgh and ancient terminal-point of a ferry which sailed to and from North Berwick, has a cave wherein MacDuff is said to have hidden from Macbeth whilst awaiting a fisherman's passage to Dunbar. Elie owes its daily bread nowadays mainly to its attractiveness as a holiday resort. Its wide, sandy bay, its fine golf course, and its rows of good hotels and discreet boarding-houses are the indications of its personality. But much of its ancient character is preserved down wynds and side-streets, and in the vicinity of the harbour; there are still a number of unpretentious little homes with crow-stepped gables and the red pantiled roofs common to Scotland's east coast counties. Of the grander houses, the Castle, built on the sea's edge in the sixteenth century, had as its occupant in May 1679, Margaret Sharp. One morning, an agitated messenger knocked at her door with dreadful news. Her father, the Episcopalian Archbishop Sharp, had been murdered on Magus Muir, three miles out of St. Andrews, the previous evening.

On the 3rd of May, nine Covenanters led by two Fife lairds, Hackson of Rathillet and Balfour of Kinloch, were searching for the newly appointed Sheriff-Depute of Fife, one Carmichael, with a view to murdering him in the name of the Protestant religion. Their search proved fruitless. During the morning, however, a boy brought them news that no less a person than Archbishop Sharp was about to cross the Muir in his coach and six.

Sharp was undoubtedly an unsavoury character—a proud, morally lax, patrician position-seeker, who used religion to prop up his own personal vanity. He had been a zealous Covenanter until he was offered an archbishopric. Thereafter, he calmly persecuted his former comrades, and even sanctioned the use of a cruel instrument of torture known as the boot. He had also recently perjured himself in the eyes of the Covenanters by promising one of their number, a young fanatic named Mitchell, a pardon if he confessed his culpability in an alleged plot against Sharp's life. The confession made, Sharp immediately had the Covenanter put to death.

On this, his last journey, the Primate halted to smoke a pipe with his friend, the minister of Ceres. The dust of that pleasant ash knocked out of his pipe-bowl, Sharp, accompanied by his

eldest daughter, climbed back into the coach and set out on the
last stretch of their journey.

James Russell, one of the nine men concerned in the deed, later
described what took place as the coach reached the summit of
Magus Muir:

"James, riding towards the coach . . . seeing the bishop
looking out at the door, cast away his cloak and cried 'Judas
be taken!' The bishop cried to the coachman to drive on;
he (James Russell) crying to the rest to come up . . . fired into
the coach driving very fast about half a mile. . . . Andrew
Henderson outran the coach, and stroke the horse in the face
with his sword; George Fleman . . . riding forward, gripping
the horses' bridles in the nearest . . . George Balfour fired
likewise, and James Russell . . . ran to the coach door and
desired the bishop to 'Come forth, Judas'.

He (Sharp) answered that he never wronged man . . . John
Balfour on horseback said: 'Sir, God is our witness that it is
not for any wrong thou hast done to me, nor yet for any fear
of what thou could do to me, but because thou hast been a
murderer of many a poor soul in the kirk of Scotland, and a
betrayer of the church, and an open enemy and persecutor of
Jesus Christ and his members . . . therefore thou shalt die!'
. . . James Russell desired him again to come forth and make
him (ready) for death, judgment and eternity. And the bishop
said 'Save my life, and I will save all yours.' James answered,
that he knew that it was not in his power either to save or
kill us, for there was no saving of his life, for the blood that
he had shed was crying to heaven for vengeance on him. . . .
John Balfour desired him again to come forth; and he answered
'I will come forth to you, for I know you are a gentleman and
will save my life; but I am gone already, and what needs more?'
Whereupon he went forth, and falling upon his knees, said
'For God's sake, save my life,' his daughter, falling on her knees,
begging his life also. But they told him that he should die, and
desired him to repent and make ready for death. . . .
He, rising off his knees, went forward; John Balfour stroke
him on the face, and Andrew Henderson stroke him on the
hand and cut it, and John Balfour rode him down. Whereupon he, lying upon his face as if he had been dead, and James
Russell hearing his daughter say to Wallace that there was life
in him yet in the time James was disarming the rest of the
bishop's men, went presently to him and cast off his hat, for it
would not cut . . . and hacked his head in pieces. William

Danziel lighted and went and thrust his sword into his belly. . . . James Russell desired his servants to take up their priest now. . . ."

The whole bloody scene dragged out for three-quarters of an hour. In the background, a solitary figure sat and watched from his horse, a cloak drawn about his face. That figure was their leader, Hackston of Rathillet. A year later, he was carried to the High Court of Edinburgh tied to a bare-backed horse, his feet to the animal's tail; and there, before his judges, he declared that he had thought it "no sin to despatch a bloody monster". He was himself despatched by law, his body being cut up into seven parts and displayed throughout the kingdom. Another of the assassins, one Guillan, also suffered death.

Stevenson wrote of Hackston: "The figure that always fixed my attention is that of Hackston of Rathillet, sitting in the saddle with the cloak about his mouth. . . . It is an old temptation with me to pluck away that cloak and see the face; to open that bosom and read the heart." Since Stevenson's day, so many Hackstons have briefly flourished that we now know what is to be found in such hearts—the fiery flames of intolerant fanaticism scorching their wearer's humanity beneath their lunatic heat!

Gillespie House once gave shelter to Charles the Second's brother James, Duke of York, when he was Governor of Scotland. The coxswain of the royal barge fell in love with an Elie girl, and the uncommonly obliging minister of Kilconquhar arranged a secret marriage. The bride was then smuggled aboard the barge in a barrel, supposed to contain a swan for Holyrood, with instructions that it was to be handled with special care. History does not tell us what befell the coopered lady in later years. The Lady's Tower which stands on a cliff east of the town has nothing to do with this lady. It was put up as a gazebo to indulge a whim of Lady Janet Anstruther of Elie House, whom Carlyle called "a coquette and a beauty".

When last I visited Elie, I came upon an old print that interested me, in one of the sea-front hotels. The picture hung in a place where the nature of its subject could never, under any circumstances, distress the ladies. The caption read: "Billy, the celebrated Rat Killing Dog performing his wonderful feat, killing one hundred rats in five minutes and a half, on 22nd April 1823, being his ninth match." There was Billy in a wall-of-death cockpit, one rat in his mouth, warily eyeing the remaining rats as they stormed the steep sides in a vain effort to escape. Half a dozen dead rats lay about him in dramatic attitudes of mortification. Severe-looking gentlemen in top-hats gazed excitedly down on this strange spectacle of competitive massacre. I do not know whether or not, in the century which lies on top of him, other mute, inglorious terriers have improved upon Billy's splendid record. On the whole, it seems unlikely.

St. Monance, named after St. Monan, is one of the most charming of all the east coast fishing villages. Fishing is still its way of life, although this is seasonally augmented by the holiday trade. In the kirk of St. Monance, which stands on the cliff's edge, there is a plaque bearing the words "We live by the sea". It has been so with the folk of this place for centuries. Their kirk, although restored in 1828, goes back to the thirteenth century, probably to about 1265, though King David the Second refounded it in the fourteenth century. It is built on the foundations of the ninth-century cell containing the saint's relics. Above the old village, and in marked contrast, a new landward community has spread along the cliff-top. Its buildings belong to the worst sort of twentieth-century domestic hideosity, laid out without any pre-considered plan.

Kellie Castle, former seat of the Earls of Kellie, and later the romantic home of Sir Robert Lorimer, consists of a number of towers linked together. The sixth Earl of Kellie (1732-1781), a pupil of the leader of the Mannheim school, Johann Stamitz, achieved some reputation as a composer, though he wrote entirely in the style of his master, using the musical clichés of the period. The English musicologist, Dr. Charles Burney, who knew Kellie well, declared that he "wanted application".

The ruins of Newark Castle jut up out of another nearby rocky headland. Anciently, this was the home of the Sandilands, the Lords Abercrombie; but, in 1649, it was sold to General David Leslie, the Cromwellian soldier who had defeated Montrose at Philipaugh four years earlier.

The Newark doocot is one of the two finest to survive.[1] In the eighteenth century, pigeons were kept in great numbers as a delicate addition to the tables of the bonnet lairds. Indeed, the possessions of a Fife laird were proverbially supposed to amount to "a pickle (little) land, mickle (much) debt, a doocot and a lawsuit". But the havoc the birds made on the grain crops and the small profit to be got from selling them, led to the gradual abolition of pigeon-breeding. The doocots themselves remain, however, a pleasing characteristic of the Fife landscape, many of them in better condition than the castles of their former owners.

Steep wynds twisting down the cliff to a sheltered harbour; red

---

[1] The other is at Rosyth Castle, near Inverkeithing.

pantile roofs contrasting with the white harling of the walls, and the wash of the blue sea beneath—such are the visual qualities of Pittenweem. Pittenweem has religious associations in St. Fillan's Cave; in the remains of the Priory above one of' the vennels which slope down to the harbour; and in the Parish Church of St. Adrian which has been in use since 1588. Of the old houses, Kellie Lodge, a "town" mansion of the Earls of Kellie, and now called "The Castle", is the grandest, though the High Street contains the former homes of other Fife Lairds which match it in grace. The Gyles, one edge of which fronts the water, was built by that Captain Cook who took King Charles the Second to France after his defeat at Worcester. Charles, on his restoration, paid a visit to Pittenweem in 1651, when he regailed himself with a feast of "great buns" washed down by ale, canary, sack, and various other sorts of wines.

Easter and Wester Anstruther face each other across the harbour, the largest of the East Neuk fishing ports. Once, the minister of Anstruther was the diarist James Melville. One day in 1588, a shipful of Spaniards arrived in the harbour. In due course, their commander, Gomez de Medina, came before Melville and the "honest men of the town" at the Tolbooth, bearing the news that his fleet of twenty craft—part of the Spanish Armada—had been stranded on the Fair Isle. There, they had undergone severe privation, and now those warriors who could still take ship threw themselves on the mercy of the burghers of Anstruther. Melville's subsequent behaviour is an interesting comment on the decline of chivalry which has accompanied the development of scientific methods of raging war. The Spaniards were given food and clothing, then sent home. On the way back to Spain, they put in at Calais, where Medina found a Scots fisher crew under arrest. In Melville's words, Gomez thereupon ". . . made great rus (praise) of Scotland to his King, took the honest men to his hous, and inquyrit for the Laird of Anstruther, for the minister, and his host, and send hame monnie commendatiouns". "But," adds the minister, commenting on the Spanish visit, "we thanked God with our hartes, that we had sein tham amang us in that forme."

The manse from which Melville set out to meet Gomez was then just about to be replaced by a new house; that which is now the oldest inhabited manse in Scotland. It may have gone up early in the 1590's. Melville is sometimes credited with building it, though about that time he moved to Kilrenny.

Anstruther has had several famous sons and at least two famous daughters. Eppie Laing went to the stake in 1635, for having caused the storm which drowned the architect of the first light-house at the Isle of May. Maggie Lauder, however, met no such inglorious end. She lives on in a lively ballad named after her, dancing to the strains of Rab the Ranter's bagpipes, still bonnie in spite of the fact that by the time of her poetic limning, she had "lived in Fife, baith maid and wife, these ten years and a quarter". The Fair and Maggie's part in it were treated rather more fully by the native poet, William Tennant (1784-1848), who eventually became Professor of Hebrew at St. Andrews University. A monument on the high road at the back of the town commemorates the fame he brought to Anstruther when, in 1812, a local bookseller brought out anonymously his poem, "Anster Fair". It is a racy piece after the manner of Byron, complete with fantastic rhymes. From all the airts the folk came flocking to Anster: on horseback, in carts, on foot and in boats:

> "Nor only was the land with crowds opprest,
>     That trample forward to th' expected fair;
> The harness'd ocean had no peace or rest,
>     So many keels her barmy bosom tear:
> For, into view, now sailing from the west,
>     With streamers idling in the bluish air,
> Appear the painted pleasure-boats unleaky,
>     Charg'd with a precious freight, the good folks of Auld
>                                        Reekie.

> They come, the cream and flower of all the Scots,
>     The children of politeness, science, wit,
> Exulting in their bench'd and gawdy boats,
>     Wherein some joking and some puking sit;
> Proudly the pageantry of carvels floats;
>     As if the salt sea frisk'd to carry it;
> The gales vie emulous their sails to wag,
>     And dally as in love with each long gilded flag.

> Upon the benches seated, I descry
>     Her gentry; knights, and lairds, and long-nail'd fops;
> Her advocates and signet-writers shy;
>     Her gen'rous merchants, faithful to their shops;
> Her lean-cheek'd tetchy critics who, O fy!
>     Hard-retching, spue upon the sails and ropes;
> Her lovely ladies, with their lips like rubies;
>     Her fiddlers, fuddlers, fools, bards, blockheads, black-
>                                  guards, boobies. . . ."

That catalogue might almost be a typical cross-section of contemporary Edinburgh society during the period of the International Festival!

Tennant was born in a house in the High Street, where many fine old vernacular dwellings still survive. The anatomist who made important discoveries on the secreting structures, and on the functioning of the human placenta, John Goodsir (1814-67), was also born in the High Street, where his father practised as a doctor. Farther along, the house still stands in which was born Dr. Thomas Chalmers (1780-1847), who led the Disruption of 1843. Easter and Wester Anstruther each have a church with a graceful seventeenth-century spire. Cellardyke, the eastern end of Anstruther, still has a thriving oilskin factory. Oilskin has been made here for over a century, and the smell of linseed oil pervades Cellardyke's narrow street.

Crail, which looks over to the Isle of May, is the oldest of all the East Neuk royal burghs. Apart from the conspicuous breaks in the old burgh streets—breaks filled by incongruous houses "borrowed" from a city suburb—care has been taken to preserve the atmosphere of the place.

On the shore may be seen the curious bottle-shaped doocot that once belonged to the nunnery, a solitary arch of which survives in a wall on the south side of Nethergate. Crail capons—sun-dried haddocks—made it famous and wealthy in the days before kippering. It is recorded that in the fourteenth century Crail supplied the Court with herring. There was a royal hunting-box in the town, of which a fragment survives near the harbour. Once, that harbour must have sheltered a bustle of ships. Now, half silted up, scarcely a dozen set out from behind its rough old breakwater for the fishing-grounds. The practice of tossing severed fish-heads back into the water gives odoriferous emphasis to the air of decayed gentility which characterizes the harbour-head surroundings.

The Market-gait retains its noble burgh character, and there are many seventeenth-century houses still in use, some of them with the marriage initials or trade symbols of the first occupants still above the door. The town house has a delightful Dutch tower. The old church is surrounded by a wealth of interesting stones, containing many quaint epitaphs which delight those who make a hobby of collecting this variety of occasional verse. A brisk walk over cliff-tops fringed by golf courses brings one to Balcomie, whose castle is now a farm; and to Fife Ness, the most easterly point of Fife. Mary of Guise landed here in 1538 on her way to St. Andrews to marry King James the Fifth. She was received by the laird of Balcomie.

V

The Howe of Fife, which runs along the valley of the River Eden, is a broad, fertile strath. The farms are large, the soil rich and the landscape soft and undulating. A few miles away, on the banks of the River Leven, the paper-making town of Leslie, where Christ's Kirk on the Green[1] is supposed to have been located, clearly belongs to the industrial "workshop" of Fife. The Howe proper begins in the south at Gateside, and rolls down to Cupar, although eastward, fertile farmlands line the banks of the Eden almost to its mouth at Guardbridge.

To the west of Gateside lies Falkland, a favourite Stewart seat and still the possessor of their partly ruined palace. The palace was built near the site of an earlier tower which was a seat of the Celtic Earls of Fife, the MacDuffs. It must have been in this tower that the son of Robert the Second was murdered by the Duke of Albany. Historians now dispute whether he was, in fact, murdered, or merely died from an illness. The traditional story is that he was killed by starvation, being reduced to gnawing his own flesh. A woman who, for a time, managed to feed him through the gratings from her own breasts is said to have been put to death when her charity was discovered.

Falkland came into the hands of James the First when, as part of his noble-taming ploy, he forfeited the Fife earldom. James the Second gave it the designation of "palace" in a charter. The next three Jameses all added to Falkland, and spent long periods in it. James the Fourth entertained the English pretender, Perkin Warbeck, there in 1495, and gave him the hand of his cousin in marriage. As a boy of 17, James the Fifth was kept a prisoner in Falkland by the Earl of Angus, until his dramatic escape by night on horseback to Stirling. An extensive rebuilder, this monarch began improvements to the palace in 1525. They were completed in 1542, the year he died. He was lying there sick, "verrie neir strangled to death by extreme melancholie" when the news was brought to him that his wife had given birth to a child at Linlithgow. Lyndsay of Pitscottie gives this moving description of the King's reaction:

"The King inquired whidder it was a man or a woman. The messinger said it was ane fair dochter. The King answered and said, ' Fareweil, it cam with ane lass and it will pass with

[1] This is the title of a vigorous poem attributed, on insufficient evidence, to James the Fifth, which depicts a rural holiday of the fifteenth century. Later stanzas were added by the eighteenth-century poet Allan Ramsay.

ane lass': and so he commendit himselff to the Almightie God, and spak little from thenforth, bot turned his back to his lordis and his face to the wall."

James the Sixth made Falkland his favourite residence. It was to Falkland that a deputation from the Commissioner of the General Assembly at Cupar, headed by Knox's successor, Andrew Melville, came in 1596. James kept interrupting the preacher with niggling observations, until Melville angrily turned on him, called him "God's silly vassal", and reminded him that there were ". . . twa kings in Scotland. Thair is Christ Jesus, the King, and his Kingdom the Kirk, whase subject King James the Saxt is, and of whose kingdom nocht a king, nor a lord, nor a heid, but a memeber." Mary, Queen of Scots, also used the palace and frequently hunted in Falkland forest, felled by Cromwell in 1652 to provide timber for his fortifications at Perth.

The east wing of Falkland palace was destroyed by fire whilst it was occupied by Cromwell's troops.[1] But the main section, partly restored by Bruce of Falkland in 1823, and further restored and richly replenished in our own day by the late Lord Bute, one of whose sons is the hereditary keeper, houses many interesting portraits of the Scottish royal family, and the only source in Scotland—a window—where Darnley is described as King of Scotland.

Richard Cameron (1648-80), the Covenanting leader, was born in a three-storeyed house which may still be seen in the village square. He fell at Aird's Moss, fighting with his Cameronians, a name later adopted by the Scottish Regiment which claims the "Lion of the Covenant" as its founder. It still holds annual outside "Conventicles", and when its soldiers go to church, lookouts are posted to give "warning" of likely "interrupters" to the divine worship. Of such meaningless theatricalities are regimental traditions made, to be observed, for the most part, by men who can have no real interest in their origins.

Falkland village retains quite a number of pleasing pantiled houses. It also has a Co-operative factory which is a real horror. Apropos this monstrosity, George Scott-Moncrieff remarks: "Co-operative architecture in Scotland merits any abuse that may be levelled against it: it combines all the dignity of fish-and-chip saloons with the popular appeal of bank buildings."

North towards the Tay, the villages are agricultural, and a number of thatched cottages are still to be seen. At Auchter-

---

[1] I was surprised to read recently (1952) that General Eisenhower thinks Cromwell's soldiers models of military virtue. Their behaviour in Scotland was abominable, and the unnecessary destruction they wrought considerable. Are we to draw a modern parallel?

muchty, where a wife, celebrated in poetry, once taught her husband a severe lesson in the ardures of the domestic rôle by changing duties with him for a day, there are still one or two practising "theekers". Here, as formerly in most parts of the Lowlands, the thatch is stapled, and not merely laid on in layers, as it is in many parts of the Western Highlands.

Lindores Loch is fringed with thick rushes. I like to think that that charming sixteenth-century piece, "The Reeds in the Loch Sayis", might have been inspired by this place:

> "Though raging storms moves us to shake,
>     And wind maks waters overflow;
> We yield thereto bot dois not break
>     And in the calm bent up we grow.
>
> So baneist men, though princes rage,
>     And prisoners, be not despairit.
> Abide the storm, whill that it 'suage,
>     For time sic causis has repairit."

One of the "causis" which time has not "repairit" is that of the Aulk Kirk in Scotland. The twelfth-century Abbey of Lindores, occupied by Black Friars, must have been one of the loveliest buildings of its kind. It overlooks the broad sweep of the Tay, its broken ruins lie in the midst of fair fields, and once there stood an orchard in its grounds. John Knox brought his godly rabble there in 1559. He himself tells the tale succinctly: "We reformed them. Their altars overthrew; their idols, vestments of idolatry and mass books we burned in their presence, and commanded them to cast away their monkish habits." Curious how religions and pseudo-religions, even in our own day, wax strongest on a diet of self-righteousness, intolerance and hate!

Newburgh, with its craggy Clachard, and its vista of the Grampian mountains thrusting up across the Tay, has a Celtic cross, the Cross of Mugdrum, and the fragment of another, MacDuff's Cross, about which Sir Walter Scott wrote an indifferent dramatic poem. It was the birthplace of two minor nineteenth-century versifiers, the brothers Alexander and John Bethune. Both died young, as a result of privation and the strain of physical overwork. John's pathetic plaint:

> "To be in life's loud bustle lost,
>     And look on creeping things
> With nothing save their wealth to boast,
>     Worshipped as lords and kings."

—to some extent reflects the way of life of Newport and Tayport, the two largest places on Fife's northern coast. Ugly, pretentious mansions and villas built out of fortunes dubiously acquired at Dundee, on the other side of the Tay, make up their importance. But between them and Newburgh lies Balmerino, where the widow of William the Lion founded a Cistercian Abbey in 1225. It, too, is surrounded by fair fields and orchards. Its end came on Christmas night, 1547, when an English Admiral, acting on the instruction of Protector Somerset, landed a force of 3,000 men to sack it. The monks put up such a defence as they were able, but the marines succeeded in burning both the Abbey and the village. Knox and his friends completed the destruction on their way back to St. Andrews from the "reforming" of Lindores.

Of the villages at the heart of the Howe of Fife, none is more attractive than Ceres, with its communal green, its humph-backit bridge, and its plain and pleasant cottages. Apart from the call made there by Archbishop Sharp on that journey which ended in his murder, Ceres lays no claims on history. But, round about it, there are famous houses, some in ruins like Craighall, a mansion built in Charles the First's day by a Lord Advocate of Covenanting leanings, Sir Thomas Hope, and once famous for its Renaissance arches and balconies; or "The Struthers", whose full name used to be "Auchteruthyrsthruthyr", and which was once a home of the Lords Lyndsay.

The country hereabouts is, indeed, Lyndsay country. For at Pitscottie, Robert Lyndsay (d. 1565?) was born. His *Chronicles of Scotland*, a continuation of John Bellenden's History,[1] covers the reigns of the Scottish sovereigns from James the First to Queen Mary, although, in the last book, another hand has continued the tale. He is not an accurate or wholly reliable historian, but he had a graphic eye for the details of a story, and has vividly preserved many such incidents in the lives of the Jameses as the death of James the Fifth, already quoted. Pitscottie is now just a cluster of agricultural cottages, with a pub where they still claim to sell porter.

The Mount Farm lies near Cupar. Here, Sir David Lyndsay of the Mount (1490-1555), Lord Lyon King-of-Arms to James the Fifth, once had his seat. A tall column, memorial not to the poet—the Scots rarely honour their poets, except Burns, in this way—but to General Sir John Hopetoun, who took over command at Corunna after the death of Sir John Moore, stands on the hill where the poet may once have sharpened his satirical muse.

---

[1] Itself translated from the Latin of Hector Boece on the instructions of James the Fifth.

Lyndsay was in some ways the most "occasional" of the Auld Makars. The occasions which drove him to write his strongest work were rarely unconnected with the religious malpractices of the Catholic churchmen of his day—simony, plurality, oppression of the poor, illiteracy and lack of chastity being the major charges. Sir Walter Scott draws this imaginative verse-portrait of Lyndsay in "Marmion":

> "He was a man of middle age;
>     In aspect manly, grave and sage,
>         As on King's errand come;
>     But in the glances of his eye,
>     A penetrating, keen and sly
>         Expression found its home;
>     The flash of that satiric rage,
>     Which, bursting on the early stage,
>     Branded the vices of the age
>         And broke the keys of Rome. . . ."

The work which undoubtedly did most to "break the keys of Rome" was Lyndsay's dramatic satire, *The Thrie Estatis*. In this extraordinary verse-play—the earliest extant example of Scottish drama—the vices appear in mortal guise and give a dramatic display of their propensities, persuading Rex Humanitas to listen to them and applaud; thereafter, they are rebuked by the equally symbolic virtues, presented to the King by the austere Divine Correction. The vigour and verve of Lyndsay's texture may fairly be seen in the first speech made by the Pardoner, who appears complete with his tray of rubbishy relics:

> "Bona dies! Bona dies!
>
> Devout people, gude day, I say yow
> Now tarry ane little while, I pray yow,
>     Till I be with you knawin:
> Wat ye weill how I am namit?
> Ane nobill man, and undefamit,
>     Gif all the suith were shawin.
> I am Sir Robert Rome-Raker,
> Ane perfyte public Pardoner,
>     Admitit by the Paip:
> Sirs, I sall schaw you, for my wage,
> My pardons, and my pilgrimage,
>     Whilk ye sall see, and graip                    [grasp

*Here is ane relict, lang and braid*
*Of Finn Macoull the richt chaft blaid,*
   *With teeth and all togidder:*
*Of Colling's cow, here is ane horn,*
*For eating of Makonnal's corn*
   *Was slain into Balquhidder.*      [slain at
*Here is ane cord, baith great and lang,*
*Whilk hangit John the Armistrang:*[1]
   *Of gude hemp saft and sound:*
*Gude halie people, I stand for'd*
*Wha ever be hangit with this cord,*
   *Needs never to be drownded.*
*The culum of Saint Bride's cow,*
*The gruntle of Saint Anthony's sow,*     [snout
   *Whilk buir his haly bell:*            [bore
*Wha ever he be hears this bell clink,*
*Give me ane ducat for til drink,*         [for to
   *He sall never gang to Hell. . . ."*

The appearance of Duncan MacRae, that comic genius among Scottish actors, as the Pardoner in the Edinburgh Festival productions of the play was one of the funniest moments I have ever witnessed on any stage. Tactfully pruned by Robert Kemp—the original lasted for nine hours, and contained interludes of an obscene sort to keep the groundlings amused while the King and his court dined—with brilliant incidental music by Cedric Thorpe Davie, and produced by Tyrone Guthrie, this four-hundred-year-old morality became overnight a widely acclaimed success. Literary historians have always tended to be patronizing towards *The Thrie Estatis*, regarded as pure literature. But the testing-place of a play is the theatre, and there, before international audiences, this play triumphantly succeeded.

It also succeeded, in a different sense, at its earlier performances in the presence of the sovereign. It was first played at Linlithgow Palace, perhaps in the Banqueting Hall, in 1540, before King James the Fifth and his queen. Sir William Eure, the English ambassador, sent home a long account of the occasion. He tells us that when the "interlude" was finished, ". . . the King did call upon the Bishop of Glasgow, being chancellor, and divers other bishops, exhorting them to reform their fashions and manners of living. . . ." For the outdoor performance at Cupar[2]

---

[1] Johnnie Armstrong was a famous Border reiver, brought to justice by James the Fifth.
[2] A third outdoor performance was again given at Greenside, near Edinburgh, in 1554.

in 1552, Lyndsay wrote a dramatized advertisement which was no doubt played in the market-place some weeks beforehand. After some appetizing horse-play between a cottar and his scolding wife, and a boastful coward Fyndlaw of the Footband, who prays God "To send us war and never peace", and is then scared out of his wits by a sheep's head on a pole, Lyndsay concludes:

> " . . . As for this day I haf nae mair to say yow,
> On Whitsun Tysday cum see our play I pray yow;
> That samen day is the Seventh day of June,
> Thairfour get up right early and disjune."  [have breakfast

Cupar itself is the seat of Fife County Council. It has a broad and spacious main street, faintly classical in its mien and suggesting a larger town than does in fact exist around it. Cupar's Mercat Cross has had an adventurous life, having been moved during the eighteenth century from its ancient site to the top of Wemyss Hall Hill. Here, in 1559, James the Fifth's widow, Mary of Guise, and the Lords of the Congregation signed a Treaty of truce, one of the conditions of which was that the French troops of the Duc d'Oisel were to be evacuated from Fife. It brought a false peace, and led the Queen to cry, " Where is now John Knox his God? My God is stronger than his, even in Fife." There, however, she was wrong. The Catholic forces were defeated within a few weeks, the Queen herself died, and Protestantism became the dominant religion in Scotland. Cupar's Cross came back to the town to mark Queen Victoria's Diamond Jubilee.

The nearby house of Hill of Tarvit, now a possession of the National Trust of Scotland, who use it to provide students of architecture with short residential courses, was built in 1696 by Sir William Bruce to replace Scotstarvit Tower, where Sir John Scott of Scotstarvit (1585-1670), brother-in-law of the poet Drummond of Hawthornden, lived out his cultured and eccentric existence. Professor David Masson, Drummond's biographer, draws a picture of one who held the hereditary post of Director of Chancery, and who became Lord of Session: " a shrewd, sagacious Scottish Lawyer and Judge of his peculiar generation, very orthodox in his morals and beliefs, but with a dash of the eccentric and humourist in his ways, and something crabbed and cynical in his temper—systematically acquisitive of lands and gear, it must be admitted, and not more scrupulous as to the means than most Scots officials of his time, but thrifty in his use of what he had acquired and with a rough sense of honour and responsibility in him after all. . . ."

Edinburgh knew him best in his respectable town garb. In Fife, he was usually to been seen in his oldest suit and top-boots, walking about his farms. His tastes ran to Latinity, and it was he who paid Blaeu of Amsterdam for the publication in 1634 of *Delitiae Poetarum Scotorum*, an anthology of the works of the Scottish Latinists, edited by Arthur Johnston, some of which have been translated into Scots in our own day by another Fifer, the traveller, poet, disputator and scholar, Douglas Young. Sir John also paid for the sixth volume of Blaeu's Atlas, containing the maps of Timothy Pont, the Scottish cartographer, which might otherwise have been lost. Sir John projected, but did not execute, a " description of our shyredom by some in everie Presbytery ", thus anticipating Sir John Sinclair's *Statistical Account* of a century and a half later; he founded the Chair of Humanity at St. Andrews; and he wrote a pamphlet, *The Staggering State of Scots Statesmen*, which, unfortunately, does not live up to its magnificent title.

## VI

Scotstarvit is not very far from St. Andrews. Those who travel by train to the " little city, worn and grey ", usually have to change from the north-bound express to a chuffing two-coach train, at the junction of Leuchars, by the edge of a R.A.F. airfield. This bleak wind-swept station stands some distance away from Leuchars village, where may be seen a very lovely church. The semi-circular apse and the arched walls are Norman. The daughter of a Celtic chief, Ness, married a Norman crusader, Robert de Quenci, who died in the Holy Land in 1192. Their son, Saier de Quenci, who died in 1220, completed the church of St. Athernase. By a stroke of good fortune, those seventeenth-century builders who added a heavy tower and belfry, did not destroy much of the original fabric. Apart from its church, Leuchars is a dull spot, though near by stands the fine mansion of Earlshall, restored by Sir Robert Lorimer. It was a Bruce of Earlshall who killed Richard Cameron at Aird's Moss, afterwards hacking off the Covenanter's head and hands and carrying them in a sack to Edinburgh.

The chuffing train[1] makes only one call between Leuchars Junction and St. Andrews—at Guardbridge, where a paper-mill sits by the side of the Eden, and an ancient bridge spans it. Then the engine swings round in a wide curve, lets out a loud wail of deference, chugs between two ancient golf courses, and slides into St. Andrews station.

[1] Now withdrawn by British Rail.

Almost everyone of any consequence in the history of Scotland has come, at one time or another, to St. Andrews. From the establishment of the Cathedral by Bishop Arnold in 1160, St. Andrews grew steadily in ecclesiastical importance. Consequently, it became the focal point of the Reformation struggles. Indeed, as politics were bound up with religion in Scotland until the end of the seventeenth century, the influence of St. Andrews men reached all over Scotland, especially after 1411, when Bishop Henry Wardlaw and Prior James Bisset founded a *Studium Generale*, which, two years later, became by Papal decree Scotland's oldest University. The oldest fragments of "antiquity" are the ruins of the tiny Culdee church above the harbour. The tower of St. Rule (or Regulus) comes next in venerability. Antiquaries have sought to identify it with the round towers of Abernethy and Brechin, attributed to the eighth and tenth centuries, while some have even sought analogy in the early campaniles of Italy. It may have been erected by Bishop Robert between 1127 and 1144, probably originally attached to a church. This same Bishop Robert also founded a Priory, whose monks formed the chapter of his see, on a site south of the Cathedral, before he died in 1159. All that remains of it now are "a few stalls standing against a garden wall, fragments of cloisters, and some humps of grass-covered masonry within the garden of a modern house". It was also he who had St. Andrews elevated to the status of a royal burgh.

It was his successor, Bishop Arnold, who caused to be begun the Cathedral, for the religious services of the Priory. This, the largest of all the Scottish Cathedrals, took one hundred and eighty years to complete, the work being carried on with loving care and reverence by a succession of prelates. It was finished by the patriot Bishop William of Lamberton, the friend and supporter of Robert the Bruce; and the great King himself was present when, on July 5th, 1318, the mighty edifice was dedicated. Rich tapestries and jewels, part of the spoil of Bannockburn, enlivened the grey walls, some of them already old and worn by the ceaseless rubbing of the salt winds. Then, in 1378, by some accident, the Cathedral was partly destroyed by fire: but it was faithfully rebuilt and restored.

Early in the sixteenth century, Prior John Hepburn built the great wall which runs along the edge of the cliff, down to the harbour, and up to the west gate. In 1512, he also founded the College of St. Leonard, which stood on the site of the present St. Leonard's Girls' School. This, then, was probably the moment of St. Andrews greatest glory. The storm of the Reformation had not yet burst. True, a Bohemian doctor, Paul Craw, had been burned as a heretic—apparently he preached principles of religious and social reform which we might nowadays call "leftish"—somewhere in St. Andrews in 1432; and the long, unhappy years of burnings and counterburnings, of torture and murder in the name of God, could be said to be in sight when the flames singed Craw's flesh. But the Churchmen in the naturally fortified medieval castle jutting out on a sea-rock built with a keen eye for defensive possibilities by Bishop Roger in 1200, were still outwardly as much in control of the religious situation as ever. Soon, they began to fight against each other. The boy Archbishop Stewart, a natural son of James the Fourth, had fallen with his father at Flodden. So many nobles had died on that bloody field, indeed, that more administrative power came into the hands of Churchmen than would otherwise have happened. Power begets the desire for still more power and, of course, corrupts. Hepburn, the building Prior, decided that he should be the next Archbishop, a decision also reached in favour of himself by Andrew Forman, Bishop of Moray, and by the poet, Bishop Gawain Douglas (?1475-1522), nephew of Archbishop Bell-the-Cat Douglas who had hanged the favourites of James the Third. The poet whose sturdy version of Virgil's *Aeneid* into Scots was the first British translation ever to be made, struck the first blow by seizing St. Andrews Castle. Prior Hepburn retook it, and, according to legend, subjected the poet to a term of imprisonment in the horrible bottle dungeon, still to be seen. A Douglas army under the Earl of Angus failed to dislodge Hepburn, though the poet was freed to resume his charge of Dunkeld. In the end, Forman was appointed by the Pope, while Hepburn was bribed out of the Castle with the offer of the abbacy of Arbroath.

The scuffling of these clerical thugs can hardly have increased the dignity of the Church in the eyes of the folk of Fife. Still less did the burning of Patrick Hamilton in 1527, on the orders of Cardinal David Beaton. Because the faggots were damp, Hamilton's agony was prolonged. He was "roasted rather than burnt", yet he remained steadfast to his principles until he lost consciousness. His main "heresy" was that "Man hath no free will to do good works before the grace of the Holy Spirit", a doctrine which leads logically to the denial of personal responsibility for one's standard of conduct. In time, Hamilton's dogma reached its logical absurdity in the state of "grace" which the "elect" amongst the Covenanters enjoyed, when not even murder could rob them of their "appointed" Heavenly places. James Hogg's *The Memoirs and Confessions of a Justified Sinner*—a novel of the most powerful psychological significance—sets out a case of that sort.

Cardinal Beaton's intrigues over the next few years are not easily unravelled. As a result of his interventions, the English King's plans to wed his son, Prince Edward, to the infant Queen Mary, when they should both reach marriageable years, were defeated; and permission to read the Bible in English, granted towards the end of James the Fifth's reign, was withdrawn. The Cardinal feared union with Reformed England, not out of patriotism, but because of its likely effects against the old religion in Scotland. An alliance with France was therefore sought instead.

Then the Cardinal started a vigorous policy of heretic-hunting; hanging and drowning men and women for, at worst, offences which would produce only a rebuke in a modern court. Beaton's death was plotted by some Scottish nobles, and backed by English gold. Henry the Eighth sent a fleet under Lord Hertford to devastate St. Andrews. Instead, the English burned and looted the Borders, then sacked and burned Edinburgh, from which Beaton, who was at Holyrood, had hastily to flee. The patriotic Reformers regarded the destruction wrought by these English expeditions as "the judgment of God".

Meanwhile, Beaton's men managed to lay hold of the most outspoken anti-Papistical speaker of the day, George Wishart. Wishart was brought to St. Andrews, arraigned before Beaton, and, on the 1st of March 1546, suspended from a chain and burnt in front of the Castle, the fire being placed in a position which enabled the Cardinal to enjoy the spectacle from a window.

Wishart's death has been reported in noble terms by John Knox. The hangman knelt before the condemned man and said . . . "'Schir, I pray yow, forgive me, for I am not guiltie of your death.' When he was come to him, he kissed his cheik, and said, 'Lo! here is a token that I forgive thee. My harte, do thyne office.' And then by and by, he was put apoun the gibbet, and hanged, and there brynt to pouder (powder). When that the people beheld the great tormenting of that innocent, they mycht not withold from piteous mourning and complaining of the innocent lamb's slawchter."

The "innocent lamb", however, even if he had not been an actual plotter in the incident which followed, was at least on friendly terms with those who murdered Cardinal Beaton, and seems unlikely to have disapproved of their intent.

Knox—who is never reliable when writing of his enemies, or about any matter which did not conform exactly to his somewhat narrow conception of "The Trewth"—says that Beaton spent his last night, May the 28th, with his mistress. The drawbridge of the Castle had been lowered to let in workmen. It also let in Norman Leslie, Kirkcaldy of Grange,[1] and James Melville, the father of the diarist. When the porter realized his error, Leslie quickly stabbed him and threw him into the fosse. The genuine workmen were then turned out again, the Cardinal's unarmed staff rounded up, and the gate locked. Beaton, disturbed by the noise, rushed to his window, saw what had happened and hastened to a secret escape-passage. He found it guarded by Kirkcaldy, so he turned back to his chamber and barricaded himself in.

Leslie then set fire to the door. The Cardinal opened it; and the murderers rushed and fell upon him. As he lay dying of his wounds, Melville reminded him of the fate of George Wishart, stabbing him again. "All is gone," cried the Cardinal, with prophetic significance, as he sank to the floor. They hung his body over the Castle wall in a blanket, then salted it, and flung it into a dungeon. Seven months later, it was buried in the Black Friars' Convent, a single arch of which still stands in the grounds of Madras College. Sir David Lyndsay, who, although he supported the principles of the Reformers, never became involved in their butchery, wrote a verse account of the affair, "The Tragedy of the Cardinal", in which Beaton is made to relate, rather sorrowfully, his own shortcomings as a warning to others. Being himself a humanist, Lyndsay gives this verdict on the murder:

> ". . . Although the loon be weil away,
> The deed was foully done."

St. Andrews Castle thereupon became the stronghold of the militant Reformers, besieged by the forces of the Regent Arran. Knox himself joined the beleaguered garrison. But not even Knox could restrain the drinking and raping which apparently went on. In the close heat of August 1547, six French galleys and two great ships of war suddenly sailed upon the scene. In conjunction with Arran's forces, the Frenchmen gave the Castle such a battering that the Reformers were forced to surrender. The spire of St. Salvator's was destroyed in the bombardment, and Knox was haled off to be chained as an oarsman in the galleys. Once, during this period of travail, he caught a distant view of St. Andrews from his bench. He vowed to come back and glorify God by destroying the places of worship there.

Eighteen months later he was released. After sojourning in England and Geneva, he returned to Scotland in 1556, but once again he was forced to quit the country.

[1] Who later changed his loyalties to Mary's side.

In 1558, Archbishop Hamilton burned a poor old recusant priest, Walter Mill, for heresy. Mill, who was over eighty, hoped he would be the last to suffer at the stake for his principles. The sight of the torment suffered by this decrepit old man so stirred the populace that his hope turned out to be true, though religious executions by other means continued until the end of the seventeenth century. Knox came back permanently to Scotland early in 1559. On the 9th of June, he preached on "the cleansing of the Temple" at Crail, repeating the incitement to destruction at Anstruther and St. Andrews on the following days. Thereupon, amid

> " . . . steir, strabush and strife,
> When, bickerin' frae the towns o' Fife,
> Great bangs of bodies, thick and rife
> Gaed to Saint Andrew's town,
> On, wi' John Calvin i' their heids,
> And hammers i' their hands, and spades,
> Enrag'd at idols, mass and beads,
> Dung the Cathedral doun."[1]

Between June 11th and 13th, the idols in the Cathedral were "dung doun", the vestments torn, and the building left a shell from which, as an afterthought, the lead was stripped off the roof. A leadless roof could not long survive the salty, penetrating powers of the north-east wind. Once it had begun to crumble down, local folk started to use the Cathedral stones, here as in so many of the other buildings destroyed by Knox's rabble, as a quarry for their houses or for the upkeep of their harbour. It was not until the late nineteenth century that Lord Bute had the tattered remains of Scotland's greatest religious edifice preserved. Now, it is in official custody and safe from further destruction, its once noble proportions marked in outline on the grass.

The shouts of the mob, many of them no doubt louts glad of a chance to destroy for destruction's sake, others representatives of those congenital "rebels" who think that being a "rebel" is in itself a "glorious thing", like the Gilbertian pirate king—the shouts of the mob as they ripped and smashed, marked the end of an old tyranny and the beginnings of a new. Before long, a gloomy reign of Calvinistic pietism blanketed out the people's fairs and, wherever it could, their songs and their dances. The new régime soon distinguished itself by burning women; not for heresy, to be sure, but for practising the non-existent crime of witchcraft. As is always the case where extremists, backed by

[1] Tennant: *John Knox, or the Dungen Doun o' the Cathedral.*

armed force, gain control, the conditions which followed were soon no better than those that had flourished before; only now, the misery was felt by different sorts of people, and more widely shared.

By the late eighteenth century, the Lowland Scot had begun to shake off the worst effects of the doleful fog of the Reformation. It drifted northwards, where it damped the vitality of the once-volatile Highlanders. It still lingers on in pockets to-day, where those curious "survivors" of the seventeenth century, the ministers of the Free Presbyterian Kirk, are fighting a bitter, losing battle to keep the people subjected beneath a set of tenets as bigoted and as absurd as the principles of African witchcraft.

Shorn of its Cathedral, St Andrews itself gradually fell into that state of decay which, in a cleanly preserved state, remains part of its character. Queen Mary used to spend holidays there, in the house still named after her. Andrew Melville, uncle of the diarist and Knox's undoubted successor as leader of the Reformed church, studied there, and eventually became Principal of St. Mary's College. The young James Graham, later the "Great Marquis" Montrose, came up to the University as a boy of fifteen. Many are the famous men and women who have followed him since. Indeed, the continuity of academic life has flowed on unbroken.

But only just. By 1697, the "decay and destitution of the town" caused the Professors to try unsuccessfully to get the University moved to Perth. St. Andrews, they claimed, was now nothing but a dirty village, the inhabitants of which were violently predisposed against the academicians.

St. Andrews supported the Hanoverian régime, and Prince Charles, when he entered the town, got few recruits. It provided Dr. Johnson with a good deal of material for his sarcastic quippery when, in 1773, Boswell brought him there. On viewing the Cathedral, he wisely observed that to differ from a man in doctrine "was no reason for pulling his house about his ears". After viewing the ruins of the city, he hoped John Knox was buried in the highway, for "I have been looking at his reformations". "Amidst all these sorrowful scenes," he announced, "I own I have no objection to dinner." He dined well with the Principal and Professors of St. Leonard's and St. Salvator's—since 1747 united into one college. One of the undergraduates, young Robert Fergusson (1750-74), who later became a spur of emulation to the muse of Burns (to whom he stands next amongst the poets of the eighteenth-century revival), was not at that august table. But he gave vent to an amusing anti-Johnsonian squib, "To the Principal and Professors of the University of St. Andrews, on their superb treat to Dr. Samuel Johnson", declaring that:

*" . . . ne'er sic surly wight as he*
*Had met wi' sic respect frae me.*
*Mind ye what Sam, the lying loun!*
*Has in his Dictioner laid doun?*
*That* Aits, *in England are a feast*
*To cow an horse, an' sican beast,*
*While in Scots ground this growth was common*
*To gust the gab o'* Man *and* Woman.
*Tak tent, ye Regents! then, an' hear*
*My list o gudely hamel gear. . . ."*

Then follows a Scots menu which "the lying loun" would undoubtedly have found a considerable strain on his not overrobust digestion.

The poet whose name is most endearingly associated with St. Andrews, however, is Andrew Lang (1844-1912). That kindly, many-talented historian and man-of-letters became the first Gifford lecturer in the University in 1888. He wrote what has remained by far the best saga of St. Andrews,[1] and in his best poem, "Alma Mater", he drew the picture of it which remains longest in the hearts of most who love her:

*" St. Andrews by the Northern Sea,*
*A haunted town it is to me!*
*A little city, worn and grey,*
*The grey North Ocean girds it round,*
*And o'er the rocks, and up the bay,*
*The long sea rollers surge and sound.*
*And still the thin and biting spray*
*Drives down the melancholy street,*
*And still endure, and still decay,*
*Towers that the salt winds vainly beat.*
*Ghost-like and shadowy they stand*
*Dim mirrored in the wet sea-sand. . . .*
*O broken minster, looking forth*
*Beyond the bay, above the town,*
*O winter of the kindly North*
*O college of the scarlet gown. . . ."*

Gentle nostalgia—that was the quality Andrew Lang conveyed best in his verse and in his more personal prose. It is also the quality which, for most of us, invests St. Andrews. For it is ultimately the student life which gives the place its prevailing

---

[1] Accused, however, by later historians of " inaccuracies ". I do not know of one historian who has not had this charge levelled at him at one time or another. Lang's delightful book is available in a modern edition.

present-day character; and student days are evanescent. During term-time, as another rhymer has it, even "the wind walks in a scarlet gown". The wan, grey streets throng with clusters of young folk, their gowns fluttering in the breeze. Bicycles lean precariously against shop-windows: tuck-shops, full to the point of steaminess, serve cakes and coffee with cheerful, harassed efficiency: and learned lovers stroll along the leafy Lade Braes, or over the cliff-tops towards the fantastic sea-spun "rock and spindle" formation at Kinkell; or down to the smooth fair sands where occasionally horses with their tweeded riders go clopping along by the water's edge. On Sundays, after service in St. Salvator's, there is the long procession of red gowns down to the harbour, the men going out along the low wall, and returning on top of the breakwater. Traditionally, this is supposed to represent the "seeing-off" of the preacher.

But, really, there is more than one St. Andrews. As a place, it has no visible means of support, apart from what it earns by purveying for the students, the tourists, and the golfers; though no doubt much of the postman's burden is made up of dividends which get lighter every year. Society, lacking a leavening of what are sometimes called "the lower classes", has atrophied, on several rather dessicated levels. There are the *rentiers,* those who live precariously on inherited fixed incomes behind an immutable façade of genteel dignity. There are the wealthy incomers; those who buy the expensive houses, of which there are many, to ease away the closing years of their lives: lives often spent quietly yet vigorously in the forces, or in colonial service abroad. The University folk form their own coteries; the townspeople, dependant for a livelihood on the summer holiday trade, make up theirs; and the social groups do not mix. A settler in St. Andrews who does not qualify for admittance into any of these groups might well find the place a mausoleum of loneliness, the ghosts of the past more warm and real than many of the living inhabitants.

It does not seem so in summer, when the Royal and Ancient Golf Club, founded in 1754, is the scene of International Golf Championships. Nor does it seem so later in the season, when the generous beach is flecked with holiday-makers. Buses continually discharge their daily loads among the dunes. Ice-cream carts are clots of garish colour amongst the prevailing green and brown of rush-grass and sand; ponies trot along sedately with sixpenny "fares" on their backs; and the cries of happy children splashing at the sea's edge mingle strangely with the sad crying of the gulls. But these things pass with the sunshine, and the loneliness is there none the less.

Sometimes, St. Andrews has seemed to me a dead city, in spite of the ever-changing colours and the different ways of living which meet together and enliven its pleasant streets: dead in a strange way. Walk out on a clear night when the last youthful reveller has hiccoughed into silence, and the moon is fretting the gaunt shape of the Cathedral's western arch. The slumbering holiday-makers become unreal; the sleeping golfers seem frivolously absurd. Only the past is real; all the power, the horror and the beauty of it; that past which once made this place great, and now keeps it a sounding shell from which the ancient memories cannot, even if they would, depart.

For me, Andrew Lang's verses evoke mainly the student aspect of St. Andrews. These other wider, stronger aspects of the place are better fixed, I think, in a poem by my friend, George Bruce, whose work so vividly captures the atmosphere of the east coast:

" Pause stranger at the porch: nothing beyond
This framing arch of stone, but scattered rocks
And sea and these on the low beach
Original to the cataclysm and the dark.

Once one man bent to the stone, another
Dropped the measuring line, a third and fourth
Together lifted and positioned the dressed stone
Making wall and arch; yet others
Settled the iron doors on squawking hinge
To shut without the querulous seas and men.
Order and virtue and love (they say)
Dwelt in the town—but that was long ago
Then the stranger at the gates, the merchants,
Missioners, the blind beggar with the dog,
The miscellaneous vendors (duly inspected)
Were welcome within the wall that held from sight
The water's brawl. All that was long ago.
Now the iron doors are down to dust,
But the stumps of hinge remain. The arch
Opens to the element—the stones dented
And stained to green and purple and rust.
Pigeons settle on the top. Stranger,
On this winter afternoon pause at the porch,
For the dark land beyond stretches
To the unapproachable element; bright
As night falls and with the allurement of peace,
Concealing under the bland feature, possession.
Not all the agitations of the world

211

*Articulate the ultimate question as do those waters*
*Confining the memorable and the forgotten;*
*Relics, records, furtive occasions—Cæsar's politics*
*And he who was drunk last night:*
*Rings, diamants, snuff boxes, warships.*
*Also the less worthy garments of worthy men.*

*Prefer then this handled stone, now ruined*
*While the sea mists wind about the arch.*
*The afternoon dwindles, night concludes,*
*The stone is damp, unyielding to the touch*
*But crumbling in the strain and stress*
*Of the years: the years winding about the arch,*
*Settling in the holes and crevices, moulding*
*The dressed stone.  Once, one man bent to it,*
*Another dropped the measuring line, a third*
*And fourth positioned to make wall and arch*
*Theirs.  Pause, stranger, at this small town's edge—*
*The European sun knew those streets*
*O Jesu parvule, Christus Victus, Christus Victor,*
*The bells singing from their towers, the waters*
*Whispering to the waters, the air tolling*
*To the air—the faith, the faith, the faith.*

*All this was long ago. The lights*
*Are out, the town is sunk in sleep,*
*The boats are rocking at the pier,*
*The vague winds beat about the streets—*
*Choir and altar and chancel are gone.*
*Under the touch the guardian stone remains.*
*Holding memory, reproving desire, securing hope*
*In the stop of water, in the lull of night*
*Before dawn kindles a new day."*

I do not think St. Andrews will ever have a "new day". It will not share in the changes which have already begun to transform parts of southern Fife.   There will be students and there will be golf; there will be holiday-makers oblivious of the past, and there will be the past itself, indefinitely suspended over the imaginations of those for whom life means more than the urgent flickering minute.   That, at least, is how I hope things will go on being with St. Andrews; for it is almost the only place known to me where the stream of Time still flows on placidly, bestowing upon those few who seek it now and then, some brief respite from the harsh and horrid pace of our own uncertain civilization.

# Chapter VII

# AYONT THE TAY

*" Oh, tell me what was on yer road, ye roarin' norlan' wind*
*As ye cam blawin' frae that land that's niver frae my mind?*
*My feet they trayvel England, but I'm deein' for the north—*
*' My man, I heard the siller tides rin up the Firth o' Forth.'*

*Aye, Wind, I ken them well eneuch, and fine they fa' and rise,*
*And fain I'd feel the creepin' mist on yonder shore that lies,*
*But tell me, ere ye passed them by, what saw ye on the way?*
*' My man, I rocked the roarin' gulls that sail abune the Tay!'*

*But saw ye naethin', leein' Wind, afore ye cam to Fife?*
*There's muckle lyin' ayont the Tay that's mair to me nor life.*[1]
*' My man, I swept the Angus braes ye haena trod for years—'*
*O Wind, forgie a hameless loon that canna see for tears! . . ."*

VIOLET JACOB.

THESE stanzas from Mrs. Violet Jacob's poem, " The Wild
Geese ", are, I think, peculiarly revealing. For they shape and
reflect that passionate local patriotism which has been a characteristic of folk from Angus and the Mearns district of Kincardineshire for a very long time. Somehow, these people of the North-
East have managed to maintain a relative isolation, the effects of
which still show in the fouth of Scots which survives on their
tongues, and in this strong regard for their native airt. Mrs.
Jacob's expression of it is clean and wholesome. Other authors,
many of them more famous in the eyes of the world, have made
of it mawkish make-believe and mincing sentimentality.

It is here in Angus that the Kailyaird School had its origins,
and it is from here that it still maintains its couthy hold on
Scottish public taste. The word kailyaird means, in Scots, a small
cabbage-patch; and the late nineteenth and early twentieth
century group of Scottish writers who earned its application to

[1] In this last chapter of the present volume, we reach the North-East.
Strictly speaking, the term North-East applied to the Scottish Lowlands is
usually meant to designate Kincardineshire, Aberdeenshire, Banffshire and
Morayshire, which together form a fertile strip of flattish country around the
eastern periphery of the Highlands. Forfarshire is perhaps a debatable
county, in that it has certain similarities both to Fife and to its northern
neighbours. Mr. John R. Allan has dealt fully with the North-East proper
in a companion volume. Angus, to give Forfarshire its older and friendlier
name, seems to me to come into my province, and it will occupy the greater
part of this chapter. For the sake of completeness, however, some general
remarks on the North-East round it off.

the products of their whimsical imaginations, did so by virtue of the narrowly parochial range of their interest, and the sniggering falsity of their human portrayals.

The rise and development of the Kailyaird School makes an interesting story; the more so since now, in the middle of the twentieth century, and hard on the heels of the Scottish Renaissance (a realist movement which strives to instil a new and native vigour into contemporary Scottish literature), we seem to be about to have to endure a Kailyaird "period" revival.

An English-born minister of Highland blood, John Watson (1850-1907), who wrote under the pen-name of "Ian MacLaren", published, in 1894, a collection of sketches of Scottish characters, which he called *Beside the Bonnie Briar Bush*. His title came from an anonymous popular song of the 1750's, and he printed two lines of it by way of preface—

*"There grows a bonnie briar bush in our kailyaird,*
*And white are the blossoms on't in our kailyaird"* . . .

The book became a best-seller, by the standards of those days. So, too, were such succeeding volumes as *The Days of Auld Lang Syne*. For a few years, Watson ministered to the parish of Logiealmond, in South Perthshire. It was this brief spell in his early career, and neither his later immensely successful ministry at Sefton Park, Liverpool, nor his astonishingly profitable American lecture-tour, that provided him with the material upon which his considerable worldly success was later based. That material was the way of life of the ordinary folk of Perthshire and Angus.

Some of you may not have been to Perthshire or Angus. No matter. You can take it from me that the folk who live there are *not* abnormally addicted either to half-witted pawkiness or to infantile quaintness.[1] Nor, from all honest account, were their hard-working fathers and grandfathers before them. The Kailyairders, being good North-British late-Victorians with an eye for the main chance, simply seized upon the comfortable dictum of the philosophical Doctor Pangloss—that all was for the best in the best of all possible worlds—and then manipulated their local characters to make them fit it. Hence the dreary procession of improbables who pass through their pages: the "wutty" provosts and kindly-scheming bylies; the doctors who

[1] The true sufferers from these diseases are surely those folk in our towns and holiday resorts who flock to patronize smugly quaint Olde Worlde Tea Shoppes, liberally ornamented with phoney-surface-beams and Birmingham brassery!

work for nothing except love of humanity; the ministers whose unctuous saintliness makes the gorge rise up in a healthy throat; the Scarlet Women who, by enticing nice mothers' sons, cause nice mothers' hearts to break tearfully in sweet-scented wee houses up the purple glens; the poverty-stricken dominies who instil simple platitudes in the minds of bent-on-getting-on boys; and of sweet-natured, dithery villagers with about as much character as a colony of rabbits.

Watson, however, was by no means the first, or the worst, offender in this public caricature of Scottish rural character. *Beside the Bonnie Briar Bush* merely brought together in readable prose the fundamentals of a phase in Scottish literature that had been moulded by social forces not altogether literary, and had already erupted in the sixteen volumes of *Modern Scottish Poets*, the contents of which were conscientiously gleaned from odd corners of local Scottish newspapers by one Edwards, and published at intervals between 1880 and 1897.

The eighteenth-century revival produced Ramsay's Scots songs and *The Gentle Shepherd*; Fergusson's racy Edinburgh poems; the great satires and songs of Burns; the ballad-collecting of David Herd, the Englishman Joseph Ritson, Sir Walter Scott and others; the backward-looking verse-tales of Scott, and the Waverley Novels; the folk-like novels and poems of James Hogg, the Ettrick Shepherd; and the Jacobite songs of Lady Nairne; but it had burnt itself out by 1835. Ramsay, Fergusson and Burns were mainly concerned with the Scotland of their own day. Scott, Hogg, and Lady Nairne, on the other hand, were much more interested in Scotland's past. In the days of the earlier writers, Scotland still retained much of its *virr*, in spite of the southern movement of the aristocracy which was one result of the Union; and the seventeenth century was still close enough to be accurately remembered by parents and grandparents. There was as yet no need to make tales about it. The romantic preoccupation of the later writers, however, concealed the gradual decline—indeed, may even possibly have provided a stimulus for their escape into history.[1]

Once the stars departed, and the historical vein could no longer be profitably sustained by their imitators, the lesser authors had no option but to turn back to "real" life. By about 1860, the significant life of Scotland was no longer that of the countryside, as it had been in Burns' time, but that of the towns. And life in the rapidly expanding, slum-creating industrial centres could

---

[1] None of which, of course, reflects in any way on the excellence of their individual achievements. Here, I am solely concerned with general tendencies.

not very well be sung about: first, because those who were its keenest victims were the only people who really knew its terrible heart, and they were hardly likely to be in a position to express themselves freely; second, because their masters and the middle minions had very different tastes, which naturally did not lean in the direction of industrial realism. They wanted something comfortably reassuring; something which was still Scottish (for they were not devoid of mild patriotism); something sentimental, countrified and "clean", which could be guaranteed to leave the reader with the reassuring impression that he was an altogether superior person to the rustic characters in the book.

It is perhaps not without significance that the leading members of the Kailyaird group were all in some way closely connected with the Church. (The course of Scottish literature is strewn with the labours of ministers who have confused poetry and piety, and who, when accurate research after fact was called for, preferred instead to indulge in irrelevant moral judgment!) Watson was a minister. So was Samuel Rutherford Crockett (1860-1914), a Galloway man with a turn for historical tale-telling which he put to racy use in *The Raiders*, though in *The Lilac Sun-Bonnet*, which also came out in 1894, he provided the best example of Kailyairdism at its worst! Several members of the group received encouragement from the Reverend Sir William Robertson Nicoll, a self-made Aberdeenshire parson, who abandoned literature in favour of journalism and publishing. While editor of the *British Weekly*, he was one of the first to discover Barrie.

Sir James Matthew Barrie[1] (1860-1937) was born at Kirriemuir in Angus, and after graduating at Edinburgh University he, too, entered the world of journalism. His first book to attract attention, *Auld Licht Idylls* (actually his second bow before the public as an author, *Better Dead* having appeared the year before, in 1887), is a vivid piece of reportage and reminiscence about his native Kirriemuir. Unfortunately, he was early blown off his brilliant course, and he altered his direction to cultivate the gentle Kailyaird breezes. An unlimited capacity for whimsy, a quite unscrupulous use of pathos, a love of snivelling sentimentality for its own sake, and a willingness to misrepresent Scots folk for the amusement of his English readers and theatre audiences—these are the sins of which he is usually and quite properly accused.

---

[1] George Blake, in an admirable little study of Barrie and the Kailyairders, examines the facts about their enormous if short-lived success, and probes the nature of the aesthetic falseness of their work in greater detail than is, of course, possible here.

Allied as they were in his plays to an expert and subtle sense of theatrecraft, Barrie's misuse of what were undoubtedly considerable gifts can only be regarded as little short of tragic. For, unless there is some unforseeable alteration in the course of the world or in the direction of public taste, it is difficult to believe that many of his plays will hold their place on the adult Scottish stage.

Yet one cannot be sure. As I have remarked already, there are signs of a revival of interest in the products of Kailyairdism, prompted, I think, mainly by linguistic considerations. It is coming about in a curious way. In spite of the brave endeavour of C. M. Grieve (Hugh MacDiarmid) and the younger Lallans Makars, our amalgam of local dialects and older literary words has not made as much progress as might reasonably have been expected. Much good work and some great work has been produced, all of it infused with a contemporary sensibility; but it shows no signs of becoming widely popular. On the other hand, there is still a fairly large public anxious to consume versifying of the Kailyaird order; pieces in which the writer, who has often elected to live the major part of his life overseas, looks forward to coming home to some wee glen in the Hielans where his bones may rest in peace; or verses celebrating country small-beer in amiable conversational jingle. On the more intellectual level, anthologizers have recently been giving this sort of thing puzzling prominence[1] (I suspect because of the notion that even if the emotions are phoney, the Scots is at least spoken Scots, "genuine" as opposed to "literary"). On a more ordinary plane, the publications which for more than half a century have purveyed Kailyairdism in prose and verse for general consumption, still emanate from Dundee.

II

We have reached Angus by a somewhat intellectual route. The usual method of approach from the south is by rail over the Tay Bridge. This bridge is the second to stand on that site. The destruction of the first Tay Bridge on the night of December 28th, 1879, still remains one of the worst of British railway disasters.

Sir Thomas Bouch's slender structure did not allow sufficient

---

[1] Undue prominence in the case of Douglas Young's *Scottish Verse: 1851-1951*, wherein the Editor offers a cabinet of linguistic curios of little literary consequence. Mr. Young's failure to distinguish between verse and minor poetry has resulted in a collection not at all representative of the best work written in the period his book covers.

"give" for the bridge to adapt itself to side winds of gale force. Judged even by the engineering standards of his own day, his design was unsound. (Stevenson, his greatest contemporary, probably knew equally little about the effects of wind pressure. But whenever he calculated that one bolt would do, he put in two!) In addition to this, owing to Bouch's lack of personal supervision, some of the workmanship was of an appallingly low standard. Doubts about the safety of the bridge were expressed in many quarters when it was first opened in May 1878; but when, in June the following year, Queen Victoria crossed it on her way to Balmoral, and knighted Bouch the following day, even the sceptics were silenced.

On the day of the tragedy, the last Sunday of the year, a great storm raged. The rain lashed against the girders, and the winds tore at the slender piers. The last grey light of a midwinter afternoon was thickening into the mirk of a wild night as the late train stood at St. Fort station, where the tickets of the passengers were taken. Here, two passengers got off the train to catch a cab to Leuchars. Seventy-five people—mostly exiles returning home for the New Year—and a spaniel dog remained on board when the guard's whistle blew, and the last lap of their journey began.

The yellow gas-lights of the compartments were not strong enough to be seen under such conditions from the northern side. But at last the engine lights were framed by the shadowy girders. The wind blew fiercer as the train crawled slowly towards the centre of the bridge. Suddenly the storm fell away, and for a few moments an eerie calm prevailed, only to be shattered by a blast of hurricane force. It struck side-on the cab bound for Leuchars, and nearly blew it over. It caused the duty-watch aboard the warship anchored beneath the bridge to turn his back on the train to avoid being blown down. It broke windows in Dundee, and sent chimney-pots crashing to the ground.

A little boy watching the progress of the train from a hill-side cottage, saw a sudden flash of red light leap down from the bridge towards the water. Excitedly, he rushed in to tell his parents, who sternly rebuked him for inventing wicked stories on the Sabbath!

The train failed to arrive at Dundee on schedule. At first, no one amongst the relatives and officials waiting to meet it suspected what had happened, although several people had seen the engine lights disappear, and the signalman's apparatus went mysteriously dead when the blast of wind struck. At last, after more than an hour of anxious peering and waiting, James Smith the station-

master, and one of his staff, crawled out along the dripping girders, while the wind did its best to pluck them off. They came upon the broken metal strands after half an hour of dangerous struggle with the storm. Later, a momentary glisk of moonlight shone through the clouds, revealing beyond all doubt that something serious had certainly happened to the bridge. But had the train gone back to St. Fort? Relatives hoped so. Still no one knew, since communication with the Fife coast was impossible. It was not until a softer wind pulled away the first wet mists of morning that the full horror of the disaster was exposed. There was not a sign of the missing train, and where the central girder of the bridge should have stood, a jagged gap yawned above the swirling waters.

It took a team of divers many weeks to recover the bodies. Some of the passengers had apparently managed to clamber out of the coaches, only to be swirled away to destruction. Most of them had been battered to death by the fall, or drowned almost immediately. The door of one of the first-class carriages was picked up by a fisherman off the coast of Norway months after the event. There was only one survivor. The little spaniel dog somehow managed to swim safely ashore.

Bouch, whose plans for the Forth Bridge had been passed—one pier, which now supports a dumb light, had in fact been built—at once lost all public confidence. A committee of investigation found that his Forth Bridge plans were even less sound than those of the ill-fated Tay Bridge, and another designer was sought. Bouch never really recovered from the effects of the shock which the news of the disaster brought on. Within a year he was dead, disgraced and degraded.

The bridge which now carries the traveller over the Tay was completed in 1887. It lacks the soaring strength of the Forth Bridge and is not, indeed, at all impressive to look at. But then, neither is the town which it most immediately serves.

Dundee stands upon one of the most glorious and exciting situations it is possible to visualize a town possessing. Across the broad mouth of the Tay lies the northern shore of Fife, undulating gently away from Newport and Tayport. Northwards, the plashing woods and dipping fields of Angus lean up towards the Grampian foothills. To the west "the silver Tay" meanders about its green inches as it flows round the Sidlaws, and through the fertile Carse of Gowrie. To the east, the North Sea sweeps to the horizon. From the top of Dundee Law, which now stands within the town, and on which there is an uncommonly hideous war memorial, the scenic panorama swings out

*Fife: Anstruther Harbour*

still farther, taking in the golden sands of Fife and Angus, and the rugged mountainous spine of the Highlands. Yet with the exception of several English Midland towns, Dundee must most surely be the ugliest city in the British Isles. Allied to this ugliness is its curious lack of communal personality. Mention Glasgow, and at once the mind's eye conjures up a vision of ship-builders, slumdom and townified Gaeldom; mention Edinburgh, and it remembers orderly architectural classicism, the cool objectivity of administration, and a thousand older vernacular overtones of history. But what does the mention of Dundee suggest? Jute; marmalade; cash registers; and the pulp press. Yet these things do not add up to a single integrated personality. Dundee somehow just does not seem to "belong".

George Blake has suggested[1] that Dundee is really a town with a western temperament—it absorbed a high proportion of Irish labourers during the heyday of its expansion—set down in the east. He points out, too, that *vis-à-vis* the English economy, Scotland is hopelessly overtowned. Dundee seems to me to be the obvious "superfluous" town. It owed its modern industrial existence in the first place to Calcutta. And it was India, so long the provider of the Jute Barons' fortunes, who ended Dundee's jute monopoly as long ago as 1870, by entering the world market herself, at first as a modest imitative competitor, later as a serious rival.

Destruction has played a large part in Dundee's stormy history. Edward the First of England burned the City's old records when he sacked the place in 1291. Thus, we are more or less dependent on unreliable secondary sources and on legend for the story that one Alpin or Elpin, King of Scots, in the year 834, made Dundee his headquarters for his war against Brude, King of Picts. Alpin is said to have marched with an army of 20,000 men against his enemies, who were in occupation of Dundee Law. Because of the dominating nature of this position, Old Dundee must have been quite indefensible. The unfortunate Alpin suffered defeat at the hands of his enemies, and was thereafter beheaded on the hill-top in full view of his beaten army.

King Malcolm the Second marshalled his forces at Dundee in 1010, before marching to defeat a Danish marauding force at Barrie. The great Malcolm Ceanmore, about 1071, built a palace for his queen there, the remains of which withstood the ravages of more than eight centuries, but fell before the picks of vandalistic nineteenth-century "improvers" who wanted the site for a factory.

[1] *The Heart of Scotland.*

David, Earl of Huntingdon and Prince of Scotland (Sir Kenneth in Scott's novel, *The Talisman*), the brother of King William
the Lion, accompanied Richard Cœur de Lion on the third
crusade in 1191. Tradition has it that as the Prince's homeward-
bound vessel neared the Scottish coast, it was overtaken by a
tempest which threatened to destroy it. Thereupon the Prince
vowed that if his life were spared, he would found a chapel at
whatever place he should come safely to shore. He landed at Dundee, where he was met by his brother, who gave him a gift of the
town, together with numerous privileges and immunities. Legend
again avers that the great tower which still stands in the city,
and round which in time three churches grew in the shape of
a cross, was built in the fulfilment of this vow. The tower,
however, is unlikely to be older than the fourteenth century,
although it may have been erected on the site of Prince David's
earlier chapel. St. Mary's, St. Paul's and St. Clement's suffered
disastrous damage by fire in 1841, and have long since given place
to "renovated" modern buildings of little or no charm. St.
John's, the fourth church, which was added much later, had a still
more chequered existence, and is no longer there at all. The
ubiquitous Sir Gilbert Scott restored the tower in 1873, when the
old clock was taken away and the peal of bells added. Public
clamour, however, insisted that the clock was brought back.

Alexander the Third confirmed Dundee's privileges and immunities, and the town grew in importance. On Alexander's
sudden death, therefore, it naturally attracted a good deal of
attention from the armies of Edward the First. The Castle was
taken in 1291. Edward himself entered the town in 1296 and in
1303, leaving behind him an English Constable as governor of
the City. Young William Wallace, according to Blind Harry,
was at that time being schooled at Dundee, where he lived with
his mother. One day young Selby, the Constable's son, "near
twenty years of age", came riding into the town with three or
four followers, bent on pleasure. Selby caught sight of Wallace,
whom he challenged in insulting tones, asking him to explain
how he came to be so grandly dressed—"Ane Ersch (Erse) mantle
it war thy kind to wear"—and demanding the surrender of his
knife. Wallace thereupon grabbed the Englishman by the collar,
and "surrendered" the knife by stabbing Selby to death. The
bloody whinger still in his hand, Wallace then fought his way
through Selby's followers, and ran to the lodging of a trusty
friend, from where he and his mother safely fled the City before
he could be caught.

Because it was the centre of the English domination, Wallace found it necessary to lay siege to the Castle once he had control of Sçots troops. The actual taking of it was left to his friend, Alexander Scrymgeour, for which success Wallace made him Constable of Dundee in place of the dead Selby. This Scrymgeour was the ancestor of the later Standard-bearers of Scotland.

The Castle was rebuilt in 1312, and its walls gave shelter to the Bruce for a night or two during 1314. There is more than a suggestion of Fate's casual irony about Bruce's main connection with Dundee. It was in the Greyfriars Monastery of Dundee, founded by the pious Lady Devorgilla, mother of John Balliol, that the Great Council of Clergy acknowledged Bruce as their King in 1309; and it was in another of her foundations, the Church of the Greyfriars at Dumfries, that the murder of the Red Comyn had earlier taken place. These were, of course, the two acts which destroyed forever the claims of the House of Balliol to the throne of Scotland.

Richard the Second attacked and burned Dundee in 1385. The army of Henry the Eighth tried to do the same thing after the Battle of Pinkie, but was disturbed at its task by news of the approach of Mary of Guise's Scots-French troops.

Dundee's later royal visitors all seem to have been entertained with great splendour, although the townsfolk were perhaps not always as loyal in their hearts as their sovereigns might have desired. James the Fifth had a magnificent six days of hospitality in 1528. Probably the Dundonians had no reservations about him. They certainly had reservations about Queen Mary, who spent two days in their midst in 1565: and they would hardly be likely to feel over-kindly towards Charles the Second when he stayed some weeks with them in 1651, immediately before his march to Worcester. James the Sixth was the Stewart sovereign whom they really seem to have gone out of their way to honour. He came to them in 1590, in 1594, and again in 1617. On this last occasion, he was welcomed with a panegyrical address and two Latin Odes of Welcome, delivered by the Town Clerk. Such a means of loyal address might well be revived. At least, it would add a certain academic interest to the platitudinous monotony of the average royal welcome-speech to-day!

The reason for the anti-royalist feeling which underlay some of these Stewart receptions was, of course, the fact that Dundee was the first town in Scotland wholeheartedly and consistently to support the Reformation. George Wishart began his ministry there in 1544, but he was driven out of the town. A plague then afflicted the inhabitants—claimed by Knox as a divine instrument of correction!—and Wishart returned at great personal risk to preach from the battlements of the Cowgate Port, those who were uninfected standing on one side, those who had the disease on the other. He had the protection then of a redoubtable Protestant provost, John Halyburton, who held office for thirty years.

The Reformers did their work in Dundee with even more than their usual zeal. The three monasteries were totally destroyed. The garden of one of them, the Greyfriars Monastery, was given to the town by Queen Mary as a burial-place, and it holds the dust of many of the City's famous sons, including that of Admiral Duncan, victor of the naval Battle of Camperdown. In later years, once it was full, this cemetery became known as "the howff" because it was used by living Dundee folk as a meeting-place wherein they could exchange views on the world's affairs without fear of neighbourly interruption.

One of the most curious literary productions of the Reformation came from Dundee. It was called *Ane compendious Booke of Godly and Spirituall Songs, collected out of sundrie partes of the Scripture with sundrie of other Ballates changed out of prophaine Sangis for avoyding of sinne and harlotrie with augmentation of sundrie gude and godlie Ballates;* and the earliest edition to survive, though almost certainly not the first, is dated 1567. The authorship of *The Gude and Godlie Ballads,* as the book is usually called now, is attributed to three brothers, James, John and Robert Wedderburn of Dundee, who were all graduates of St. Andrew's University.

The idea of *ballatis* of a religious order which ordinary folk could sing was not original, having been tried out with some success in Germany, Sweden and France. But the Wedderburns were the first to provide such material for the use of the Reformers in Scotland.

None of the Wedderburns apparently possessed much poetic talent.[1] The principle upon which they worked was to adapt a popular set of folk-words in such a way that, ostensibly at any rate, they carried a religious significance. As the historian J. H. Millar points out,[2] "While a mere hymn set to a secular tune would have been a feeble instrument for conversion or edification, the combination of hymn pasquinade might well prove irresistible, and the faint suggestion of the profane or illicit, so dear to a certain type of religious mind, could not fail to stimulate curiosity. It is certainly the daring employment of what we may fairly call

---

[1] Professor Mitchell, who recovered the 1567 copy and edited it for the Scottish Text Society, thinks otherwise.
[2] *A Literary History of Scotland.*

parody or burlesque that engages and detains our interest in these singular compositions."

Singular they certainly are. One of them goes:

> " With huntis up, with huntis up,
>     It is now perfite day,
> Jesus, our King, is gain hunting,
>     Wha lykis to speid thay may.
>
> Ane cursit fox lay hid in rox,
>     This lang and mony ane day,
> Devouring scheip, whill he mycht creip,
>     Nane mycht him schaip away.          [escape
>
> It did him gude to laip the blude
>     Of young and tender lambs,
> Nane culd miss, for all was his,
>     The young ains, with their damms.
>
> The hunter is Christ, that hunts in haste,
>     The hunds are Peter and Paul,
> The Paip is the Fox, Rome is the rox,
>     That rub us on the gall."

It is easy to see how that sort of racy nonsense made its mass appeal; probably much the same sort of appeal as " The Red Flag " makes amongst followers of the extreme Left to-day.

A particularly delicious ballat begins:

> " God send every Priest ane wyfe
>     And every Nun ane man
> That they micht live that haly lyfe
>     At first the Kirk began.
>
> Sanct Peter, whom nane can reprufe
>     His lyfe in marriage led;
> All guid Priests whom God did luve
>     Thai marryit wyffis had. . . ."

Robert, the Vicar of Dundee, may well have been the author of this effusion, because by then he had already acquired two daughters by a female with whom, as Millar delicately puts it, he had " formed a connection ".

Only one piece in the whole collection fused into a real poem:

> *" All my luve, leave me not,*
> *Leave me not, leave me not,*
> *All my luve, leave me not,*
> *Thus mine alone;*
> *With ane burding on my back*        [burden
> *I may not bear it, I am sa waik,*
> *Luve, this burding fra me tak,*
> *Or else I am gane. . . ."*

It is not difficult to imagine the nature of the "burding" of which the female singer wished to be relieved in the original. But, by happy chance, the Wedderburns managed to overlay the grossness of the old song, and produce a hymn of sincere and ardent tenderness. There are not many such hymns in the whole range of Scottish literature.

Because of its undeviating staunchness in the cause of Reform, Dundee earned its sobriquet of "the Scottish Geneva". Naturally, it became a stronghold of the Covenanters, and a thorn in the side of Charles the First. The Marquis of Montrose, with an army of seven hundred and fifty Highlanders and Irishmen stormed it and broke open the gates. His men then swarmed into the City, scattering in search of plunder. A Covenanting minister, the Reverend James Kirkton,[1] who was naturally biased against Montrose, tells us that: "The behaviour of his soldiers was to give no quarter in the field, and ordinarily, wherever they came in the country, they deflowered the women and butchered the poor men, not contenting themselves with common slaughter except they barbarously mangled the carcase." Whether or not this was how the royalist troops were behaving on this occasion, news was received that a Covenanting army, under General Baillie and General Harvie, was hastening to the relief of Dundee, and Montrose's army beat a helter-skelter retreat. The extrication of his force is said to have caused the Marquis to exercise every whit of his leadership. His retreat northwards up the coast, only to find every road but the one he had travelled blocked by Baillie's troops, and his subsequent successful break-out by doubling back over his tracks—the one manœuvre Baillie was naturally not expecting—remains one of the outstanding military feats in Scots history.

Five years later, in April 1650, when Montrose, wounded and

[1] *The Secret and True History of the Church of Scotland from the Reformation to the year 1678.*

defeated, was being ignominiously carried a prisoner to Edinburgh, a halt was made at Dundee. It is much to their honour that some of the citizens, overlooking the sacking he had given their city in the days of his success, saw that his wounds were properly dressed and that he was provided with clothes becoming to his rank.

The following year, during the early stages of Cromwell's usurpation, members of the nobility, believing (with a singular lack of military judgment) that it would be a safer refuge than any of the southern towns, flocked to Dundee for sanctuary. One of those refugees was the Earl of Buccleuch, who lodged in the Luckenbooths at the east end of the High Street. There, his daughter was born: Ann Scott, who later became wife to the unfortunate Duke of Monmouth, from which union sprang the present line of Buccleuchs. Duchess Ann plays a conspicuous part in Scott's verse-romance, "The Lay of the Last Minstrel".

Needless to say, Cromwell did not overlook Dundee. He ordered General Monk to deal with it, and, in 1651, the indefensible city fell once again. Major-General Lumsden, the royalist commander, put up a stout defence, until his garrison was finally driven back into the old tower. From there, it surrendered. As the men marched out, honourably defeated, Monk had them rounded up in the churchyard; then he issued orders for them to be slain in cold blood. Two royalist regiments who found themselves trapped in the Fishergait, also surrendered, only to meet a similar fate. Then began that slaughter of the unarmed townsfolk which forms one of the thickest stains on Monk's reputation. A sixth of Dundee's population fell to the naked sword. Tradition has it that in the end, what caused the General to call a halt to the massacre was the glimpse he caught in Thorter Row of a naked babe sucking its dead mother's breast.

The most famous of all Dundee's sons was John Graham of Claverhouse (c. 1648-89). He was born in Claverhouse Castle, which stands on the opposite side of the Duchty Water to Mains Castle. Claverhouse,[1] who was created Viscount Dundee in 1687, became famous and dreaded as the bloodiest of all those who hunted the Covenanters. His nickname, "Bonnie Dundee", is said to have been bestowed on him ironically to stress the contrast between his outward comeliness and his inward hideousness.

Shortly before his victory at Killiecrankie in 1689—a victory which cost him his life, and was the last serious blow struck in the

[1] It would not be unfair to call him the Royalist's Monk. Between these parties of the extreme Right and Left, there was little to choose when it came to brutality.

cause of James the Seventh and Second—Claverhouse descended upon Dundee with the intention of sacking it. He did, in fact, burn the suburb of Hilltown, but he is said to have been repelled by a body of armed burgesses who had foreknowledge of his coming. More probably, Claverhouse withdrew on finding that he had come up against opposition, and went off in search of more important foes.

During the first Jacobite rising, Graham of Duntroon proclaimed the Old Chevalier, King of Great Britain to the townsfolk of Dundee. The following January, on a cold, grey Friday morning, the Chevalier arrived in person with a train of three hundred gentlemen. He spent the night in the mansion of Stewart of Grantully. The whole visit was an unfortunate misjudgment. The Chevalier was suffering from an attack of the ague. Sheriffmuir had already ended his hopes two months before; and, although a contemporary report tells us that he had to remain for over an hour in the market-place while his friends kissed his hand and the townsfolk cheered, it cannot have been much other than curiosity which prompted most of the populace to turn out.

The Young Chevalier was temporarily more successful, for under the leadership of Sir John Kinloch, a Jacobite force of about six hundred soldiers took Dundee on the 7th of September 1745, and held it until the 14th of January 1746.

Thereafter, Dundee was never again called upon to give proof of its indefensibility. But the spirit of destruction seems to have got into the blood of the Dundonians. No longer having foes to destroy their best buildings, they took this work upon themselves. No revengeful conqueror could have been more thorough. The Palace has gone; so has " Our Lady Workstair's Land ", a fine old mansion dating from about 1500; so have the Luckenbooths, in which both Monk and the Old Chevalier lodged; so have all the old mansions in the Seagate, where the Guthries, the Afflecks, the Brigtons, and other such old Dundee families had their homes. Gone, too, is the Old Custom House, wherein the novelist, James Grant (1822-1887), set much of his once-famous tale, *The Yellow Frigate*. About twenty old churches have been carefully destroyed. Worst of all, the dignified Town House built by William Adam in 1734 was demolished between the two World Wars, for no real reason at all. Apart from the Old Tower and the nearby castles of Dudhope and Broughty Ferry, Dundee can now boast of having not a single old building still standing, and very few new ones worth a second glance.

Here, indeed, practical philistinism has worked itself out to its logical conclusion. Dundee publishes the least progressive of Scotland's native-owned daily newspapers, and is one of the biggest production centres in Britain of postcards, popular journals and "comics". Its slums are not a whit less sordid than those of Glasgow, though those of the larger city have attracted an unfair share of public approbation because of their greater size. According to C. M. Grieve (whose earlier castigations of Scottish evils were by no means as illogical as have been so many of his later Communistical outbursts), "Dundee Art Gallery is a byword. Public money has been wasted on worthless pictures in vicious taste, and atrocious pictures of ex-Lord Provosts and other public men form a large part of the collection. . . . The same thing applies to the private collections of the Jute Barons, and other wealthy Dundonians."

It seems possible, however, that Dundee reached its nadir of intellectual debasement during the "'thirties". The breath of national recovery, which is stirring in so many Scottish quarters, has not passed by Dundee. New light industries have taken root, and gone some way towards solving the city's unemployment problem caused by the decay of the jute industry. For some years, too, Dundee Repertory Company has been building up a taste for good theatre in the town.[1] Even the College, founded in 1866 by the munificence of the Baxter family, and at present part of St. Andrews University, has been aspiring to separate status.

The Dundonian whose reputation spread farthest around the world was probably the historian, Hector Boece, Boyce or Boethius (1465-c. 1536). He was born at Dundee, and after graduating at the University of Paris, he occupied the chair of Philosophy at Montaigu College, until in 1500 he was appointed by Bishop Elphinstone to be the first Principal and Professor of Divinity at King's College, Aberdeen. Later, he became rector at Tyrie, and for the last nine years of his life, he received a pension from his sovereign. His fame rests on his *Scotorum Historia ab illius gentis origine*, the seventeen books of which were first published in Paris in 1527. On the orders of James the Fifth, the work was translated into Scots by John Bellenden. It

---

[1] Scottish Drama, still in its infancy at the time of the Reformation, was actively discouraged by the Kirk for more than three hundred years. Its modern nascene dates only from the 1920's. "John Brandane" (Dr. McIntyre, 1869-1939), "James Bridie" (Dr. O. H. Mavor, 1888-1951), Joe Corrie, Robert Kemp and Robert Maclellan are the brightest stars in its still somewhat limited galaxy. Barrie's name might be added, although he wrote mainly for the London stage. Some doubts exist as to whether or not the Communist Ewan MacColl, author of *Uranium 235*, is in fact a Scot at all. Scotland's theatrical tradition rests entirely on Lyndsay's *The Thrie Estatis*; Ramsay's *The Gentle Shepherd* and Home's *Douglas*.

contains one of those ingenious medieval theories which seek to show how the Scots are directly descended from Biblical races. It also abounds in traditional legendary material, including the story of Macbeth, which Holinshed borrowed for his " Chronicle ", where Shakespeare found it.

Sir George Mackenzie (1636-91) was also a Dundonian. He earned one reputation as a lawyer with his *Institutions of the Laws of Scotland*, published in 1684: another as " Bluidy Mackenzie ", the relentless criminal prosecutor before whom came many a captured Covenanter; and yet another as a public man for the part he played in the founding of the Advocates Library in Edinburgh.

The Reverend John Glasse (1695-1773), founder of the Glassites,[1] was a native of Dundee. That flamboyant character, the Reverend George Gilfillan (1813-78), though actually born at Comrie, lived out his working life as a Secession preacher in Dundee. Thus it came about that when, in addition to his fiery preaching, he took to literature, and, from about 1849 to 1854, held undisputed sway as the most influential critic of the age, Dundee became the centre towards which young poets directed their manuscripts, and sometimes also their persons.

The flood-tide of Victorian optimism was then at its height. A new age was at hand—or so the poets thought. Gilfillan went so far as to believe that Christ was about to reappear—possibly in Dundee! Gilfillan was a seeker-out and, by his way of it, an improver of youthful genius. But he was also a lamentable vulgarian, and, like so many other Scottish ministers who have dabbled in literature, quite unable to distinguish between the rival claims of pietism and poetry.

Nowadays, few ever read his best book,[2] *A Gallery of Literary Portraits*, though it is preserved in the Everyman Library. Smith, Dobell, and the forgotten minor members of the " Spasmodic School "—so called because of the ease with which they dropped into bathos—were Gilfillan's special *protégés*. They all received their *congé* at the hands of Professor William Aytoun, of the Blackwood Group, in his satire *Firmillian; A Spasmodic Tragedy*, by T. Percy Jones. Gilfillan naturally came in for the hardest knocks.

At one point in the " drama ", two rival poets are arguing on the top of a plinth. One of them is mad with jealousy because the poems of the other have gone into a second edition. Mean-

---

[1] See Chapter V.

[2] His huge edition of *British Poets*, major and minor, provided a valuable service in its day, and in the case of the obscurer figures, is still useful.

while, the gowned figure of Apollodorus (alias Gilfillan) enters, declaiming:

> *" Why do men call me a presumptuous cur,*
> *A vapouring blockhead, and a turgid fool,*
> *A common nuisance, and a charlatan?*
> *I've dashed into the sea of metaphor*
> *With as strong paddles as the sturdiest ship*
> *That churns Medusae into liquid light,*
> *And hashed at every object in my way.*
> *My ends are public. I have talked of men*
> *As my familiars, whom I never saw.*
> *Nay—more to raise my credit—I have penned*
> *Epistles to the great ones of the land,*
> *When some attack might make them slightly sore,*
> *Assuring them, in faith, it was not I.*
> *What was their answer? Marry, shortly this:*
> *' Who, in the name of Zernebock, are you?'*
> *I have reviewed myself incessantly—*
> *Yea, made a contract with a kindred soul*
> *For mutual interchange of puffery.*
> *Gods—how we blew each other! But, 'tis past—*
> *Those halcyon days are gone; and I suspect,*
> *That in some fit of loathing or disgust,*
> *As Samuel turned from Eli's coarser son,*
> *Mine ancient playmate hath deserted me. . . ."*

The " death " of Apollodorus is cruelly witty.

> *" I do beseech thee, send me a poet down,*
> *Let him descend, e'en as a meteor falls . . ."*

he cries in contemplative ecstasy. At this point up in the gallery of the plinth, the less popular poet seizes his rival, who begs for mercy on the grounds that a third edition of his poems has been called for and he must live to see it through the press. Maddened beyond endurance at this additional mortification, his adversary pushes him over the edge. He falls on top of Apollodorus, crushing him to death.

In some ways, the pathetic William McGonagall (1830-*c*. 1903), pedlar, weaver and ham-elocutionist who made a meagre living by giving " performances " up and down the country; butt for the cruel wit of University undergraduates; possessor of the Order of the White Elephant; and, in his own words, " poet and tragedian ", is exactly the sort of representative literary figure with whom Dundee might have been expected to become associated.

Two Scottish writers have preserved descriptions of McGonagall's "performances". Neil Munro was present at a meeting of a "pseudo-Literary Society in Dennistoun", where the Bard appeared. He was "of middle height, shaven and puckered visage, long lyart locks, and a general aspect of being kippered like an East Coast herring. . . . On his entry there was vociferous cheering, which he gravely acknowledged by repeated bowing. There was not the slightest evidence that he suspected any irony in the ovation. . . . At the start of the proceedings the Secretary read a series of telegrams and letters of apology for absence, ostensibly from some of the most distinguished literary men in England. . . . All of them expressed the loftiest admiration for the guest of the evening. . . ."

Thereupon "the guest of the evening" played his part, while his baiters became more and more drunk. (McGonagall was a total abstainer, and therefore must often have had the last laugh, since nothing is so irritatingly absurd to one who is not drunk as the witless, fuddled antics of those who are!) Finally, he was told he was to have a presentation. "With agreeable expectancy, he stood up to receive it at the chairman's hands, and there was suddenly produced for him on a salver an enormous sausage of many pounds weight, all decorated with ribbons! . . . It was pathetic to see the instant disillusionment of one, who a moment before was unsuspicious, at the fact that he was merely a laughing-stock for a convivial company of dubious taste. There was a tremor in his voice when he protested that he felt hurt and insulted by such a presentation as certainly no other poet in history had been offered. . . ." However, his feelings were gradually soothed, and: "A few days later, McGonagall wrote back from Dundee expressing his contrition for his touchiness about the sausage, which he now handsomely declared was the best he had ever tasted."

William Power's picture of McGonagall comes from the latter end of the "knight's" life. He appeared in the long-since demolished Albion Halls in Glasgow. Says Power:

"He was an old man, but with his athletic though slightly stooping figure and his dark hair, he did not look more than forty-five: and he appeared to have been shaved the night before. He wore a Highland dress of Rob Roy tartan and boy's size. After reciting some of his own poems, to an accompaniment of whistles and cat-calls, the Bard armed himself with a most dangerous-looking broadsword, and strode up and down the platform, declaiming 'Clarence's Dream' and 'Give me another horse—Bind up my wounds.' His voice rose to a howl. He thrust and slashed at imaginary foes. A shower of apples and oranges fell on the platform. Almost before they touched it, they were met by the fell edge of McGonagall's claymore and cut to pieces. The Bard was beaded with perspiration and orange juice. The audience yelled with delight; McGonagall yelled louder still, with a fury which I fancy was not wholly feigned. It was like a squalid travesty of the wildest scene of *Don Quixote* and *Orlando Furioso*. I left the hall early, saddened and disgusted."

As Hugh MacDiarmid has pointed out in an amusing essay on the Bard, McGonagall was not a bad poet. He simply wasn't a poet at all. His "verse" shows little grammatical awareness; despises the rules of prosody; is utterly incapable of generating any serious emotion and abounds in trite details and observations. There is no bathos because there are no heights from which a descent may be made. The only admirable quality which McGonagall's work possesses is its desperate sincerity. Because of this, I find his outpourings painful, and the innumerable would-be witty later parodies of it, a display of utter witlessness in the worst possible taste. No sensitive man can laugh with wholesomeness at such naïvety as this:

" *Beautiful new railway bridge of the silvery Tay*
 *With your strong brick piers and buttresses in so good array,*
 *And your thirteen central girders, which seems to my eye*
 *Strong enough all windy storms to defy.*
 *As I gaze upon thee my heart feels gay,*
 *Because thou art the greatest railway bridge of the present day,*
 *And can be seen for miles away,*
 *From north, south, east or west, of the Tay. . . ."*

or this:

" *The man that gets drunk is little else than a fool*
 *And is in the habit, no doubt, of advocating Home Rule.*
 *And the best of Home Rule for him, so far as I can understand*
 *Is the abolition of strong drink from the land.*

 *And the men that get drunk, in general, wants Home Rule,*
 *But such men, I think, should keep their heads cool,*
 *And try to learn more sense, I most earnestly pray*
 *And help to get strong drink abolished without delay."*

Whether or not McGonagall was mad from the start, or merely a victim of his own early posturings as a poet, matters not at all now. His fame is that of an eccentric whose huge failure, because of his intense sincerity, assumes a tragic quality. It is this aspect of the man that James Bridie has gone some way towards honouring in his play, *Gog and MacGog*.

So far as I am aware, Dundee has not produced a single poet of any consequence; but William Montgomerie and his wife Norah, who have lived there for many years, are the editors of those two delightful modern collections of Scots Children's Verse, *Scottish Nursery Rhymes* and *Sandy Candy*.

### III

Dundee apart, Angus falls naturally into three divisions: the coastal towns and villages; the landward towns in their pastoral settings; and the glens of the north-east corner, where the mountainous core of Scotland rests its rugged flanks.

On the stretch of coastline which lies between Dundee and Arbroath, the traveller moves through the suburban solidarity of Broughty Ferry—originally the northern terminus of a ferry-service to Tayport in Fife—through Monifieth, with its golf course, round Buddon Ness and so into Carnoustie. As an urban outlet, Carnoustie is to Dundee what Helensburgh is to Glasgow. Carnoustie is also a championship golfing centre. North of Carnoustie, the coastline becomes rocky. Easthaven is a quiet little fishing port in a coign of the cliffs, fringed with tilled fields. Looking out over the sea, some lines of Violet Jacob came into my head, as poems of hers so often do in Angus:

> "*The lang lift lies abune the warld,*
> *On ilka windless day*
> *The ships creep doon the ocean line*
> *Sma' on the band o' grey;*
> *And the lang sigh heaved upon the sand*
> *Comes pechin' up tae me*
> *And speils the cliffs tae whaur ye stand*          [climbs
> *I' the neep-fields by the sea. . . ."*

Arbroath, or Aberbrothock as it once was called, has preserved in the parish of the nearly new kirk of St. Vigean's, the Dooster Stone, which is said to contain the only extant legible Pictish inscription. The township clustered around the mouth of the Brothock Water was thus most probably once a Pictish settlement.

About 1178, William the Lion founded the great red-stone Abbey—in which he and his queen were in due course buried—and raised Arbroath to the status of a burgh of regality, in 1186.[1] The Abbey was dedicated to Saint Mary and Saint Thomas à Becket. Its monks were originally of the Tyronesian order. The Abbott's Harbour at Old Shorehead—a wooden pier projecting from Danger Point—was erected in 1394 as a result of an agreement made between the Abbot and the burgesses of the town.

Arbroath Abbey grew in importance, and many of its incumbents became leaders in the clerical and political life of Scotland. So it came about that it was from Arbroath Abbey on the 6th of April 1320, when Edward of England was trying to persuade the Pope to excommunicate Robert the Bruce, that the magnificent Declaration of Arbroath was despatched to His Holiness Pope John XXII by the nobles and commoners of Scotland (the second and third estates) met together in Parliament there.

" By reason of his desert as of his right, the Providence of God, the lawful succession . . . and our common and just consent have made him our King, because through him our salvation has been wrought. Yet even him, if he yielded our cause to England, we should cast out as the enemy of us all, and choose another King who should defend us; for so long as a mere hundred of us live, we will never surrender to the dominion of England. What we fight for is not glory, nor wealth, nor honour; but freedom, that no good man yields save with his life."[2]

God knows, we have not lived up to the inspiration of these ringing words in the centuries that have come between us and their utterance! But in dark and drublie times, when those who believe in Scotland have been cast down and are full of despair, the trumpet call of the Declaration of Independence has served, and still does serve, as a rallying signal to the weary of heart.

A scene of a very different order took place outside the Abbey a hundred and twenty-five years later—one of those disgusting clerical brawls which helped to bring the Auld Kirk into popular disrepute. The monks of the Abbey appointed the Master of Crawford[3] to be their Chief Justiciar, or supreme judge in

[1] James the Sixth made it a royal burgh in 1599.
[2] Dr. Agnes Mure Mackenzie's translation of the original Latin.
[3] The style and title used of the presumptive heir to the Scottish peerage. When this man in due course became the 4th Earl he was known as the Tiger Earl or Earl Beardie. It was his alliance with the Douglas against James the Second that led that monarch to murder the Douglas in Stirling Castle. The Tiger Earl eventually made his peace with the King and became a loyal servant.

Fife: "St. Andrews by the Northern Sea"

civil affairs, a position he already held in relation to the Abbey of Scone, in Perthshire. Young Crawford, however, insisted on maintaining a huge train of followers, which the monastery was expected to pay for. Because of this, and because his general conduct caused him to be, in the words of an old historian, "uneasy to the convent", the Chapter shortly afterwards deposed him, and appointed Alexander Ogilvie of Inverquharitie[1] to be his successor. The Master, however, refused to surrender his appointment, and promptly took forcible possession of town and Abbey. His friend, the Earl of Douglas, sent along a hundred Clydesdale men to assist him, and the Hamiltons added their quota of troops.

Meanwhile, the Ogilvies found unexpected support from the arrival at Inverquharitie of Sir Alexander Seton, Lord of Gordon and afterwards Earl of Huntly. He and his men were to spend the night on their way to Strathbogie. By an ancient Scottish custom, the host's quarrel also became the guest's quarrel, so long as the host's meat lay undigested in the guest's stomach. Together with some assistance from other friendly barons, the Ogilvie army marched for Arbroath on the 13th of January 1445, with the intention of recapturing the town. When they arrived, however, they found the forces of the Lindsays, Crawford's retainers, drawn up in battle order before the gates.

The respective commanders gave orders for their forces to engage, and combat was just about to be joined when the Master's father, the third Earl of Crawford, an old man with flowing white hair, himself excommunicated for his raids against clerical land in Fife, rushed between the lines with the intention of preventing the conflict between his son and his wife's family. But, before he had time to speak, an Ogilvie who did not recognize him ran the old Earl through the mouth and neck with his spear. He fell from his horse, mortally wounded.

This sight so enraged the Lindsays that they rushed in to the charge. A bloody battle ensued, in which the Lindsays were the victors. Their casualties numbered about a hundred; the Ogilvies lost over five hundred. Seton and Inverquharitie's brother escaped by flight. Inverquharitie was wounded and taken prisoner. He was carried to Finhaven Castle, the old Earl of Crawford's seat. When his widow learned that one of her kinsman's soldiers had wounded her husband to the point of death, she rushed to the chamber where the wounded man lay and smothered him with a pillow.

The old Earl lingered on for a week in fearful agony. No one

[1] " Qu ", in Middle Scots, is pronounced like " w ".

*Angus: Arbroath Abbey*

dared touch his body for four days after his death, until Bishop Kennedy of St. Andrews could be persuaded to lift the excommunication and pronounce forgiveness over his ashes.

The family feud which resulted from this affray dreed on until the time of the Reformation. One Abbot of Arbroath, tired of the ancient wrangle, wished heartily "that every future Lindsay should be poorer than his father", a prophesy which came true. For, although the Lindsays once owned large tracts of Angus, the Ogilvies—the direct male descendants of the old Celtic Maormors of the province—retained their ancestral seat long after the castles of the Lindsays had changed hands or crumbled into ruin.

The last Abbot of Arbroath was the infamous Cardinal Beaton, who was also and at the same time Archbishop of St. Andrews, a flagrant piece of wealth-grabbing which helped to confirm his unpopularity.

The friends of John Knox "reformed" the old Abbey in the usual manner, and thereafter it became a quarry. In view of this, the surviving remains are remarkably extensive. They featured in a surprising drama a few years ago.

On the 26th of December 1950, Scots folk were astonished to read over their breakfast-tables that the Coronation Stone had been removed from its place under the throne in Westminster Abbey. Scottish Nationalists had for years talked of "returning" their Stone of Destiny—Lia Fail, traditionally the pillow of Jacob, brought to Ireland in the fifth century B.C., and thence to Scotland, from where it was taken by Edward the First as a symbol of conquest: for upon it the Kings of Scotland were crowned. But the difficulties of removing such a cumbersome piece of masonry without being detected had hitherto proved insurmountable. On this occasion, however, five young Scots successfully got it out of the Abbey and carried it home to Scotland in a small car. There, it was found to have sustained a crack at some previous stage in its adventurous career. It was secretly repaired by a Glasgow monumental sculptor.

Meanwhile, the police of Great Britain began a nation-wide search for the adventurers. In England, the affair caused a considerable amount of indignation, the breaking-into a holy place being regarded in some quarters as sacrilege. In Scotland, those with Episcopalian or ultra-pro-Union sympathies, echoed the English horror. But the majority of Scots, including even douce business men who could not for a moment be suspected of harbouring "nationalist" sympathies, privately hoped that neither the stone nor its "liberators" would be discovered. The feeling of the few—that the proper resting-place for the Stone, except when in use during coronations, was in Scotland, possibly in Edinburgh's St. Giles' Cathedral—became a general sentiment: and the Church of Scotland, while not condoning the act of removal, supported such a view.

In the end, moderate public opinion in Scotland (at any rate, as mirrored in the national newspapers) urged that the best way to secure the legal return of the stone to Scotland was to give it back voluntarily: the theory being that the English authorities, impressed by the trusting nature of the gesture, would generously fall in with Scotland's wishes. So on April 14th, 1951, the stone was secretly laid by the altar of Arbroath Abbey.

Those who had complained of sacrilege became strangely dumb when the police took possession of it and promptly locked it in a Forfar cell, before taking it back to London in a plain van. In the end, England, as usual, let down moderate Scottish opinion, and gave excellent publicity material to the extremists who thought that the Stone ought to have been destroyed rather than surrendered. The Stone was hidden in a secret place in Westminster Abbey until public clamour had died down. Then, cynically, it was produced, dusted, and replaced in its former position, to the accompaniment of a superfluity of those meaningless, unctuous apologies for their existence which Scottish M.P.'s of both major parties can so easily drool out whenever London occasion demands, regardless of the true feelings of their constituents.

Wisely, the authorities took no action against Ian Hamilton and his daring companions. Martyrdom might have given the relationship between the two countries an ugly jar. In one sense, the exploit succeeded, for, in forcing its way into the English newspapers which rarely carry information about Scottish affairs, it at least made the English aware that a strong desire for some form of Home Rule within the United Kingdom framework does exist in Scotland. In another sense, picturesque though the adventure was, since it gained nothing but such publicity, it could be said to have failed in its object.

In any case, as my friend Douglas Young pointed out at the time, the Stone is probably a fake. There is no reason to suppose that, in the first place, the Stone delivered up to Edward the First was the genuine Lia Fail, and quite a lot of ground for believing that it was not!

One other connection with the Abbey of Arbroath still exists. Out in the North Sea, lying opposite the harbour of the town, the jagged fins of a dangerous reef rip the surface of the waters.

Here, medieval monks fastened a bell which, swayed by the motion of the waves, warned mariners of their danger.

One day, however, Sir Ralph the Rover, a high-spirited marauder whose "mirth was wickedness", as Robert Southey tells us, cut the bell away to "plague the Abbot of Aberbrothak". Then the Rover sailed across the seas in search of plunder.

At last, heavy with booty, he sailed home towards Scotland's shores. As he approached the east coast, a storm sprang up, and visibility shrank to a few yards. Master and crew lost their bearings in the fog.

> "They hear no sound, the swell is strong;
> Though the wind hath fallen, they drift along,
> Till the vessel strikes with a shivering shock—
> 'Oh Christ! it is the Inchcape Rock!'
>
> Sir Ralph the Rover tore his hair;
> He curst himself in his despair;
> The waves rush in on every side,
> The ship is sinking beneath the tide.
>
> But even in his dying fear
> One dreadful sound could the Rover hear,
> A sound as if with the Inchcape Bell,
> The Devil below was ringing his knell."

Arbroath built itself a new harbour in 1725, and a still larger harbour in 1841. The hand-spinning of Osnaburghs began in 1736. In 1820, the mechanical weaving of linen created a flourishing minor industry in the place, and with it the accompanying bleach-fields. A tanning factory also set itself up at about this time.

An alarming interruption to the way of life of this douce north-east port occurred on the evening of May the 23rd, 1781. A French privateer, commanded by one Fall, suddenly appeared off the coast, and ordered the magistrates of Arbroath to come aboard and make terms. Naturally, the civic dignitaries were a little unwilling to risk their staid persons in this way; so, instead, they sent to Fall a delaying message asking what his terms of ransom might be. At the same time, they sent hot-foot to Montrose a messenger with an urgent request for military assistance.

Fall demanded £30,000, and six civic chiefs as hostages until the money was paid. His message concluded: "Be speedy, or

I shoot your town away directly, and I set fire to it. I am, gentleman, your servant. . . ."

Shortly afterwards, a detachment of troops from Montrose having duly arrived, the magistrates set Fall at defiance. The pirate then did his best to shoot their town away with heated shot; not, fortunately, with enough accuracy of aim to damage more than a few chimney-pots.

Arbroath was the scene of the labours of James Phillip (?1656-?1713), son of the proprietor of the smallholding of Almer's Close. He developed into the romantic scholar who joined the army of Claverhouse in 1689, and became his standard-bearer. His unfinished Latin epic, *The Graemeid*, notable mainly for the violence of the author's pro-Claverhouse feelings, is one of the most curious products of Scottish Latinity.

One other literary association distinguishes Arbroath: Scott made it the model for "Fairport" in his novel, *The Antiquary*, Auchmithie, the fishing village which clings to the rocky coast three and a half miles north of Arbroath being his "Musselcrag".

Lunan Bay, where Walter Mill (1476-1558), the last of the Reformation martyrs to die at the stake, was priest for forty years, lies between Arbroath and Montrose. It has a long low sandy beach, the curve of which in summer is filled with youthful holiday-makers.

Montrose (*moine t'rois,* moss on the peninsula) stands on a peninsula which juts southwards, at the estuary of the South Esk. To the west of the town, the river swells into a broad tidal loch known as Montrose Basin. At high tide, the loch is full; at low tide, there is only a river surrounded by a wide expanse of mud. As long ago as 1670, attempts were made to reclaim the Basin with a bulwark, known locally as Drainer's Dyke. Alas, however, the drainers worked in vain; for no sooner was their dyke completed than an uncivil local witch, Meggie Cowie—one of the last of her kind in the district—raised a fearsome storm that breached and destroyed the drainers' labours!

Two earlier townships, not a trace of which has remained—Celurea, mentioned by Boece, and Salork, mentioned in a charter of Malcolm the Fourth's time—probably stood higher up the Basin. But in the reign of the latter monarch, mills and salt-pans had been established at Montrose. Towards the end of the century, William the Lion lived for a time in the castle there. This castle, which then stood on the Forthill near the site of the present Infirmary, sheltered Edward the First of England from the 7th till the 21st of July 1296. Andrew of Wyntoun, Blind Harry, and a local nineteenth-century poetaster, Balfour, erroneously allege that John Balliol "rendered quietly the realm of Scotland" to the English tyrant at Montrose Castle, just as Froissart wrongly claims Montrose to have been the port from which Sir James Douglas sailed for the Holy Land with the heart of Robert the Bruce. Actually, Strathcathro saw Balliol's humiliation; and Berwick was the Douglas's port of embarkation. In any case, Wallace destroyed Montrose Castle the year after Edward's residence in it, and it was never rebuilt.

The Erskines of Dun—the family from which the poetess, Mrs. Violet Jacob, sprang—shortly before the Reformation got on to bad terms with the folk of Montrose, apparently over the matter of constantly increasing rents. But the laird, a convinced Protestant, became something of a popular leader in the north-east during the Reformation. Amongst his other activities, he established a school in Montrose where Greek was taught for the first time in Scotland. To teach this language he brought over from France Pierre de Marsiliers, who circulated the Greek testament amongst his pupils, on which account he was summoned to appear before the Bishop of Brechin in 1538 on a charge of heresy. Instead of facing up to the inevitable consequences of such an interview, Marsiliers fled to England. Marsilier's pupils included George Wishart, who later became his assistant, and Andrew Melville, Knox's successor, who was born at Baldowie, in a neighbouring parish.

Dun's leadership proved quite capable of standing up to the test of enemy belligerency; for when an English ship, bent on carrying out as much casual destruction as possible, sent a midnight landing-party ashore at Montrose in 1548, the invaders were driven back into the sea by a rapidly mustered citizen "Home Guard" with Dun at their head.

James Graham, fifth Earl and first Marquis of Montrose (1612-50), and one of the finest of the Scottish cavalier poets, was born at Old Montrose, in the parish of Maryton. After his educations at St. Andrews, and an unfortunate interview with Charles the First in 1636, at which the King, ill-advised by his useless favourite, Hamilton, treated his future champion with contempt, the "Great Marquis" joined the national movement of the Covenant, and assisted at the signing of that document in 1638. Thereafter, he three times occupied Aberdeen for the Covenanters, defeating the Royalist forces of Viscount Aboyne at the Bridge of Dee in 1639. But the following year, it became clear to him that Argyll the "Glied Earl", as he was nicknamed because of his squint, was using the Covenant as a pretext for forming an anti-Royalist political junto within the Scottish Parliament. This

Montrose could not tolerate, although to the end of his days he remained true to the Covenant in religious principle. His brilliant victories for Charles the First, by which he virtually conquered Scotland, were nullified by that monarch's English defeats and eventual capitulation to the Scots Covenanting army at Newcastle. Charles the Second, for whom Montrose also fought, betrayed this great soldier by urging him to campaign against the "rebels" at the same time that he himself was surreptitiously treating with Argyll, into whose hands Montrose was finally betrayed by a greedy impoverished laird, MacLeod of Assynt. Montrose's greatest victory of all was in the noble manner of his death. As the grim procession moved towards the Tolbooth of Edinburgh, Argyll gloated through a shutter of a house in the Canongate of Edinburgh, where he was celebrating the wedding of his son. Twice before, Argyll had fled before Montrose and his army. Even now, he dared not look his noble foe in the face. Time brought its revenge; for, in due course, Charles the Second brought justice to bear on Argyll for his unscrupulous personal manœuvrings and bloody persecutions. He, too, died at the Tolbooth, though he was granted a comparatively clean beheading under the blade of the Maiden. His severed head was also stuck upon a spike above the great gate.

Montrose's birthplace gave to his family three successive titles: that of Earl in 1505—the first Earl was killed on Flodden Field— Marquis in 1644; and Duke in 1707. Now, the family seats are at Buchanan, in Stirlingshire, and Arran. No territorial connection with the district of the family origin has been preserved.

James, the Old Chevalier, *de jure* though not *de facto*, King of Scotland, Ireland and England, made his exit from Scotland with the Earl of Mar in 1716, through the back door of the town house of the Duke of Montrose—the same house in which the "Great Marquis" was supposed to have been born—which once stood at the south end of the High Street. It was from this house that James wrote a remarkable letter to the then Duke of Argyll:

"... Among the manifold mortifications I have had in this unfortunate expedition, that of being forced to burn several villages, etc., as the only expedient left me for the publick security was not the smallest. It was indeed forced upon me by the violence with which my rebellious subjects acted against me, and what they, as the first authors of it, must be answerable for, and not I; however, as I cannot think of leaving this country without making some provision to repair that loss, I have there-

fore consigned to the Magistrates of ————[1] the sum of
————, desiring and requiring of you, if not as an obedient
subject, at least as a lover of your country, to take care that it
be employed to the designed use, that I may at least have
the satisfaction of having been the destruction and ruin of
none, at a time I came to free all."

At the moment of worst adversity, this most tactless and witless
of the later Stewarts shows a courtesy and grace of mind of which
the Hanoverians were incapable and which, even at this late date,
is strangely touching.

During the early stages of the '45, the Jacobites took possession
of Montrose. The Duke of Cumberland was in the town on the
10th of June the following year. This being the birthday of the
Old Chevalier, many of the Jacobite ladies paraded themselves in
white dresses, while the children lit bonfires in the street. The
Hanoverian Governor, having no wish to punish women and
children, overlooked the matter. Not so Cumberland. The
Governor was dismissed and punished, and one or two of the
offending boys were publicly whipped. Amongst these juvenile
patriots who thus suffered for the Cause was Thomas Coutts
(1735-1822), who, with his brother, later became the founder
of the famous banking concern of Coutts and Company.

Dr. Johnson and Boswell paid a visit to Montrose in 1773,
on their way north from Edinburgh to the Hebrides. There,
the incident of the lemonade, described by Boswell, took
place:

" We found a sorry inn where I myself saw another waiter
put a lump of sugar with his fingers into Dr. Johnson's lemonade, for which he called him ' Rascal '. It put me in great glee
that our landlord was an Englishman. I rallied the Doctor
upon this and he grew quiet. . . ."

Boswell also reported that they " went and saw the town hall,
where is a good dancing-room and other rooms for tea-drinking.
The appearance of the town from it is very well; but many of the
houses are built with their ends to the street, which looks awk-
ward." Very few of these " side-on " houses are still standing,
although a number of them can still be seen in villages on the
north-east coast. The idea behind such an arrangement was pre-

[1] Place and amount were left blank, for General Gordon, his senior commander, to fill in, the amount being the balance left over after the expenses
of the Jacobite army had been met.

sumably to offer the least possible surface of the building to the force of the easterly gales that whip across the North Sea in winter.

Disasters and near-disasters overtook the early bridges across the South Esk. Up until the end of the eighteenth century, a ferry between Montrose and Inchbrayock[1] carried the traffic. The timber span, constructed between 1793-96, incorporated a lifting drawbridge which allowed the passage of ships. Unfortunately, the narrowing of the navigable channel which this device necessitated increased the force of the current, and, in spite of several attempts to shore up what was then regarded as a remarkable invention, the whole bridge became so shaken that it had to be taken down.

The next bridge was a chain suspension one, completed in 1829. It stood the strains put upon it until the summer of 1838, when a large crowd assembled to watch a boat-race. In the excitement of the moment, a section of the onlookers suddenly rushed to one end of the bridge, causing the upper chain to snap. As it whipped free of its tension, it killed several people. Others were lurched towards the water but, fortunately, the under chain held and a major tragedy was averted. The bridge was thereupon repaired, but an October gale tore up the roadway across it a few months later. It was therefore strengthened in design by the addition of new supports.

The viaduct which carries the Arbroath-Montrose railway over the river was erected in 1882-3 to replace the original bridge completed only two years before. This first bridge had been built to a modification of the plans for Bouch's Tay Bridge, and after the Tay Bridge disaster, the Board of Trade refused to license the Montrose structure for the carriage of passenger traffic.

When Pennant visited Montrose in 1776, the manufacture of sailcloth was the principle industry of the town, as it had been since about 1745. Sail-making gradually gave place to flax-spinning. In 1805, a spinning factory was built at Ford's Mill. It was equipped with one of Boulton and Watt's new steam-engines, and the man who was in charge of it during its first year of operation was George Stephenson, the inventor of the locomotive. During that year, Stephenson recorded that he managed to save the astonishing sum of £28 off what cannot have been a very large wage.

Rope-making, machine-making, ship-building and brewing—all these things have been carried on at Montrose, behind the dreep-

[1] Named after an old church dedicated to St. Braoch.

ing haars of winter, and the swinging light of Scurdyness. There was once a considerable foreign trade with Norwegian and Baltic ports. One of the town's thoroughfares is still called Baltic Street, of which Violet Jacob sang:

> " Oh, Baltic Street is cauld an' bare
> An' mebbe no sae grand,
> But ye'll feel the smell i' the caller air
> O' kippers on the land. . . ."

That smell of kippers reminds us that fishing is still one of Montrose's main occupations. It has also become a much-favoured holiday resort. Apart from the visits of Burns in 1787, and Queen Victoria in 1848, amongst its most distinguished holiday-makers must have been the Scottish composer, Francis George Scott, and the poet, Edwin Muir. In the mid 'twenties, C. M. Grieve (" Hugh MacDiarmid ") was employed on the staff of the local paper, the *Montrose Review*. Many must have been the nights when these three friends and familiars of the " Scottish Renaissance " Movement got together in Montrose.

According to Scott, it was in Montrose that the unfortunate schism between Muir and Grieve, between literature in Anglo-Scottish and literature in Lallans,[1] or Scots, broke out. Muir, in *Scott and Scotland*, a study of the achievements and influence of Sir Walter Scott, had given his opinion of the future of Scottish literature in a passage which no doubt will become familiar to historians of Scottish letters:

" . . . the chief requisite of a literature is a homogeneous language in which everything can be expressed that a people wishes to express. Scotland once had such a language, but we cannot return to it: to think so is to misunderstand history. That language still exists, in forms of varying debasement, in our numerous Scottish dialects; but these cannot utter the full mind of a people on all the levels of discourse. Consequently, when we insist on using dialect for restricted literary purposes we are being true not to the idea of Scotland but to provincialism. . . . If we are to have a complete and homogeneous Scottish literature it is necessary that we should have a complete and homogeneous language. Two such languages exist in Scotland, and two only. The one is Gaelic and the other English. . . . And of these two alternatives English is the only

[1] Burns' word, not Douglas Young's. " They spak their thochts is guid braid lallan, like you and me ", wrote the Ayrshire bard.

practicable one at present. . . . To say this is to say that Scotland can only create a national literature by writing English. . . ."

To Grieve, whose reputation by 1930, when Muir's book was published, already rested firmly on fifty or sixty exquisite Scots lyrics written in a language which borrowed from the past and created an amalgam of dialects to replace the lost " core " of the auld Scots tongue, such a criticism must have seemed to hack at the very foundations of his future fame. Instead of producing a cool, logical case in defence of Scots, Grieve launched a literary and personal attack against Muir and his work; a tirade which he kept up sporadically for over a decade, sickening the reading public with its violent irrelevancies, and perhaps inculcating the tirading habit in his own mind to such an extent that the man who began his career as an inspired lyric poet now appears likely to end it as a ranting politician, whose dream-like conception of the Communist state bears as much relation to the inhuman reality as Peregrine Pickles' ludicrous feast in the manner of the ancients probably did to Julius Caesar's Saturday suppers.

A reasonable case could have been brought against Muir's case, as against all such generalizations. The Scots tongue, after all, had lost its " core " by the late seventeenth century. Yet, over a hundred years later, in spite of the fact that the aristocracy (then the section of society whose influence mattered most) had mainly taken to speaking English, the Scots language had still enough *virr* in it to produce Ramsay, Fergusson and Burns. Furthermore, the early demise of Scots literature has been prophesied over and over again for something like four centuries. Yet good work in Scots has always kept on appearing.

It may be counter-argued, of course, that in Burns' day Scots was still the speech of what, for want of a better term, we may call the " working classes ". From this line of thought, Grieve has sought to " prove " that Scots poetry is essentially " working-class " in its orientation. Theoretically, it is then fairly simple to ally it with " the workers' struggle " (which, in Grieve's philosophy, seems to mean the policies of Soviet Russia), and with the inborn rebellious instincts of the human heart by which those who cannot, or will not, adjust themselves to the ways of an ordered society, seek to bring about its destruction. Much of the so-called Communism of Grieve's later versifying and of the " workers-break-your-bonds " droolings of those whom the " leader " of the Scots literary movement now sees fit to attach importance, seems to me to have significance not as literature

—precious little of it is that!—but purely and simply as political evidence of a clinical sort.

The palpable distortions, the half-truths, the advocacy of hate as a more effective motive force than love, the hysterical anti-Englishness, and the sheer intolerant narrowness of sympathy displaced by Communist writers seeking to appropriate the Renaissance Movement in Scotland to themselves, may either be evidence of a sick society, or merely of individual minds sickened and thickened by their own frustrations. In any case, their influence is so small that they would be of little account, were it not that they represent also a serious sickening of Scottish literature, and go some way towards supporting Muir's theory that Scots as a language for literature has no long-term future. For if Scots has to make its last stand as the lingo of unintellectual Communism (masquerading as oppressed Freedom), then all Grieve's earlier protestations anent the need for establishing homogeneity of national expression are reduced to absurdity.

The B.B.C. in Scotland has done noble work in striving to make known the achievements of Scots, both ancient and modern. So, too, in a smaller way, has the Saltire Society. But such forces as the Anglifying influences of the London-controlled Television[1] and press, together with that relentless and, possibly, inevitable educational levelling of speech—which, at any rate, seems to have become a non-reversible British trend—are year by year crushing out the fouth of Scots spoken even in the North-East, where dialect has for long retained its strongest hold.

Fulminations and political mis-representations can obviously do nothing to alter this situation. The only hope is to broaden the basis of Scots, so that it may become not only "respectable" again, but so beloved that the ordinary people of Lowland Scotland will be no more prepared to let it go than were the peasants of Norway when, towards the end of the nineteenth century, they welded their mountain dialects into Landsmaal, the better to withstand the pressure of Danish. Can such a hope have much expectation of realization at this hour of the day?

IV

Of the inland towns in Angus, only three are of any size—Brechin, Forfar and Kirriemuir.

Brechin—called after Brachan or Brychan, a Celtic prince of the sixth century—although nowadays officially only a royal

[1] True in 1953 but not in 1973, with B.B.C. Scotland, Scottish Television, Border Television and Grampian Television in existence.

burgh, is entitled to be called a city by virtue of its ancient position as a seat of ecclesiastical government. It climbs up the northern bank of the River Esk, and from the southern side of the river still presents a picturesque appearance. " Picturesque ", that term so over-worked by descriptive writers of a century ago, and by word-lame guide-book compilers of to-day, has become almost a modern sneer, especially when used in conjunction with " picture-postcard ". No such debased meaning is intended here, for the sylvan qualities of Brechin in summer, set as it is amidst thick foliage, and rising out of the silvery Esk, spanned by a very old two-arched bridge, do suggest the proper meaning of " picturesque "—of pleasing beauty; such as would make a " picture ". Brechin has, in fact, provided many photographers and artists with " pictures ".

Kenneth Mac Malcolm (971-95) founded a monastery and a Culdee College there, dedicated to the Holy Trinity. By 1153, Brechin was the charge of a bishop. In 1218, Culdees and the chapter were still in existence, working and worshipping side by side, but, by 1248, the chapter alone survived.

The Cathedral, founded about 1150, when Brechin was made a See by David the First,[1] has been added to at various periods, and reduced again by " improvers " in 1806-8. The old building was a plain cruciform structure with an aisleless choir in early First Pointed style; north and south transepts and an aisled five-bayed nave in a mixture of late First Pointed and early Second Pointed, in which latter style the north-west tower was also built. The " improvers " reduced the length of the choir, demolished the transepts and rebuilt the aisles flush with the nave. As a result of their efforts, little of the original building now survives except the octagonal clustered piers, the gabled west front, and the squat five-storied tower which was built by Bishop Patrick in the middle of the fourteenth century.

Attached to the south-west angle of the Cathedral stands the Round Tower, built about 1000. Just under eighty-seven feet high and capped with a hexagonal spire added in the sixteenth century, this round tower is the finest Scottish example of a structure common enough in Ireland.[2] In the Vennel, too, the ruins of the *maison dieu* or *hospitium* founded by William of Brechin in 1256, still stand.

Only one story of religious embroilment comes down to us, through an account by the Presbyterian minister, Robert Baillie.

[1] Brechin still is a See of the Episcopal Church of Scotland.
[2] Other Scottish examples are at Abernethy in Perthshire, and on Egilshay, in the Orkneys.

When Archbishop Laud's Service-book was ordered to be read in Scottish churches in 1637, the Bishop "one Sunday, when other feeble cowards couched . . . went to the pulpit with his pistols, his servants, and as the report goes, his wife with weapons. He closed the doors and read his service. But when he was done, he could scarce get to his house—all flocked about him; and had he not fled, he might have been killed." Baillie adds grimly, "Since, he durst not try that ploy over again."

Although the annals of the Episcopal See are comparatively uneventful, the town had its share of secular "tullziement". The Danes are supposed to have burned the whole place in 1012. Brechin Castle withstood the siege of Edward the First in 1303. Unfortunately, after three gallant weeks, Sir Thomas Maule, the Scottish commander, was killed by a stray arrow, and thereafter the garrison surrendered. From the Maule family, the Castle descended to the Dalhousies in 1782, one of whom was a friend and admirer of Burns. The poet's correspondence with George Thomson, the folk-song collector, is now in the Castle library. At the Battle of Brechin Muir, fought in 1452, near the Hare Cairn in the nearby parish of Logiepert, the Earl of Huntly defeated the Earl of Argyll's rebellion against James the Second. In 1645, both town and Castle were harried by Montrose. The fourth Earl of Panmure and Lord Maule proclaimed James the Eighth at Brechin in 1715, for which misjudgment his estates were forfeited, although they were bought back again by the family in 1764.

To-day, while still preserving its sylvan appearance, Brechin's industries include the manufacture of linen, flax-spinning, rope-making, distilling, paper-making, and, in a small way, iron-founding.

Forfar, the county town, lies at the foot of a basin formed by the surrounding slopes, in the centre of the southern half of Angus. Malcolm Ceann Mor had a castle on Castlehill, where, according to both Hector Boece and George Buchanan, that Parliament met which first conferred "modern" surnames and titles upon the Scottish nobility. Queen Margaret also had a royal residence in the Inch of Forfar loch.[1] Their former presence is still commemorated by such ancient local names as King's Muir, Queen's Wall, the Palace Dykes, and so on.

King David the First elevated the town to the dignity of a royal burgh, and three later sovereigns—William the Lion,

[1] Both royal residences and the title-conferring Parliament may well be figments of successive local investigations developed by the credulous early historians.

Alexander the Second and Robert the Second—all held parliament there. Most of the town was burnt down in 1244 in a disastrous fire. After having been "refused" admission to the Castle by its keeper, Gilbert de Umfraville, in 1291, Edward the First forced admission on his second visit to Forfar five years later, staying in it for the best part of a week. Finally, in 1308, while "stuffit all with Inglismen", the Scots troops of Bruce took back the Castle and destroyed it. It was never rebuilt.

During the Civil War, Forfar remained loyal to Charles the First. As a reward for its good conduct, Charles the Second confirmed the town's ancient status, and, in 1684, presented it with its Mercat Cross. In 1830, this cross was removed to the site of the old Castle, where it still stands. Another relic of past conflicts is the "branks" or witch's bridle, a metal head-cage which, when fastened, forces a spur into the mouth of the wearer so that he or she cannot move the tongue. It was used to prevent a condemned victim from declaiming his innocence on the way to the stake. The bridle was salvaged from the ashes after the execution.

The story of the Forfar Cow has become famous to the point of legend. It is preserved for us in its original form in a diary kept by Sir John Lauder, Lord Fountainhall (1646-1722), a Presbyterian legalist of considerable integrity who, like Montrose, remained also a staunch Royalist.

"In the reknowned town of Forfar," he tells us, "ane who had many kine. . . left the tub wherein he had milked them, by neglect, at his door. By comes a neighbour's cow, who, being damned thirsty, comes the high way to the tub and takes a very hearty draught. In the mean time comes he that ought (owns) the milk, and seeing the damage that was done him, to the Toun Council he goes, maks a very grievous complaint, (and) demands that he that owns the cow that had drunk his milk, pay him. The Council was exceedingly troubled with this demand, never in their remembrance having had the like case through their fingers. After much debate on both sides, a sutor (cobbler) stands up, and shows that he had light upon a medium to make up the difference. He asks whether it was a standing drink or not that the cow took. . . . They, replying: 'How could she take it but standing,' he replied that it was a most sure thing in that country, known to them all, that none ever paid for a standing drink. They, following his decision . . . cleared the cow with its owner from paying ought, as having taken only a standing drink."

Later writers have ventured to improve the tale by crediting the cow with alcoholic tastes, and making the "standing drink" a bowl of browst left outside the local ale-wife's door.

To-day, Forfar lives by its linen and jute manufactures, its bleaching and its position as a market town. It is a douce grey place, unimaginative and unbeautiful; but here there may still be heard, as is fitting in the place where Scotland's most famous lexicographer, Dr. John Jamieson (1759-1838), was a Secession minister for seventeen years, a goodly fouth of north-east Scots.

The only other town of any size in Angus is Kirriemuir, Barrie's birthplace and resting-place, out of which he made his Thrums. The original Secession church of the Auld Lichts, founded in 1803, was rebuilt in 1843. Kirriemuir has no significant history of its own, though in Kirriemuir Parish there still stands the fifteenth-century Inverquharity Castle, seat of that branch of the Ogilvies who became involved in the fracas with the Lindsays which resulted in the smothering of Alexander Ogilvy of Inverquharity at Finhaven in 1446. A later Alexander fell into Covenanting hands at the Battle of Philiphaugh and was executed at Glasgow in 1646. A Jacobite Ogilvy of this family followed James the Seventh, and wrote the song "It was a' for our rightfu' King".

The Grampian Mountains invade the eastern hinterland of Angus. They fall sharply down each side of Glen Doll and the White Water, and penetrate, though less massively, through Glen Clova, reaching almost to Kirriemuir. Craig Mellon towers above Glen Doll. To the right of the mountain, a valley pathway leads over to Deeside. In both these Glens, though particularly in Glen Clova, through which flows the South Esk, the pasture-land is rich; yet either because of their relative inaccessibility, or because they "lead" nowhere and the modern motorist has a preference for "circular tour" roads, not many people come to pree their quiet border-land beauty.

V

Where, in the north, do the lowlands of Scotland end? If height of hill be the principal criterion, at the Pentland Firth. For a hill-less strip runs right up the east coast of Scotland beyond Angus—through Kincardine, that loamy fertile county where, in the guise of Lewis Grassic Gibbon, J. Leslie Mitchell (1901-35) found inspiration for his great trilogy, A Scots Quair, and through

it interpreted the "speak" of the good earth[1] in his lilting
Scots-laden prose; through Aberdeenshire, with its glittering
granite city and its hard-working practical farmers and business
men, and the fisherfolk who keep their own communities along
its coasts; through Banffshire, with its sharp blending of Highland
and Lowland sceneries, and its rich cluster of distilleries; through
fertile Moray and golden Nairn (where Dr. Johnson thought
the Highlands began because there he first heard the "Erse"
tongue!); through the Black Isle, the easternmost strip of Ross
and Cromarty, and so into what Ivor Brown has called the "Dead
Vast" of Sutherland and Caithness.

Of course, height of hill is not the only factor to be considered
in settling the Lowland boundaries. Native characteristics are
also of some account. In the long run, however, it is the hills
that have played the most significant part in moulding Highland
character. A man from the North-East and a man from Stirlingshire will have in common many attributes of thought and speech
and habit. Both will have more than a man from, say, Skye or
the Lews.

Yet, in the end, there is a central core of common nationality
in all Scots which transcends such artificial division as Highland
and Lowland. Basically, we are all Celts. Our common Celtic
ancestry reaches back over thousands of years, and, by sheer force
of accumulation, makes all later "modern" regional differences
caused by Scandinavian, Norman, Saxon or English influence of
but superficial account. Once, Gaelic was the language of most
of our country. Now, even in the Highlands, it is receding. Its
very recession serves to stress these false divisions which have
always been, and still are, excellent material for politicians who
do not wish us well to play upon.

I do not think that in the Scotland of the future Gaelic can
ever again be the national language, any more than Lallans is
likely, so to speak, to go into reverse and reconquer Lowland
Scotland. But of one thing I am sure. Somehow or other, if
Scotland is ever again to regain her intellectual nationhood, she
will have to learn to sublimate her endless internal dissensions
and dividing differences, and speak with one voice. I think it
will be an Anglo-Scottish voice she will find, just as the Ireland
that has arisen out of its old heroic Gaelic ashes has an Anglo-
Irish voice. The old languages may be doomed; but their
influences and the noble values they created must be made to
mould, and so live on in, the new.

[1] With an admixture of Communist theory for which Kincardine must not
be blamed, however.

# INDEX

# INDEX

"Spasmodic School" of literature, 229
Spiers, Alexander, of Elderslie, 15
Spittal's Hospital, Stirling, 138
*Staggering State of Scots Statesmen*, 202
Standing Stones of Orwell, 155
Stephenson, George, 243
Stevenson, Robert Louis, 175; Hackston of Rathillet, on, 190
Stevenson, Thomas, 56
Stewart, Archbishop, 204; Doune Castle, 108; Falkirk, 2nd battle of, 130
Stewart, Sir John, of Bonkill, 125
Stewart, Prince Charles Edward, xiv, 8; Falkirk, 124; Glasgow sojourn, 15
Stewart, Royal, origin of, 57, 70
Stirling, 120; coat of arms, 131; Coeur de Lion, 132; Cowane Mansion, 137; derivation of, 124; Falkirk, 2nd battle of, 130; Heading Hill, 72, 132; "Ludgings", 137; Macky, John, on, 131; Mar's Wark, 137; Pictish stronghold, 131; Smith, Alexander, on, 98; Smith Institute, 136; Spittal's Hospital, 138
Stirling Brig, 140
Stirling Castle, 130; Damien's flying failure, 133; William Douglas, murder of, 132; King Egfrid, 131; James III, 133; James VI, 135; Mar, Earls of, 142; Mary, Queen of Scots, 135
Stirlingshire, 98-139; Industrial area, 122; Loch Lomond Islands, 98; Pass of Balmaha, 98
Stockwell, 6
Straloch, Gordon of, 36
Strathaven, 38
Strathblane, 118
Strathclyde, 5, 70
Strathendrick, 114
Strone, 38, 55
*Summer in Scotland*, Brown, 27
*Summer in Skye*, Smith, 27
Sugar, West Indian, 46
Surnames conferred, Forfar parliament, 248

Tarbet, 90; Alexander Rodgers, 96
Tassie, James, 16
Tay, 140, 213-52; Abbey of Lindores, 197

Tay Bridge, 172; destruction of, 217
Taylor, John (the Water-Poet), 171
"Tears of Scotland", Smollett, 82
Teith, River, 106
Telfer, Mrs. Alexander, 87
Telford, Thomas, 89
Tennant, William, 193
*Testament of Cresseid*, Henryson, 169
Thatch, in Lowlands, 197
*The Thrie Estatis*, Lyndsay, 199, 200, 228
Thistle Trust, 136
Thomson, Alexander, 119
Thomson, James, 18, 48
Thomson, Janet, 155
Thoresby, Ralph, 12
Tiger Earl of Crawford, 132, 234
Tillicoultry, distillery, 147; St. Serf, 163
Timber trade, 45
Tobacco trade, 14, 15; Greenock, 46
*Tour of the Hebrides*, Boswell, 27
Torryburn, Fife, 175
Trade, 13; boots, 22; bottle, 141; brewing, 141, 243; bricks, 123; coal, Clackmannan, 151, Dunfermline, 171; Dysart, 183; West Fife, 170; cotton, 16, 21; cotton dyeing, 85; distilling, 141, Brechin, 248, "John Haig", 171, Tillicoultry, 147; flax, 170; glass, 15; ironworks, 123, 248; jute, 220, Dundee, 228, Forfar, 250; linen, 170, Arbroath, 238, Forfar, 250, Kirkcaldy, 180; mining, 140-1; paper, 141, Brechin, 248, Fife, 171; pottery, 15; ropemaking, 243, Montrose, 243, Brechin, 248; sailcloth, Montrose, 243; shipbuilding, Clyde, 20, 21, 22, Montrose, 243; tanning, 15, 238; timber, 45; tobacco, 14; Turkey Red, 84, 85
Trossachs, 105-7, 111
Trout, 150, 155
Turgot, Bishop, 165, 167
Turkey Red, dyeing, 84, 85
Turnbull, Bishop William, 6

United Turkey Red Limited, 85
*Uranium 235*, MacColl, 228
Urquhart, Sir Thomas, of Cromarty, 113

265